A Medium Seen Otherwise

A Medium Seen Otherwise

Photography in Documentary Film

Roger Hallas

OXFORD
UNIVERSITY PRESS

OXFORD
UNIVERSITY PRESS

Oxford University Press is a department of the University of Oxford. It furthers
the University's objective of excellence in research, scholarship, and education
by publishing worldwide. Oxford is a registered trade mark of Oxford University
Press in the UK and certain other countries.

Published in the United States of America by Oxford University Press
198 Madison Avenue, New York, NY 10016, United States of America.

Library of Congress Cataloging-in-Publication Data
Names: Hallas, Roger, author.
Title: A medium seen otherwise : photography in documentary film / Roger Hallas.
Description: New York : Oxford University Press, 2023. |
Includes bibliographical references and index.
Identifiers: LCCN 2023006058 (print) | LCCN 2023006059 (ebook) |
ISBN 9780190057770 (paperback) | ISBN 9780190057763 (hardback) |
ISBN 9780190057794 (epub)
Subjects: LCSH: Documentary films—History. |
Photography in motion pictures.
Classification: LCC PN1995.9.D6 H245 2023 (print) |
LCC PN1995.9.D6 (ebook) | DDC 070.1/8—dc23/eng/20230306
LC record available at https://lccn.loc.gov/2023006058
LC ebook record available at https://lccn.loc.gov/2023006059

DOI: 10.1093/oso/9780190057763.001.0001

Paperback printed by Marquis Book Printing, Canada
Hardback printed by Bridgeport National Bindery, Inc., United States of America

To M. B., and in memory of my father, Tony Hallas

Contents

Acknowledgments

In the long journey of writing this book, I have benefitted from the support, inspiration, and critical feedback of many people, as well as the financial assistance and research time provided by several institutions.

The College of Arts of Sciences at Syracuse University provided a semester of research leave followed by a Faculty Fellowship from the Humanities Center. I am enormously grateful to the George A. and Eliza Howard Foundation for the fellowship that permitted me to take another semester of research leave to complete the main research for this book (and to my colleague Dympna Callaghan, who first told me about the fellowship). I would like to thank Erin Mackie and Coran Klaver as departmental chairs who have been incredibly supportive during the process of writing this book. Thanks are also due to Vivian May, director of the Humanities Center, and Associate Deans Gerry Greenberg and Alan Middleton. Some production costs for the book were supported by subventions from the College and the Department of English.

At Oxford University Press, Norm Hirschy has been an absolutely stellar editor, without whose support, patience, and guidance I would not have been able to complete this tome. Rada Radojicic and Hemalatha Arumugam have masterfully steered this book through the production process. Michele Combs has once again produced an excellent index for me. The anonymous readers for the press provided meticulous and constructive feedback for my revision process. I am grateful to all the filmmakers, distributors, and archivists who have provided access to films and documents. Akram Zaatari has very generously allowed me to use a frame capture from his film *On Photography, Dispossession and Times of Struggle* (2017) as the basis for the book's cover.

Many scholars have engaged with my research and writing of this book. Frances Guerin gave me important direction early on as I was figuring out the shape of the project, while my dear colleague, mentor, and friend at Syracuse, Steve Cohan, has consistently provided a sharp eye and supportive voice along the whole process. I have also benefited greatly from feedback and conversations with other Syracuse colleagues: Will Scheibel, Chris Hanson, Mike Goode, Crystal Bartolovich, Chris Forster, Patricia Roylance, Susan Edmunds, Carol Fadda, Kendall Phillips, Tula Goenka, Doug Dubois, Lucy Mulroney, and Kathy Everly. Within film studies, I must thank Patricia Zimmermann, Jonathan Kahana, Anabelle Honess Roe, Jessica Scarlata, Amy Shore, Shawn Shimpach, Carla Marcantonio, Jennifer Horne, Emma Sandon, Marsha Gordon, Scott MacDonald, Rebecca Baron, Jaimie Baron, Paige Sarlin, Karen Redrobe, Joan Hawkins, Tess Takahashi, and Pooja Rangan. A special shout-out to Joshua Malitsky for inviting me to talk at the Center for Documentary Research and Practice at Indiana University Bloomington, which allowed me to test drive my arguments early in the project. I benefitted from my students' generative discussions in two graduate seminars (*Film, Photography, and the Documentary Idea* and *Writing and Filming Photography*). A special thanks must be extended to my dear friend Trisha Ziff, whose documentary film *Chevolution* (2008) first got me thinking about photography documentaries. Her films and our conversations have deepened and elaborated my understanding of the relationship between film and photography.

The long journey of writing this book could not have been completed without the personal encouragement and nourishment (both literally and figuratively) of friends and family, including Ingrid Hallas, Jenny Ward, Joan Grummant, Petra Hammerl Mistry, Nina Rueschen, Andrea Verdoorn, Jolynn Parker, Liz Horn, and the Fee and Brightman families. My academic career owes such much to the intellectual, emotional, and financial support of my late parents, Tony and Brigitte Hallas. My father was a great amateur photographer whose passion for the medium taught me how the camera could allow you to see the world anew. If my cinephilia was born on Saturday afternoons watching classical Hollywood movies on BBC2 in the early 1980s, then my photophilia began even earlier, when I spent weekend nights in the darkroom developing the pictures that I'd taken with Dad's borrowed camera. The knowledge of photographic history and aesthetics that I learned from him proved immensely valuable when I first became seriously interested in film studies as an undergraduate student. It brings me great joy to return to this earlier passion, but my only regret is that Dad passed away before I was able to complete this book. I thus dedicate it to his memory.

My greatest gratitude must go to Matthew Fee, my beloved husband, intellectual accomplice, and cinematic soulmate. His eternal inspiration, enduring patience, and boundless generosity nurtured me every day, especially when I feel doubt or frustration. He has shared his keen insights into the films I discuss and provided tremendously valuable feedback on the draft chapters of the book, which now bears the profound imprint of his sage input.

An earlier version of the book's introduction was published under the title "A Medium Seen Otherwise" in *Social Research* 89, no. 4 (2022): 975–1000.

About the Companion Website

Oxford University Press has created a website to accompany *A Medium Seen Otherwise: Photography in Documentary Film*. It includes thirty-nine short clips of the films discussed in the book. These are indicated by the symbol [▶] in the text. https://global.oup.com/us/companion.websites/9780190057770/

Introduction

Having undergone profound material, aesthetic, and institutional transformations since the arrival of digital technologies, photography and film frequently intersect in the processes of convergence (the shared technological basis of diverse media in digital code) and remediation (the mutual reshaping of old and new media). However, the foundational relations between film and photography have a long history extending well back into the nineteenth century. This history includes many acclaimed practitioners who have worked in both media, such as Albert Kahn, Helen Levitt, Agnès Varda, Chris Marker, Robert Frank, Wim Wenders, Abbas Kiarostami, and Fiona Tan, but it also involves a range of intermedial forms that combine elements of both media, such as the film still, the film photonovel, and the photofilm. These hybrid forms were long neglected critically because they were considered marginal forms of paratextuality or deviations from medium specificity—the idea that a medium must be deployed according to its own specific capacities compared to other media.[1]

The broader intermediality between photography and film takes many forms: from the invention of cinema through photographic technologies to the creation of digital media forms that integrate film and photography, such as the webdocumentary; and also on the level of media practice, from the incorporation of photographs into film to the mutual influence between filmmakers and photographers.[2] For example, Magnum Photos, the world's most prestigious photo agency, has long recognized, innovated, and exploited the aesthetic, political, and commercial possibilities of such intermedial relations between photography and film. From its earliest years in the late 1940s, co-founder Robert Capa nurtured his Hollywood connections to fiscally support the agency through exclusive access to film sets, subsequently elevating behind-the-scenes film stills with the aesthetic prestige of photojournalistic modernism.[3] Since the late 1980s, the agency has undertaken a variety of initiatives around its photographers' relationship to cinema, including documentaries about the agency, a program of short films by its photographers, archive-driven publications on its film work, an exhibition on cinema's inspiration for its photographers, and a series of web documentaries.[4]

Much of the scholarship on the various intermedial relations between photography and film asserts that they challenge dominant conceptions of both media since their intermediality inevitably generates some form of critical self-reflexivity, which challenges the orthodoxies of medium specificity. As David Green summarizes, "each becomes open to critique and analysis by subjecting it to terms of reference drawn from the other."[5] For many contemporary filmmakers and artists, photographic

A Medium Seen Otherwise. Roger Hallas, Oxford University Press. © Oxford University Press 2023.
DOI: 10.1093/oso/9780190057763.003.0001

stillness becomes a means to rupture conventional conceptions of cinematic time and space, while cinematic qualities such as sequence and motion engender strategies to critically interrogate our ideas of photographic time.

As a "research axis" for diverse theoretical, historical, and interpretative inquiries rather than an all-encompassing theory of media, intermediality emerged out of European literary theory, media studies, and philosophy during the 1990s, arriving in Anglo-American film studies in the 2010s.[6] While it draws from and engages with scholarship on adaptation, intertextuality, hybridity, transmediality, remediation, and multimediality, intermedial studies not only emphasizes the imperative to move beyond studying media as "isolated monads," it also calls for the recognition of *both* the similarities and differences *between* media.[7] As Lars Elleström notes, "intermediality must be understood as a bridge between media differences that is founded on medial similarities."[8] The relationship between film and photography favors such an intermedial approach due to what Marion Schmid has aptly called photography's "umbilical relationship" to film.[9] The individual film frame, or photogram, is a still photographic image which dissolves into the virtual image of the projected motion picture. Moreover, as lens-based media, film and photography share fundamental material and perceptual aspects, such as the frame, depth of field, and indexicality. Film historiography since the late 1980s has complicated the historical narrative of cinema's birth from photography by situating the emergence of cinema in relation to a wide range of non-photographic technologies, including the magic lantern, the panorama, theatrical melodrama, the museum, the train, optical toys, the gramophone, and the shop window.[10] Yet film retains a crucial intermedial relation to photography, as demonstrated by the abundance of scholarship to emerge on the topic in the twenty-first century, precisely at the historical moment when the future of cinema came into question.[11] As David Campany has observed, in gradually losing its stable mode of collective viewing on a large screen, film in the post-cinematic age moves closer to the dispersed condition of photography, which has always been distributed over a multitude of material forms, including books, reports, albums, magazines, postcards, posters, murals, exhibitions, and archives.[12]

Film and photography have long held complex intermedial relations around the concept and practice of documentary. Coined in the early nineteenth century, the adjective "documentary" drew from the eighteenth-century meaning of "document" as something written that provides evidence or information.[13] As Brian Winston points out, film carried over the evidentiary assumptions established early on around photography as a document: "The photograph was received, from the beginning, as a document and therefore as evidence. This evidentiary status was passed to the cinematograph and is the source of the ideological power of documentary film" (14). When John Grierson transformed the adjective into a noun to describe an emergent mode of non-fiction cinema imbued with strong narrative and rhetorical effects, he coined his now legendary, but paradoxical, definition of documentary as "the creative treatment of actuality" (14). As documentary became a transmedial practice in the 1930s extending from film and photography into theater and literature in Europe and the United States, its dialectical tensions proliferated beyond actuality/creativity to include the related tensions between objective/subjective, machine/human, and politics/aesthetics.[14] Although photographs were incorporated into documentary theater and literature of the 1930s, it was not until the postwar period when documentary film began to make use of photographs. Such intermedial incorporation engendered opportunities for the creative treatment of photographs in film, potentially opening up a different lens on our understanding of each medium. Indeed, Philippe Dubois contends that "the best *lens on* photography" will be found beyond photography: "to grasp something of photography we must enter through the door of cinema (though it may end up being the opposite)."[15]

A Medium Seen Otherwise examines the innovative incorporation of photography into documentary film, attending to the various ways in which this specific manifestation of intermediality permits us to see both photography and documentary film otherwise. I use the adverb "otherwise" deliberately here for the implications of its multiple meanings. It does not merely denote "in a different way," but also "in other respects" or "apart from that," which emphatically positions difference in relation to similarity. Thus, while the incorporation of photography into documentary film engenders new perspectives on both, these emerge from the complex play of similarity, as well as difference, between film and photography. For instance, the shared reliance on framing and composition through a camera lens permits documentary film to perform what I call an aesthetic mimicry of photographers' distinctive ways of capturing the world, which can facilitate critical perspectives on their practices. The third meaning of otherwise also resonates here: "in circumstances different from those present or considered." To place photography within documentary film can create some unique dynamics that are neither present nor considered outside of their intermedial juncture. For example, editing together photographic images with film footage in which movement is absent or barely perceptible can generate an uncanny temporal ambiguity, potentially serving several rhetorical purposes.

In this book, I therefore do not aim to reinforce old arguments about medium specificity in relation to film or photography, for, as much scholarship of the past several decades has demonstrated, both media have long been thoroughly intermedial, that is to say, imbricated in one another discursively, institutionally, and materially. Moreover, neither film nor photography can be defined through a singular ontology of medium specificity as each medium has existed in diverse manifestations. What interests me most in this project is the *specificity* of the intermedial encounter between film and photography when the latter is incorporated into documentary film.

Since the technological foundation of cinema in the photogram must be concealed from the viewer for the film medium's illusory power to be manifested, the presence of photographs and their stillness within films can often markedly shift or disrupt the film viewer's experience. As Garrett Stewart contends, "In roving past or fixating upon photographs, cinema undergoes—which is to say stages—a pregnant suspension. The motion picture stalls upon a glimpse of its own origin and negation at once."[16] In such moments, cinema is snagged by the eruption of its "specular unconscious" (1).

Indeed, some of the major works of Structural Film within North American avant-garde cinema of the late 1960s and early 1970s, such as Michael Snow's *Wavelength* (1967), Morgan Fisher's *Production Stills* (1970), and Hollis Frampton's *nostalgia* (1971), center around the presentation of photographs precisely for what such disruption can illuminate about the material and perceptual foundations of film as a medium.

The incorporation of photographs within narrative cinema and documentary films tends to be more episodic: moments in a scene or short sequences within a larger narrative or rhetorical flow. For Raymond Bellour, the appearance of the photograph in narrative cinema establishes the possibility for the film spectator to become "pensive": "The photo subtracts me from the fiction of the cinema, even if it forms part of the film, even if it adds to it. Creating a distance, another time, the photograph permits me to reflect on cinema."[17] If the presence of photography in narrative cinema has generated significant scholarly consideration, its appearance in documentary film has attracted considerably less attention.[18] Does photography thus cause more or less disturbance within the viewing experience of documentary film? A brief comparison of the opening moments of Michael Haneke's narrative feature *Code Unknown* (2000) and Yance Ford's documentary *Strong Island* (2017) will allow me to consider this question, specifically in relation to the impact of the photographs on narrative and rhetorical address within the films, as well as how narrative and documentary film differently reframe the significance of photographs displaced from their original contexts of production and circulation.

Early in *Code Unknown*, documentary photographs interrupt the fictional diegesis. At the end of a searing, eight-minute-long take that moves back and forth along a Parisian street, Amadou (Ona Lu Yenke), a young Frenchman of African descent, is arrested after trying to remonstrate Jean (Alexandre Hamidi), a white teenager from the country, for throwing his trash at a Romanian pan handler (Luminita Gheorghiu). Following a cut to black, a series of sixteen color documentary photographs from a war zone appear in full frame as a male voiceover reads what sounds like a fragment of a letter to his partner, which describes his experiences in Kosovo; he then confirms his return to Paris and apologizes for his behavior before leaving on assignment (Video 0.1 ▶) (Figure 0.1). The fragmentary information of the correspondence allows us to deduce that the photographer on the voiceover is Georges (Thierry Neuvic), Jean's older brother and the boyfriend of Anne (Juliette Binoche), who has tried to help Jean in the previous scene. The photographs appear to be real photojournalistic images that capture the wrenching trauma of war and genocide in the Balkans: corpse-strewn landscapes, distraught grieving relatives, and injured civilians caught in the line of fire. For audiences at the time of the film's original release, the visual and thematic specificities of these Balkan war photographs would have been immediately familiar as contemporary news images. Many of the photographs show subjects with plaintive, pleading looks at the camera or gesturing for aid to someone beyond the frame. After this sequence of still images, the film cuts back to the flow of the fictional narrative.

I didn't know what to say.

Figure 0.1 Photojournalist Georges (Thierry Neuvic) reads a letter to Anne (Juliette Binoche) over a series of war photographs from Kosovo in *Code Unknown* (Michael Haneke, 2000).

The photographic sequence jars for several reasons. First, the narrative flow of the moving image has been stilled by photographic images. Moreover, movement is doubly arrested since many of the photographs contain urgent actions, such as carrying wounded bodies or frantic gestures for assistance, that have been frozen by the photojournalist's camera. The rapid movement of the editing from one shot/photograph to the next contrasts with both the photographs' arrested movement and the previous scene's spatio-temporal integrity within the long take. Second, the obvious nonfictional status of the images rips us from the fictional diegesis of the film, despite the voiceover that is situated in that world, albeit through epistolary mediation. Presented in full frame, the photographs literally have no place in the diegesis. We can infer from the voiceover that these are Georges' photographs, partially suturing the rupture of the real into the fiction, but the film does not situate them in relation to any character who could be looking at them. Georges' epistolary voiceover may imply that Anne is looking at them as she reads his letter, but the film never confirms this visually, nor aurally.[19] The images address us directly as if we are watching a photographic slide show. Even if we do not recognize the photographs as those of the renowned French war photographer Luc Delahaye taken in Bosnia-Herzogovina during the Balkan Wars of the early 1990s, our perception of their documentary status complicates their incorporation into the fictional narrative.[20]

Haneke deploys the disjuncture between stillness and motion, and fiction and documentary, as a narrational strategy of modernist art cinema to amplify the ethical frame of the film. If the multi-character, fictional narrative of *Code Unknown* explores the ethical dimensions of everyday encounters in a multicultural European city, then the rupture of the fictional diegesis by Delahaye's photographs confronts us with the question of the ethical responsibility toward the other in contemporary Europe far more directly, if only momentarily, than the analog of fictional narrative. But in addressing viewers directly, such a rupture pushes them to contemplate the world beyond the fictionality of the diegesis, which can just as easily lead to a greater attention to the fictional construction of the narrative as it can to a heightened ethical charge of the real within the film.

Photographs also appear early in *Strong Island*, Yance Ford's first-person documentary about the 1992 murder of his brother, William Ford, and the deep histories of structural racism that led to his murder case never going to trial. The documentary opens with three separate conversations framed in different ways: an observational scene records Ford's telephone conversation with the former prosecutor who refuses to discuss why William's murder never went to trial, a talking head interview with William's mother Barbara in her kitchen recalls her initial belief after the funeral that justice would be served for her slain son, and a direct-address to the camera by Yance in extreme close-up outlines his fundamental goal for the film: he wants to know all the reasons why the case never made it out of the grand jury while refusing "to accept that someone else gets to say who William was." After the title credit, Barbara's talking-head narration of their family history is interwoven with shots of Yance's hands carefully placing various family snapshots on a neutral white surface (Video 0.2 ▶) (Figure 0.2).

To suture talking-head testimony with family photographs (or home movies) through sound bridge transitions to voiceover narration has become an extremely common narrational device in documentary film since the 1970s. Such shifts from moving to still images are entirely naturalized within the documentary viewing

Figure 0.2 Director Yance Ford carefully places family photographs in front of the camera in *Strong Island* (2017).

experience for several reasons. Documentary filmmakers often animate these images by panning across and zooming in and out of the photograph to immerse the viewer into the still image, to generate emotional intensification of voiceover testimony, or to literalize the cognitive movement of memory. But more fundamentally, this shift fails to automatically cause cognitive disruption because documentary film relies on what Bill Nichols calls "evidentiary editing" rather than the spatial and temporal relations that structure narrative film editing: "a documentary film can sustain far more gaps, fissures, cracks, and jumps in the visual appearance of its world even though it represents the familiar, historical world."[21] Moreover, Nichols contends that this "intermittent representation of people and places" can be seen as one of documentary film's distinguishing characteristics (19). In fact, this quality of incorporating diverse sources points to documentary's profound tendency toward both intertextuality and intermediality. The possible discontinuities across the visual track apply not only to the spatial and temporal relations across diverse footage, but also between other indices of difference in the film's presentation of evidence, such as new footage/found footage, color/monochrome, film/video, analog/digital, live-action/animation, indexical/non-indexical, text/image, and still/moving. Documentary film prioritizes rhetorical over narrative continuity, in which the spoken word of the soundtrack plays a particularly important role in the rhetorical integration of diverse sources of visual evidence. As Nichols notes, "Arguments require a logic that words are able to bear far more easily than images" (21). Indeed, photographs only become evidence of something through their entry into discourse.

Visual evidence in a documentary film is simultaneously representational and presentational: it lays claims to represent the historical world (primarily through indexical images), but it is also marshalled and presented as evidence for an argument to the documentary's viewer, who oscillates "between a recognition of historical reality and the recognition of an argument about it" (28). Some forms of visual evidence, such as observational film footage, are more regularly naturalized as representational (unobtrusively documenting a profilmic reality). Photographs, on the other hand, retain a stronger trace of their presentational status within documentary film because the viewer recognizes them as the incorporation of a different medium, one marked by stillness and muteness. Through these characteristics they always bear the stamp of external evidence—images produced elsewhere, at other times, and for other purposes. Even when filmmakers, such as Ken Burns, attempt to render photographs more cinematic—and thus more representational—through the application of sound effects and camera movement across the still image, these techniques only partially mask photography's medial difference. The viewer's recognition of that difference is not marked by the shock or disruption that they experience with fictional narrative cinema, but they do nevertheless register its variance cognitively.

In this sense, the incorporation of photographs into documentary film generates a viewer experience similar to what Jaimie Baron has called "the archive effect."[22] In resituating "the archival document" as "an *experience of reception* rather than an indication of official sanction or storage location," Baron argues:

> This reformulation of archival footage and other indexical archival documents as a *relationship* produced between particular elements of a film and the film's viewer allows us to account not only for emergent types of archives and the diverse documents held within them but also for the ways in which certain documents from the past—whether found in an official archive, a family basement, or online—may be imbued by the viewer with various evidentiary values as they are appropriated and repurposed in new films. By looking at the ways in which found audiovisual documents function within the films that appropriate them and at the various relationships established between the viewer of these films and the documents mobilized within them, we may come closer to an understanding of how these films generate particular conceptions of the past and, ultimately, of history itself. (7–8, emphasis in original)

With very few exceptions, documentaries incorporate photographs as found evidence, even when the photographs have been taken by the filmmakers themselves. They stimulate a doubled mode of viewing that is simultaneously cinematic and photographic. Whereas Baron is primarily concerned with the incorporation of archival moving images into documentary and experimental films and videos, my concern in this book is specifically engaged with the intermedial relations between film and photography. Thus, in addition to examining how such intermediality enables particular understandings of historical reality within documentary film, I am primarily engaged with exploring how it permits us to see photography, and also documentary film, through a different lens. This is not merely a matter of medial reflexivity, but also political reflexivity.[23]

In contrast to Ken Burns's cinematic rendering of photographs, Yance Ford foregrounds the act of presenting photographs as evidence in *Strong Island* as his hands carefully arrange the family snapshots on a blank white surface. These overhead shots are intercut with shallow-focus, low-angle close-ups of Ford's face looking down and his hands sorting through bundles of photographs. The photographs become visual objects in the mise-en-scène of a profilmic reality in the present, albeit a relatively abstract one—visually reminiscent of Elizaveta Svilova's editing room scenes in Dziga Vertov's *Man with a Movie Camera* (1929). Like Svilova, Ford's hands acknowledge the act of assemblage in the film's construction, yet his haptic gestures exceed cinematic self-reflexivity, for they also express an affective relation to the snapshots as cherished photographic objects. There is a protective, deliberative tenderness to the way in which his hands position each family photograph within the frame—these are not just images that mean, but objects that matter. Tory Jeffay reads Ford's presentation of the photographs as a strategy of Black annotation and redaction to protect against the "invasive visibility" of the documentary camera that has historically spectacularized Black bodies: "Ford [...] allows us to see the image, but only in relation to himself, his body, his gaze."[24] By emphasizing the materiality of the photographs, *Strong Island* exceeds their conventional incorporation into documentary film as visual evidence authenticated by their photographic indexicality. The documentary recognizes that the relations photography engenders *in* the world through its materiality are as significant as the visual representation *of* the world that it generates in photographic images. As this book will show, Ford's film is not alone in this regard.

Photography's technological reproducibility has lent it to intermedial incorporation into other media since its earliest days with the publication of William Henry Fox Talbot's book *The Pencil of Nature* (1844), which contained twenty-four photographs. The development and refinement of halftone printing brought about a technological revolution in the intermedial distribution of photography by the end of the century, as it spread to newspapers, magazines, posters, and other print media. By the early twentieth century, the rise of the illustrated press and the photobook enabled new modes of experiencing photography through seriality, montage, word-image relations, and graphic design. Given the intensive intermedial preoccupations of the European avant-garde in the 1920s, film played a significant role in this visual reimagination of the printed page as artists, graphic designers, and photographers drew inspiration from the relativity of time, space, and movement in cinema, perhaps most extensively articulated by László Moholy-Nagy in his book *Painting, Photography, Film* (1925).[25]

Sequence and arrangement within and across pages fomented new possibilities for photographic narrative and rhetoric, creating a "para-cinema of the page."[26] As David Campany notes, "Moving images transformed the nature of the photographic image, turning its stillness into *arrestedness*," an instantaneity that would later be most famously articulated by Henri Cartier Bresson as "the decisive moment" (12). Photographic arrestedness appears in 1920s avant-garde films, such as *Man with the Movie Camera* and *Paris qui dort* (René Clair, 1924), not as the photograph, but as the freeze frame that suspends cinematic motion and splits time between the frozen instant within the frame and the continuing duration of the projected image. Even in Robert Siodmak and Edgar Ulmer's *People on Sunday* (1930), which includes a scene depicting an itinerant photographer at a lakeshore, freeze frames come to stand in for the photographs he is taking—a self-reflexive nod via photography to the film's capacity to capture the contingency of everyday life in late 1920s Berlin.[27] Although Campany argues that "it is difficult to imagine a freeze frame resistant to a photographic reading," the insertion of photographs into film do generate spectatorial dynamics that are distinct from freeze frames (54). The photograph exists as a physical object in the historical world beyond the film; it becomes a virtual image of a material image in a film, whereas the freeze frame remains a particular manifestation of the virtual film image. Thus, the intermedial temporality of the filmed photograph incorporates not only the arrested moment in the photographic image (Roland Barthes' "that-has-been") and the duration of the projected film, but also the temporalities of the photograph's profilmic presence before the film camera and its material history as an object.[28] The intermedial incorporation of photography into documentary film therefore multiplies the already complex temporality of each medium as it oscillates between presentational and representational modes. This tension between the photograph as object and as image allows it to transcend its normative documentary function as mere indexical evidence or visual illustration.

To historicize some of the key stylistic tropes that developed around this particular form of intermediality, I devote some of the first three chapters to films from the mid-twentieth century when photography began to appear in and become the subject of documentary films. However, this book is not intended as a comprehensive history of photography's incorporation into documentary film, nor do I attempt to address all types of photography. My primary interest lies in examining how documentary and vernacular forms of photography are taken up by documentary films.[29] Such films may both enact and illuminate the passage of photography from one discursive frame to another. My focus remains on late twentieth century and early twenty-first century documentaries that incorporate such photography in a substantive way, because either they are about the medium itself or their use of photography is fundamental to their historical or political project. Thus, they fall primarily into the subgenres of the political, historical, and art documentary.

I attend to this period for several reasons. The significant turn to the reflexive and performative modes of documentary in the 1980s and beyond foregrounded the ideological interrogation of documentary representation itself, which encouraged inventive engagements with photography in documentary film, particularly in relation to the political dimensions of affect. At the same time, photojournalists were experiencing a fundamental transformation of their media ecology as the illustrated press waned in face of the challenges first embodied by the twenty-four-hour cable news cycle and later by the Internet. Just as photojournalists and documentary photographers increasingly turned to gallery exhibition at a moment when the global art world was enthralled with the category of the documentary, they also recognized the documentary feature film as a viable platform to widen the distribution and public visibility of their work. On the institutional level, this period saw the establishment of new television channels, such as Britain's Channel Four and the Franco-German collaboration Arte, which carried major mandates for developing innovative arts television (including significant attention to photography). Moreover, the proliferation of cable and satellite television, and eventually streaming platforms, increased the demand for diversified documentary content for niche markets, such as arts programming.

Indeed, documentaries about photography have primarily been produced and distributed as art documentaries, with photographer profiles constituting the most prolific and popular subgenre. Even documentaries about photographic technologies, such as the three films about Polaroid photography (*Time Zero: The Last Year of Polaroid Film* [Grant Hamilton, 2012], *Instant Dreams* [Willem Baptist, 2017], and *An Impossible Project* [Jens Meurer, 2020]), commonly focus on the aesthetic uses of technology. While the vast majority of photography documentaries focus on specific photographers, other subgenres of the photography documentary, aside from photographic technologies, include: a) the history of the medium (e.g., the BBC series *The*

Genius of Photography [Tim Kirby, 2007] and the Arte series *Photo* [Stan Neumann, 2011–3]); b) specific photographic histories (e.g., *Britain in Focus: A Photographic History* [Alastair Laurence, Chloe Penman, and Francis Welch, 2017] and *Through A Lens Darkly: Black Photographers and the Emergence of a People* [Thomas Allen Harris, 2014]); (c) ethnographies of photography as a social practice (e.g., *Photo Wallahs* [Judith and David MacDougall, 1992] on photography in a North Indian hill town, and *Wedding Through Camera Eyes* [Kijung Lee, 2002] on Korean wedding photography); d) photographic genres (e.g., *Everybody Street* [Cheryl Dunn, 2013] on street photography, and *Icon: Music Through the Lens* [Dick Curruthers, 2021] on music photography); and e) iconic photographs (e.g., *Chevolution* [Trisha Ziff, 2008] on the Korda photograph of Che Guevara, and *El Dia Que Me Quieras* [*The Day You'll Love Me*, Leandro Katz, 1998] on Che's deathbed photograph).[30] As I have argued in *Documenting the Visual Arts*, art documentaries have received scant scholarly attention in either documentary studies or art history, both of which treat them as largely second-order representations.[31] Concerned that they hew too close to the merely panegyric, documentary studies has shown greater interest in films and television programs that are seen to be more directly addressing the social and the political, whereas art history methodologically prioritizes proximity to its object of study, namely the original work of art. Yet, it is precisely the intermediality of such documentaries that allows them to do interesting and innovative things.

Art documentaries present photographs as evidence of aesthetic practice for the viewer to contemplate and judge, usually in full frame to maintain the aesthetic integrity of the image. If close-ups and camera movement are employed to isolate a detail, they function as much to highlight and interpret an aesthetic element of the presented photograph as to immerse the viewer into the represented world. The predominantly representational moments in photography documentaries observe the production, circulation, and display of photographs, recognizing photography as a social practice as much as an aesthetic medium. By shifting from photographs as the representation of the world to the representation of photographic practices within the world, such scenes reorient attention from the photographic image to photography as an event and the photograph as a physical object with its own material history. Both moves recenter the political and social dynamics of photography within the art documentary. Political and historical documentaries that make extensive use of photography, such as Rithy Panh's *S21: The Khmer Rouge Killing Machine* (2003), are also often concerned with what can be done with photographs as much as they are with deploying them as indexical evidence for the viewer. Through its capacity to record in duration and dynamic space the social actions and relations engendered by photography, documentary film permits us to see the medium in a new light that reflects two recent, and interrelated, methodological turns within photography studies: toward the material life of photographic objects and the event of photography.

Over the last two decades, a materialist turn in photography studies undertaken by visual anthropologists and photographic historians, such as Elizabeth Edwards, Christopher Pinney, Elspeth Brown, Thy Pu, and Geoffrey Batchen, has insisted that photographs are objects as much as they are images.[32] To even experience them as forms of disembodied vision or as visual signs, we must simultaneously encounter their very materiality as objects, whether that be the illuminated screen of a mobile phone that instantaneously "opens up" a digital photograph with the touch of a finger, a family snapshot that is tenderly held in the hand as a memory it provokes is verbalized, or a photo essay in a news magazine that is distractedly scanned as fingers leaf through its pages at a rapid pace. As Batchen notes, the daguerreotype, one of the earliest photographic technologies, foregrounds this very "thingness of the visual." For its image to be seen, the daguerreotype must be angled at forty-five degrees: "Hand and eye must work as one if a daguerreotype is to be brought into visibility, the look of the image comes only with the feel for its materiality."[33]

Photographic materiality manifests itself in two principal ways, what Elizabeth Edwards and Janice Hart call "the plasticity of the image" and "the presentational form."[34] In analog photography, the plasticity of the image includes the chemistry of the photosensitive surface, the paper on which the image is printed, and any visual embellishments applied to the visual surface. Given the ubiquity of digital photography within contemporary screen cultures, its plasticity primarily resides in electronic illumination, the heat and vibration generated by the computer drive, and the imperceptible mobility of the rescanning signal. For Edwards and Hart, presentational forms refer to the physical objects through which photographs are experienced, such as *cartes de visite*, cabinet cards, albums, mounts, and frames. Digital convergence bifurcates the presentational forms of digital photography between software applications (such as Instagram, Twitter, and Photos) and the hardware devices (such as mobile phones, laptops, and tablets) in which they are embedded. The intersection of visual content and presentational forms shapes our behavior toward and treatment of photographs, what Edwards calls "appropriateness."[35] For instance, whereas a framed photograph of a deceased family member may be positioned in a privileged place in the home, adorned with flowers and candles, and picked up by its beholder, an art photograph will be printed and framed at a larger scale, hung on a wall in isolation from other objects, and viewed at an appropriate contemplative distance. Yet, that same art photograph reproduced as an exhibition postcard could also be randomly attached to a refrigerator door as a memento of a gallery visit. As Margaret Olin contends, "The fact that a photograph, once taken, can become a visual presence in our world does not only mean that we look at photographs. We also are *with* photographs; and we spend time in their presence."[36] The sense of presence prompts us to interact with them as social objects.

Examining presentational forms thus encourages us to attend to what people do with photographs and to how photographs generate affect, meaning, and value through the social relations engaged, and also initiated, through their circulation and display. Although the visual remains the primary sense mobilized in the apprehension of photographic objects, other senses, particularly hearing and touch, also play significant roles. Family photo albums, for example, produce meaning and affect through their incitement to the oral narration of familial histories.[37] If it is the visual content that initiates engagement with a photograph, argues Edwards, then "it is touch, voice, gesture, sound, and even smell, which activate the networks between people and the photographic thing."[38] The observational capacity of film to document in duration and dynamic space, as well as in sound and image, render it particularly well suited to recording and preserving such multisensory social behavior around photographic objects. Similarly, this capacity lends film to a fuller documentation of the event of photography.

In her reconceptualization of photography as event, Ariella Azoulay challenges a pervasive theoretical assumption about the medium, namely that the photographic frame aligns photographer, camera, photograph, and viewer through its construction of a gaze that fuses visual and ideological perspective. Azoulay contends that this conception places photography "at the service of two masters": the photographer and the photograph.[39] The medium is dependent on the existence of the photograph, which is the end goal of the photographer's activity: "Thus, for approximately 150 years, photography was conceptualized from the perspective of the individual positioned behind the lens—the one who can see the world, shapes it into a photograph of his own creation, and displays it to others" (12). Although Roland Barthes' celebrated notion of the punctum, "a kind of residue neglected by the photographer" (12), contested the hegemony of the photographer, the punctum remains for Barthes an affective experience for the viewer. Azoulay, however, insists on a political ontology for photography: "What characterizes the new relations that emerge between people through the mediation of photography?" (13).

Rather than treat the camera and the photograph as tools for mediating the photographer's aesthetic and ideological vision, Azoulay insists that they enable photography as "a special form of encounter between participants where none of them possesses a sovereign status" (17), which is to say that no one party involved in such an encounter has sole control over its meaning. By understanding the photograph as the trace of such an encounter, Azoulay moves beyond what she deems the "dead-end discussion" of "inside and outside," which revolve around "those standing in front of the camera and behind it at the moment the photograph is taken, and inside and outside the frame at the moment the photograph is viewed."[40] This inside/outside model posits a separation of the photographer and the viewer from the world, objectifying it into an image in the viewfinder and the subsequent photograph. Azoulay rejects this fixity to what is potentially visible within the photograph, which reduces the viewer to pursuing an act of aesthetic judgment, to determine if "the photograph succeeds in arousing a desired effect or experience."[41] By making the photographer solely responsible for both the photograph and how it represents the photographed, the dominant conceptualization of photography spares the viewer from any responsibility toward what can be seen in the photograph.

Azoulay advocates for a shift from "looking at" photographs to "watching" them (14). Acknowledging the association of watching with moving images, she wants to reinscribe duration and movement into the interpretation of photographs. If looking at a photograph entails the immediate and exhaustive viewing of a stable, stationary object that is seen in its entirety on first look, then watching a photograph involves the prolonged and careful scanning of the image in order "to reconstruct the photographic situation, the encounter that took place 'there'" (171). It is to reveal the photograph as "a montage of the heterogeneous viewpoints of those who participated in the act of photography" (383). To reconstruct the photographic situation from the photograph is not an act of aesthetic appreciation but a civic skill, "a tool of a struggle or an obligation to others to struggle against injuries inflicted on those others, citizen and non-citizen alike—others who are governed along with the spectators" (14). Both the camera and the photograph play significant roles as objects around which this political ontology of photography as a "human being-with-others" takes place.[42] Photography is thus, for Azoulay, a space of political relations and a practice of citizenship beyond the ruling power of the state.

Azoulay makes a distinction between the photographed event (that which the photographer wishes to capture in the frame) and the event of photography, which entails all the relations initiated first by the presence of the camera and second by the existence of the photograph produced by it.[43] Unlike the photographed event, the event of photography is open-ended, always subject to new potential relations formed by the next spectatorial encounter with the photograph. Documentary film is particularly apt for examining the event of photography because the mobility and duration inscribed in the act of recording by the film camera produces a fuller documentation of the relations created by the presence of the photographic camera or that of the photograph it generates. Moreover, the capacities of film and sound editing permit documentary film to explore those relations across the spatio-temporal differences between those two presences (of the camera and the photograph). Put simply, the relativity of time and space in film enable it to better illuminate the relations among the photographer, the camera, the photographed, the photograph, and the viewer.

Documentary film has provided photographers with a medium that permits them to interrogate the dynamics of their practice in potentially new ways, particularly in relation to photographic materiality and the event of photography. The documentary films of Magnum photographer Susan Meiselas offer a prime example. Meiselas turned to filmmaking in the mid-1980s to work through continuing questions and concerns she had about the photographs she took of the Sandinista Revolution in Nicaragua. Although Meiselas had been successful in placing her photographs of the revolution internationally in high-profile publications, she grew dissatisfied with what she considered the decontextualizing and fragmenting frameworks of the news press. Her 1981 photobook *Nicaragua, June 1978–July 1979* was an attempt to "gather them back, make sense of them and give them coherence—as well as permanence."[44] However, Martha Rosler famously criticized the book for what she claimed to be multiple forms of decontextualization: the separation of the captions from the photographic plates, the exoticizing use of color, and the construction of a completed linear narrative of revolution.[45] Although Meiselas began her response to this critique and her own professional quandaries through a gallery installation, *Meditations* (1982), which compared the different discursive frameworks in which her photographs had been employed, it was in documentary filmmaking that she was able to more fully engage these challenges. Meiselas collaborated on three documentaries: *Voyages* (1985), an essay film made with Marc Karlin for UK's Channel Four; *Pictures from a Revolution* (1991), a documentary feature made with Alfred Guzzetti and Richard P. Rogers about her return to Nicaragua a decade after the revolution; and *Reframing History* (2006), a twelve-minute short film made with Guzzetti about the public installation of her photographs in Nicaragua on the twenty-fifth anniversary of the revolution. *Voyages* and *Pictures from a Revolution* exemplify the two principal approaches to seeing photography otherwise through documentary film. Whereas one emphasizes a presentational address through its placement of the photographic image within an abstract cinematic time and space, the other prioritizes a representational address in the film camera's observation of profilmic interactions with photographic objects and cameras.

    Voyages presents the photographs from Meiselas's photobook suspended in an abstract three-dimensional black space as the camera moves across and between them (Video 0.3 ⏵) (Figure 0.3). Although the mise-en-scène positions the photographs as objects in space, its abstract quality diminishes our perception of their actual materiality. Contrary to the immersive camera movement of Ken Burns, Karlin's camera

Figure 0.3 The camera moves through an abstract three-dimensional space filled with Susan Meiselas's photographs from Nicaragua in *Voyages* (Susan Meiselas and Marc Karlin, 1985).

embodies a roving, restless, and irregular movement across the surface of the images (often with hairpin turns). Such motion denies the revelation of the photograph's full frame and frequently glides across the borders between two photographs. This fragmentation of the image suspends the photographer's framing of the event, allowing us an opportunity to carefully "watch" the photograph for other gazes inscribed within in it, which escape being subsumed into the photographer's gaze as we hardly ever see the full frame of the photograph. Clearly inspired by Chris Marker's *Sans Soleil* (1982), Karlin's voiceover reads a letter from Meiselas reflecting upon the ethical and political quandaries she felt about her photographic practice in Nicaragua, particularly her relationship to the world she is photographing. Occasionally Karlin switches to summarizing her thoughts in the third person. The epistolary mode and switches in pronoun here emphasize the question of relationality, which Meiselas consistently reinforces in her letter: "Sometimes, I think that a photograph is instead of a relationship, and yet, a photograph is a relationship." The interaction between the voiceover and the movement across images in abstract space posit multiple possible relationships. Meiselas has suggested that it simulates the photographer's relation to the world they are documenting: "we are repeating the feeling of things moving, almost like you are moving in space and time as other things are moving around you and you freeze the moment. We are trying to give a feeling of just that—you see a fraction of something and then you make a frame, you have eliminated a number of things."[46] But we may also read this movement through an abstract space of photographs as the space of memory (visualizing Meiselas's recollection) or even on a more abstract level as the realm of images, which Meiselas invokes in her reflections: "If you go to Nicaragua, like me, you may cling onto images which are already pictures inside your own head. A collection of all the thousands of images you've already seen. You can't help it, despite your better instincts." *Voyages* thus demonstrates the rich possibilities to watch photography (in Azoulay's sense) from combining an aesthetically complex presentation of photographs in an abstract cinematic space with a multifaceted voiceover.

Taking an altogether more observational (and therefore representational) approach, *Pictures from a Revolution* follows Meiselas's search to find the photographic subjects from her book a decade later to hear about their perspectives on the photographic encounter and their lives in the intervening years. She thus transforms her photobook from a documentary account of the revolutionary past into a guide for navigating the present as she uses it to direct her journey around the country. It also becomes an identification manual as she asks local people in the street to help identify the names of those depicted in the photographs, which she scribbles on the page margins of the dog-eared photobook. At each such encounter with the photographic object, touch, gesture, and voice elaborate the visual apprehension of the image with affective responses and the articulation of memory (Video 0.4 ▶) (Figure 0.4). The production of the film both instigates and documents new encounters with the photographs, thus perpetuating and extending the event of photography. These filmed conversations around the physical object of the photobook not only enhance our capacity to "watch" the photograph, in Azoulay's sense of reconstructing the relations

Figure 0.4 Susan Meiselas asks a Nicaraguan woman to recount her experience of the moment when the photograph was taken in *Pictures of a Revolution* (Susan Meiselas, Alfred Guzzetti, and Richard P. Rogers, 1991).

engendered by its taking, but they also document how photographs can incite oral narration well beyond that of the historical moment represented in the image (as the photograph's subjects narrate their subsequent lives in relation to the revolution). The embalmed dynamism of revolutionary action in the photographs causes melancholy in many of the people Meiselas interviews as they reflect upon the continuation of struggle and suffering through the war against the US-backed Contras, raising the success or the end of the revolution as a question.

If, as Edwards contends, "photographs allow histories or stories to emerge in socially interactive ways that would not have emerged in that particular figuration if the photograph had not existed," then documentary films like *Pictures from a Revolution* are able to extend the event of photography by preserving and disseminating these ephemeral encounters.[47] Meiselas further exploited the intermedial capacities of film to augment her photography when Aperture published a new edition of *Nicaragua* in 2008 with a DVD copy of the documentary, while the 2016 edition included links to a mobile app that allowed readers to scan photographs in the book to view related clips from *Pictures from a Revolution* and *Reframing History*. My brief discussion of Meiselas's films points to just some of the ways in which the formal aspects of documentary film, including profilmic observation, voiceover, and camera movement over static images, enable us to see photography otherwise, as the following chapters will elaborate. Although both films are structured around the reflections of the photographer on her practices, their differing presentational and representational strategies allow contemplation of both the various gazes that construct the event of photography and the multisensory interactions enacted around photographs as social objects. In this regard, Meiselas's films exemplify one of the principal arguments of this book—documentary film can elucidate the materiality and event of photography, subtly decentering both the photographer and the photographic image, even when the latter are the ostensible subjects of the film.

I have organized the chapters of the book around how documentary films have engaged key aspects of photography: the photographic image, the photograph as object, the photographer, the photo archive, and the photographic genre of the portrait.[48] Beginning in the mid-twentieth century, Chapter 1 analyzes the roles of cinematography and editing in documentary film's incorporation of photographic images as historical evidence. Historical documentaries of the 1950s established contrastive strategies for integrating photographic images, which would lay the foundations for two distinct traditions within postwar documentary film practice: a disjunctive one that plays with the tension between the cinematic and the photographic, and an integrative one that attempts to render the photographic image more cinematic. While the modernism of the disjunctive strategy would find its fullest manifestation in the 1960s photofilm, the narrative immersion of the integrative strategy was enhanced and popularized in the 1990s by the documentaries of Ken Burns. Digital special effects have generated new visual strategies for rendering photographs more cinematic, but they can also paradoxically produce uncanny effects that draw greater attention to the visual artifice of the digitally altered photograph.

Chapter 2 examines how photographic materiality impacts the central question of the representability of violence in documentaries about war, conflict, and atrocity. The material objecthood of vernacular photographs here plays as significant a role in producing their meaning and value as the indexical quality of the images themselves. Such documentary films engage with three facets of photographic materiality. The first section analyzes three films about rediscovered photo albums made by German perpetrators during World War Two. Their emphatic "foundness" promises rare photographic evidence of genocide and atrocity, but simultaneously begets an opacity given that the oral narration central to the production of meaning for any photo album is irrecoverable in these cases. The second section turns to the physical handling of photographs as forms of social and political action in documentaries about the photography of political conflict in Northern Ireland, Chile, and Argentina. Bodily gestures toward photographic objects facilitate a range of political meanings captured by the documentary film camera, from destabilizing the public/private division to bearing witness to the disappeared by an embodied performance of habeas corpus. The final section addresses metadata as a specific component of digital photography's materiality in two documentaries that pursue the forensic investigation of human-rights violations through a digitally rendered mise-en-scène of photographs.

Chapter 3 explores how documentary film tackles the challenge of filming photographers at work. Whereas filming other types of visual artists, such as painters or sculptors, allows viewers to witness the cumulative process of the work's aesthetic creation, filming photography must address the challenge of the medium's predominant reliance on instantaneous capture (particularly in photojournalism). Since the durational quality of film actually makes it easier to miss the "decisive moment" captured by the documentary photographer's camera, photographer documentaries have long turned to imitating the photographer's aesthetic through their cinematography. The chapter analyzes films about contemporary documentary photographers that have transformed such "aesthetic mimicry" from a popularized form of aesthetic apprenticeship into diverse opportunities for opening up critical and ethical engagement with the photographer's practice, permitting new perspectives on the event of photography to emerge.

Chapter 4 continues the concern with photographic authorship from the previous chapter while also returning to issues of photographic materiality as it considers documentaries about archival recovery and discovery. As the global art world increasingly embraced photography and recognized it as a legitimate art commodity in the late twentieth century, curators and dealers were eager to discover new photographic artists in the dispersed, non-institutional archives of vernacular photography, particularly those of commercial studio photographers. Documentaries about such archival discoveries address questions of legitimation in relation to not only the photographer but also the curator, dealer, or collector who claims to have discovered them. The photographers and their discoverers become parallel protagonists in narratives—both affirmative and critical—about commodification, ownership, exploitation, and cultural recognition. The latter half of the chapter analyzes documentaries that are committed to forms of cultural and physical restitution, films that critically challenge and reverse the art world's appropriation of amateur, studio, and press photography by returning the photographs to their original cultural contexts. Moreover, given their recognition of what gets lost within the prevailing processes of archivization, such films ultimately raise the question of how preservation might be rethought and what role documentary film may play in its reconceptualization.

The final chapter brings together the major themes of the book through a consideration of documentary film's engagement with arguably photography's most prevalent genre: the portrait. Allan Sekula has posited the history of photographic portraiture as "a shadow archive" which encompassed two dialectically opposed but mutually informing traditions of modern subjectification: the "honorific" portrait, which functioned as a method of bourgeois self-affirmation, and the "repressive" portrait, which served to categorize, pathologize, and discipline bodies within the institutions of modernity.[49] Documentary filmmakers have long faced the challenge of how to use photographic portraits from the repressive tradition to bear witness to historical trauma without merely replicating their ideological function. The films in the chapter address this quandary by tapping into a fundamental and transmedial dynamic of the visual portrait, its capacity to stimulate iconic presence (the presence-absence of its depicted subject).[50] Such presence-absence becomes the foundation for any inter-subjective encounter to occur among the photographer, the photographed subject, the filmmaker, the filmed subject, and the viewer. Ultimately, the documentaries in this chapter illuminate not only how film can document what people do with photographic portraits to bear witness, but how the virtual time and space of a documentary film can itself become the site in which such testimonial acts are performed.

The book concludes with a reflection on its central themes and briefly considers what documentary film can illuminate about the transformation of photography in the age of social media.

1
Photographic Images in Documentary Film

Documentary films only began to incorporate photographs as substantial elements after World War Two, relatively late compared to the use of other static visual forms, such as maps, drawings, and paintings. For instance, maps appear in Robert Flaherty's seminal documentary film *Nanook of the North* (1922), which situates its narrative through a map of northern Canada that begins as a static element but is then animated with the use of shading and a moving arrow. Although the film does not include any photographs, Nanook (Allakariallak) is nevertheless introduced as the film's principal character through a shot that clearly invokes the visual address of photographic portraiture, while also maintaining the durational quality of cinema: he stands relatively still in a medium shot smiling directly at the camera.[1] Unlike the map, the insertion of photographic stillness into early documentary film risked unmasking the photogram as the basis of the cinematic illusion given the technological similarities between photogram and photograph. Thus, when Dziga Vertov's *Man with a Movie Camera* (1929) and Robert Siodmak and Edgar G. Ulmer's *People on Sunday* (1930) famously expose the photogram through freeze-frames in scenes involving, respectively, a film editor and a commercial photographer, it is in a modernist pursuit of self-reflexively interrogating medium specificity—of cinema for Vertov and of photography for Siodmak and Ulmer.

The eventual appearance in documentary film of actual photographs, rather than the photograms of film frames, drew substantially from the techniques for filming paintings developed by the *film d'art* or art documentary during its "golden age" in the late 1940s and early 1950s.[2] Filmmakers such as Luciano Emmer, Henri Stork, and Alain Resnais deployed zooms, pans, close-ups, and classical *découpage* to animate and, thereby, further narrativize the paintings of Renaissance and modernist masters.[3] As Steven Jacobs notes, these films generated considerable critical debate about their potential capacity to actually generate "new *filmic* artworks," rather than merely functioning as straightforward reproductive tools for art history.[4] André Bazin engages this debate with his essay "Painting and Cinema," in which he contrasts the centripetal quality of the picture frame with the centrifugal quality of the film screen: a painting "polarizes space inwards" by masking and isolating a specific portion of reality, whereas film shows us "part of something prolonged indefinitely into the universe."[5] Bazin contends that whenever Emmer and Resnais filmed a painting without ever showing its frame, it would take on the spatial properties of cinema and

A Medium Seen Otherwise. Roger Hallas, Oxford University Press. © Oxford University Press 2023.
DOI: 10.1093/oso/9780190057763.003.0002

therefore become "part of that 'picturable' world that lies beyond it on all sides" (166). Although Bazin cites Resnais' eighteen-minute film *Van Gogh* (1948) as supporting evidence, his argument only holds true for the first half of the film. Resnais draws from Van Gogh's entire oeuvre to construct the dramatic narrative of the artist's life story. In the sections devoted to Van Gogh's time in Holland and Paris, Resnais arranges shots of the paintings and their details according to the logic of continuity editing, thus constructing an objectively coherent narrative space, albeit with static images. As Van Gogh's mental state becomes more erratic and his aesthetic more abstract and expressive in Provence and Auvers-sur-Oise, the film's editing and camera movement turn increasingly disjunctive, reflecting the artist's subjective turmoil through repetition, alternation, rapid cutting, extreme close-ups, and accelerated camera movement. Resnais' *Van Gogh* thus provides two contrasting models for the incorporation of still images into documentary film: one deployed cinematography and editing according to continuity conventions, in order to assure the viewer's smooth immersion into the historical world, whereas the other used them to foreground the autonomous expressive capacities of individual images and the potential meanings produced by their emphatic and disjunctive combination.

In this first chapter, I examine how documentary film began to incorporate photographs through these differing deployments of cinematography and editing, which would broadly parallel their use in modernist and classical narrative cinema. The first tradition, inaugurated by Resnais' *Night and Fog* (1955), would pursue a self-conscious modernist *presentation* of, and engagement with, photographs as images of the historical world, while the second, initiated by Colin Low and Wolf Koenig's *City of Gold* (1957), would treat photographs as visual *representation* for enabling spectatorial immersion within the historical world. Separated by less than two years, *Night and Fog* and *City of Gold* share several key characteristics as postwar documentary short films: the exploration of a historical event involving mass movement and the creation of unprecedented human environments, the combination of archival photographs and contemporary film footage of the historical site, and an elegiac voice-over commentary to frame and bind the images. Yet the differences between the two films are ultimately more significant since they constitute the roots of two tendencies in documentary film's dynamic incorporation of photographic images during the following decades. Although both films combine innovative cinematography and editing in their filming of photographs, Low and Koenig prioritize cinematography and Resnais editing. *City of Gold* animates photographs through its seamless camera movements over and into them as the film works to immerse its viewers into the distant past, whereas *Night and Fog* continually juxtaposes stasis and movement in the relation between shots, which draws viewers' attention to the photograph as image, as representational form, and as historical sign. Although both films bear qualities of the historical documentary and the essay film, *City of Gold* set the precedent for the historical documentary's incorporation of archival photographs, while *Night and Fog* heavily influenced the aesthetic exploitation of photography in the modernist essay film.

Sound, particularly voiceover, also plays a critical role in both of these trajectories. As a supplement to the muteness of photography, sound design in these documentaries helps situate the viewer in relation to their photographs. Yet, as with cinematography and editing, sound functions in contrastive ways in the two films. Voiceovers and music in the essay film draw attention to the presentation of an image to be viewed by the audience. Sound is thus situated outside of the image. It places the photograph within a conversation between the narrator and the viewer. Sound in historical documentary functions in a far more integrative fashion. Voice, sound effects, and music are frequently presented as though they emanate from inside the image. They function to smooth the viewer's immersion into the historical world depicted in the photograph. Although this chapter focuses primarily on cinematography and editing, sound design remains a significant concern throughout my analyses, given its role in positioning the viewer cognitively and affectively in relation to the screen image—either in representational terms that immerse and suture viewers *into* the image or in presentational terms that engage them *with* the image.

Beginning with *Night and Fog*, this chapter charts each of these two trajectories across the following decades, analyzing the essayistic photofilms of Agnès Varda and Chris Marker, and then Ken Burns's historical documentary series *The Civil War* (1990). Whereas the modernist photofilm self-consciously engages its viewers with the question of photography's representational dynamics, particularly its claim to produce visual truth, the historical documentary exemplified by Burns's series purposefully occludes the mediating aspects of photographic representation in the service of greater viewer immersion into the past. The chapter concludes by assessing the promise of digital special effects to augment such viewer immersion in twenty-first-century historical documentaries. Through an examination of the 2½D parallax effect pioneered in *The Kid Stays in the Picture* (Brett Morgen and Natalie Burstein, 2002) and its subsequent application in *Men at Lunch* (Seán Ó Cualáin, 2012), I illuminate how such digitally rendered illusions of enhanced depth can paradoxically generate greater awareness among viewers of the representational dynamics in which they find themselves while watching these documentaries.

Intermedial Ambiguity

Widely acknowledged as one of the seminal and most influential examples of the essay film, *Night and Fog* is often analyzed in terms of the oppositions that structure its aesthetic organization: color/black and white, past/present, presence/absence, stillness/movement, film/photography, cinematography/editing, sound/image, and subjective/objective.[6] The most frequently discussed aesthetic aspects of the film are the exterior and interior long-take shots of the Auschwitz and Majdanek concentration camps, which Resnais' crew captured in majestic tracking shots on Eastmancolor. Sandy Flitterman-Lewis sees them fulfilling two important functions: on the one hand, they provide the viewer with time and space to contemplate the subject of the film, and, on the other, they render the gaze of the camera self-consciously visible and, through its impression of embodied movement, also the gaze of the viewer.[7] The film's editing brings the interrogative tendencies of such essayistic movement to bear onto the rapidly cut black-and-white shots that combine photographic stills and filmed footage. Jean Cayrol's voiceover commentary consistently amplifies this skepticism about the capacity of the visual image to access the truth of the event: "The reality of these camps, despised by those who built them, and unfathomable to those who endured them—what hope do we have of truly capturing this reality?"[8]

Although the film contains only twenty-eight color shots, they each last on average about 20 seconds, whereas the average length of the 279 black-and-white shots is only 4½ seconds.[9] The stark contrast between the cinematography of the color shots (long takes and camera movement) and the editing of the black-and-white shots (short takes and abrupt cuts) reinforces the perception that this chromatic distinction embodies a dialectical opposition between past and present.[10] As Sylvie Lindeperg points out, the relatively rapid editing of the black-and-white shots permits Resnais to integrate a wide range of images: archival footage and new footage, fiction and non-fiction, film and photography, images taken within the camp system and images taken after their liberation.[11] That Night and Fog integrates still photographic images with cinematic moving images is hardly surprising given the context of the film's genesis. In 1954, Olga Wormser and Henri Michel of the Comité d'Histoire de la Deuxième Guerre Mondiale commissioned Resnais to direct an educational film based on the organization's exhibition "Resistance, Liberation, Deportation," which included many archival photographs as well as material objects from the camps. Resnais selected many photographs from the exhibition before he and his team began to search in archives in France, Poland, and the Netherlands.

Faced with a looming production deadline and denied access to important archives, such as the Imperial War Museum and French military archives, Resnais felt frustration at what he perceived to be inadequate archival resources for the film and wished they could have had an additional year for research. However, visual archives had yet to properly organize, caption, and catalogue the scattered corpus of photographs from the war, and historians had yet to recognize the degree to which the Nazis restricted photographic or filmic documentation of the extermination camps (and thus how rare photographic evidence from inside the camps would actually be).[12] Moreover, Night and Fog was made decades before historians and filmmakers considered the images produced during the Nazi era and those made after the liberation of the camps as two categorically distinct bodies of visual evidence. In its attempt to address the concentration camp as a system, the film largely employs archival images as broadly illustrative rather than strictly referential to specific historical locations and times. The lyricism of Cayrol's voiceover further enables this suture of diverse archival sources through its capacity to abstract and universalize.

Despite the "jerky and chopped" momentum of the archival sequences, Night and Fog fluidly integrates photographs with archival film footage through several aesthetic strategies.[13] First, rather than rapidly alternate back and forth between color and black-and-white, Resnais creates substantial assemblages of diverse black-and-white images, which work to obscure the differences among their sources and material qualities. Second, the lack of camera movement in most of the black-and-white film footage binds it to the accompanying photographic stills, especially in contrast to the almost continuous camera movement of the color footage. Third, the majority of the black-and-white shots—whether photographs or moving images—remain on the screen for only several seconds, thus homogenizing the viewer's perceptual attention to each type of shot. And finally, as Lindeperg observes, the slight camera tremble in the shots of photographs also helps to smooth their insertion into the archival footage (98). Only one single shot in the film provides camera movement over a photograph when the camera tilts up to reveal the face of a Kapo in Auschwitz. The almost complete absence of camera movement over still images is a clear aesthetic decision on Resnais' part, especially in light of his extensive use of camera movement across paintings in his previous *films d'art*, *Van Gogh* and *Guernica* (1950). Such static framing of still photographs not only accentuates the dynamism of the color shots, but also places greater visual emphasis on the editing of the black-and-white sequences as each straight cut assaults the viewer with one shocking image after another.[14] Moreover, Resnais' editing of still photographs in *Night and Fog* was shaped by two aesthetic relationships: on the one hand, between photograph and voiceover and, on the other, between filmic and photographic images.

Many archival sequences in the film present a series of images sharing the same categorical content. For instance, the history of deportation to the camps is illustrated by several photographs of mass deportation from different locations, beginning with the now-iconic photograph of the young boy with his hands in the air from the Warsaw ghetto, as the voiceover intones, "Seized in Warsaw." Three further photographs of deportation follow while the voiceover continues, "deported from Lodz, Prague, Brussels, Athens, Zagreb, Odessa, or Rome." Parataxis structures both sound and image, but the voiceover is no longer identifying the singular referentiality of the image, as it did in the first shot of the sequence. The three photographs function as visual condensation, standing in paradigmatically for all the places of deportation.[15] Later in the film, Resnais uses parataxis to articulate the hierarchy of the camp power structure. The Kapo appears through the close-up portrait of his identification photo, followed by a photograph of an SS officer several feet from the camera and then a photograph of a camp commandant posing on an observation point on the walls of his camp. The growing distance between camera and subject in each image visually emphasizes the voiceover's explanation of the separation between victim and perpetrator.

Resnais' most innovative application of visual and verbal parataxis occurs when he uses photographs to illuminate the deception of appearances in the camps. When a series of photographs of differently designed watchtowers are presented during the sequence on the construction of the camps, the voiceover wryly comments, "No specific style, it's left to the imagination. Alpine style. Garage style. Japanese style. No style." The banality of design choice obscures the brutal function of the structure.

The critical ironic distance between image and voice is further heightened in the following sequence, which presents several photographs of various architectural structures built in the camps, including gateways, walls, and barracks, while the voiceover recites a list of their future inhabitants: "Meanwhile, Burger, a German worker, Stern, a Jewish student in Amsterdam, Schmulski, a merchant in Krakow, and Annette, a schoolgirl in Bordeaux, go about their daily lives, not knowing a place is being prepared for them hundreds of miles away." Emptied of human presence and matched to the voiceover's identification of individual future victims, the photographs come to bear witness to the systematic planning of inhumanity.

Resnais' editing experiments with the relationship between photographic and filmic images take a number of forms. Several of the transitions between the color and black-and-white sequences exploit the cut between movement and stasis. For instance, in a sequence examining the cleft between inside and outside the camp, a camera located in one of the watchtowers pans fluidly around the empty camp interior as the voiceover notes the arbitrary risk of execution in the face of camp guards' boredom. The film then cuts to a black-and-white photograph of a prisoner's corpse splayed across a barbed-wire fence at Mauthausen. The dialectical force of this cut draws from several visual characteristics: the shift from color to black and white, from film to photograph, and from bodily absence to presence. The photograph's stasis is all the more striking since the prisoner's body is caught in arrested motion, not temporarily by the camera, but permanently by the gun. Such failed escapes or successful suicides were left to hang on the camp fences for long periods and systematically documented by the *Erkennungsdienst*, the camp's photographic identification unit.[16]

Alternately, within the black-and-white assemblages, Resnais consistently blurs the boundaries between stasis and movement as the shots shift between photographs and filmed footage. Many shots that depict spaces, objects, and human bodies remain fundamentally ambiguous as to whether one is perceiving film footage marked by profilmic stasis or a filmed still photograph, an effect that I call intermedial ambiguity. This perceptual ambiguity is intermedial in the sense that the viewer remains caught in the spectatorial dynamics of both film and photography. Although Resnais clearly adopts this effect for its potential to produce cognitive dissonance, it can just as easily generate a smooth, integrative transition from one medium to another, as we will see in relation to *City of Gold* later in the chapter. A sequence representing a surgical block at Auschwitz exemplifies the film's ambiguous, unsettling depiction of the emptied spaces of the camps after liberation. It begins with a portrait photograph of an SS doctor followed by film footage of a "terrifying nurse." The next shot presents a highly ambiguous wide-angle view of an empty operating theater. Although the image lacks any movement, the perception of depth, the even illumination, and the crispness of the image all suggest that it might be film footage rather than a filmed photograph.[17] The voiceover accentuates the focus on perceptual ambivalence: "But what's behind the façade? Pointless operations, amputations, and experimental mutilations." The following two shots of other surgical facilities are more apparently photographs—physical blemishes are visible on the surface of the images, which also appear spatially flatter.[18] The subsequent three film shots from Soviet newsreels present the diabolical paradox of an operating table with a guillotine, again through an ambivalent visual stasis that asks: what in fact is here before our eyes? In this and other sequences, *Night and Fog* deploys intermedial ambiguity—this unsettling equivocality between film and photograph—to amplify the perverse, deceptive reality of the camp system and any attempt to represent it. Appearance cannot be trusted; sheer unmitigated terror lies beneath the banal surface of the image.

Intermedial ambiguity functions somewhat differently in the film's presentation of objects in the camps, which are shot in either close-ups of single objects or long shots of innumerable masses. These close-ups include shots of camp insignia, handwritten paper scraps, and wooden figures secretly crafted by prisoners. Emma Wilson contends that Resnais presents these markers of "deathly codification" and "human resistance and creativity" in a profoundly haptic manner that shows a "tactile appreciation of their surface and substance."[19] This haptic quality complicates the very temporality of these images: "they are more properly present images of past evidence that insists, remains present, obtrudes in its very materiality" (107). Although they are mostly filmed shots of objects from the Auschwitz Museum, the blunt immobility of both camera and object permits us to potentially misrecognize them as photographs, thus further complicating their temporality. Later in the film, Resnais introduces a series of shots showing the vast mass of objects collected from the prisoners sent to the gas chambers: spectacles, combs, shaving brushes, cooking pots, and clothing. Beginning with Cayrol's caustically ironic words, "Everything was saved," this sequence of filmed photographs of objects related to the care and nourishment of the body immediately follows the color tracking shots past the ovens in Majdanek. The initial shots completely fill the screen with the amassed objects, foreclosing any sense of depth or finitude, and thus, also fueling intermedial ambiguity. Perspective emerges in the latter shots where the architecture of the room holding the objects becomes visible. The sequence ends with a complex mobile shot of the vast mass of women's hair displayed in the Auschwitz Museum, where the camera movement embodies the impossible desire to make sense of what is being seen. As Wilson notes, "the image—which has appeared horribly tactile—morphs into unassimilable abstraction" (108–9).

Similar to its framing of objects, *Night and Fog* generates intermedial ambiguity around both individual human bodies and human masses. The hospital sequence of the film begins with photographs of the figure of the *Muselmann*—the prisoner on the threshold between life and death—whose body barely moves (Video 1.1 ▶). Inside the infirmary, film footage of prisoners in beds reveal only the slight flicker of eyelids or the slow heaving of a chest (Figure 1.1). The sequence concludes with a shocking, yet visually ambivalent, photograph of a man in a bed staring directly into the camera with a wide-eyed, anguished look. Is this emaciated *Muselmann* dead or alive (Figure 1.2)? The voiceover suggests, but does not confirm, the former: "In the end, each inmate resembles the next: body of indeterminate age that dies with its eyes wide open." Just as bodies become indeterminate from one another, so does the distinction between life and death. Drawing on Giorgio Agamben's discussion of the

Figure 1.1 Film footage of *Muselmänner* in the camp infirmary in *Night and Fog* (Alain Resnais, 1955).

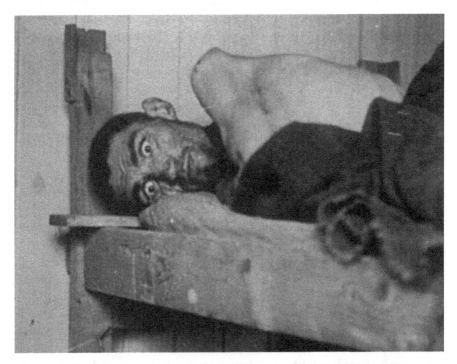

Figure 1.2 The double ambiguity of the *Muselmann* between life/death and film/photograph in *Night and Fog* (Alain Resnais, 1955).

Muselmann, Wilson reads the "category disturbance" and "uncanny hesitation" produced by the "nauseating" interplay between stillness and motion in such sequences as "riskily imitating the cognitive disturbance and impossibility that the *Muselmann* embodies" (102).

As the film turns to the disposal of corpses after extermination in the gas chamber, Resnais alternates once again between film and photograph, as well as between individual corpses and masses. The first two static film shots (from newsreels) pair a facial close-up of an open-eyed female corpse with a massive pile of corpses, in which only a single body can be individually distinguished from the tangle of emaciated limbs. The third shot returns to a photograph, one of the four so-called *Sonderkommando* photographs, which secretly document the final stages of mass extermination at Auschwitz.[20] As Lindeperg indicates, the singularity and historical significance of these four blurry photographs as the only surviving photographic evidence of mass extermination at Auschwitz were not yet recognized in the mid-1950s, thus Resnais integrates this unique photograph with diverse film footage taken by the allied forces after the liberation of the camps (105–11). The photograph depicts the burning of corpses just removed from the gas chambers by the *Sonderkommando.* The original photograph was framed by a window or doorway, implying its secret production and a foregrounding of the perspective of its unknown photographer. Although reproductions of this image normally remove the dark frame, Resnais cropped it even tighter, thus drawing our attention to the *Sonderkommando* member on the left as he swings his left arm to throw another corpse onto the smoking pyre (Figure 1.3). The following film shot initially appears to present a closer view, yet what we see is Soviet newsreel footage shot after liberation of a burning corpse (Figure 1.4). Several further shots contrast the petrified agony of incinerated corpses with the gentle movement of the smoke wafting from the pyre. Unsettling our perception of both time and space, movement here arises in film from petrified stillness, or it is frozen by the photographic camera's instantaneous capture of a living body in motion.

As the film turns to the liberation of the camps, Resnais constructs a shocking eruption of bodily movement from various Soviet, French, and British newsreel footage shot at Dachau, Bergen-Belsen, and other camps. The opening shot of this film sequence presents a long shot of corpses strewn across the ground at Bergen-Belsen. The visual mastery of this establishing shot matches the confident exposition of the voiceover, "When the allies open the doors ... " But the voice falls silent over the static medium shots and medium close-ups of petrified, entangled corpses that follow. Given the abundant co-presence of photographic and movie cameras immediately following the liberation of the camps, these precisely framed static shots could easily be mistaken for photographs taken by photojournalists like Lee Miller. With each shot, the camera distance shortens, culminating in a tightly framed close-up of a young woman's sunken face. Suddenly, the camera pulls back to "a grotesque image of mobility," a long shot of a bulldozer at Bergen-Belsen shunting a mass of corpses.[21] After such sustained contemplation of inert bodies, their eruption into motion confounds our visual and ethical perception. The bodies in motion appear most human

Figure 1.3 Secretly taken photograph of the *Sonderkommando* removing corpses from the gas chamber at Auschwitz, August 1944 in *Night and Fog* (Alain Resnais, 1955).

Figure 1.4 Burning corpse from Soviet newsreel footage after liberation in *Night and Fog* (Alain Resnais, 1955).

in the first couple of shots as arms and legs passively and perversely stroke the bodies beneath them. As they begin to be churned up with earth and then eventually pushed into a mass grave, their humanity disintegrates into the bare objecthood of bodily remains. Including arguably the most notorious shots in *Night and Fog*, perhaps due to the frequent misconception that the footage shows Nazi bulldozers rather than British ones, this sequence represents the culmination of the intermedial ambiguity developed throughout the film. Wilson aptly characterizes this process as "a bid to unsettle how and what we see, to make the visceral shudder of the indeterminacy of living and dead matter, a moment of unknowing and undoing of the viewer, key to the viewing of the film" (102).

The final archival images in the film return to intermedial ambiguity for one last time. After repeated denials of responsibility from a Kapo and several SS officers, Resnais cuts to a clearly cropped photograph of a Dachau prisoner deep in re-flection as the voiceover asks the question, "Then, who is responsible?" A fellow inmate behind the man holds what appears to be a piece of bread, thus suggesting, though not necessarily confirming, that this is an image of a camp survivor after liberation. The three film shots of corpses from Dachau that follow implicate him in an ethical responsibility to bear witness for what they cannot, namely their an-nihilation. But in contrast to the earlier sequence, in which the mass of corpses be-come increasingly de-individuated and less recognizably human, the succession of these three shots gradually allows individual human bodies to come into view. The third and final shot centers on a male corpse whose tilted head and outstretched arm reclaim the figuration of pathos from the indeterminate human remains that surround it.

For *Night and Fog* to end by posing the moral question of responsibility to the viewer reiterates its essayistic quality. The structure of the essay film, explains Laura Rascaroli, is one of "constant interpellation," in which "each spectator, as an indi-vidual and not as a member of an anonymous, collective audience, is called upon to engage in a dialogical relationship with the enunciator, hence to become active, intellectually and emotionally, and interact with the text."[22] A fundamental means of the essay film to engage its viewer is through a presentational mode, posing dif-ficult questions about the world and the images of it, and refusing clear-cut answers about their relationship. Moreover, as Timothy Corrigan notes, the historical trau-matic ruptures of total global war, the Holocaust, and Hiroshima/Nagasaki galva-nized postwar documentary with "an essayistic imperative to question and debate not only a new world but also the very terms by which we subjectively inhabit, publicly stage, and experientially think that world."[23] If Corrigan defines the essay film around such a "tripartite structure of subjectivity, public experience and thinking," then we can consider the intermedial ambiguity generated by Resnais' editing of film footage and photographs to be an essayistic strategy as significant as Cayrol's searching voice-over; it generates critical thought (around the impossibility of representation) by unmooring the perceiving subject (of the individual viewer) in relation to the public documentation of atrocity. The intermedial ambiguity between film and photography in *Night and Fog* thus amplifies its skeptical interrogation of whether the truth of the Nazi concentration camps can ever be adequately represented.

Engaging the Image

Resnais' application of photography to the essayistic was shared by several of his key collaborators in the *Groupe des Trente* (Group of Thirty), a body of filmmakers and producers formed in 1953 (including Resnais, Chris Marker, Agnès Varda, and Alexandre Astruc), who advocated for institutional support for the short film as a critical and innovative "hothouse" for postwar French cinema.[24] The concision of the short film required that it could only present a "fragmentary testing and provisional engagement with a subject," thus rendering it highly suitable to the creation of essay films, which both characteristically resist totalizing thought and embrace experimental form.[25] Varda and Marker both worked as photographers during their early careers and the medium of photography would remain a significant intellectual preoccupation for their subsequent work with the moving image.[26] In the early 1960s, their intermedial engagement with these two media manifested an experimentation with films whose visual tracks consisted entirely (or almost entirely) of still photographs. Although Marker's science-fiction narrative *La jetée* (1962) is undoubtedly the most influential of the "photofilms" of the 1960s, both Marker and Varda each made important contributions to the documentary photofilm: Varda's *Salut les Cubains* (1963) documents her trip to witness post-revolutionary Cuba, while Marker's *Si j'avais quatre dromadaires* (*If I Had Four Camels*, 1966) explores a decade's worth of Marker's own travel across the globe.

The emergence of the documentary photofilm in the early 1960s occurs within the context of multiple intermedial dynamics at play in Europe, Japan, and the United States. First, institutional support for the short film from state agencies and public television relied on concepts of "quality" that enabled writers, photographers, and other artists access to film production.[27] Second, shared commitments to modernist experimentation with narrative brought together writers and filmmakers, such as Resnais and Alain Robbe-Grillet, who published a *ciné-roman* version of their film *L'année dernière á Marienbad* (*Last Year at Marienbad*, 1961), combining the screenplay with selected frame captures from the film to create a new literary genre. Third, with the publication of William Klein's *Life is Good and Good For You in New York: Trance, Witness, Revels* (1956), Ed van der Elsken's *Love on the Left Bank* (1956), and Robert Frank's *The Americans* (1958–9), the photobook achieved a visual quality and structure that was highly cinematic; all three photographers would become filmmakers by the early 1960s.[28] And finally, the development of the automated 35mm slide projector made the machine ubiquitous in middle class homes and professional settings by the end of the 1960s. Although the illustrated slide lecture, as one of the precursors of documentary film, predates photography, the automation of slide projection in machines, such as Kodak's legendary Carousel model (1961), rendered the experience of viewing still photographs closer to the cinematic by embedding the embalmed past moment of the individual photograph in the present tense of the slideshow's newly automated temporal flow.[29]

Although they were never to be become a prolific genre, even after a revival beginning in the 1980s, photofilms were certainly an international phenomenon in the 1960s.[30] Inspired by Resnais' cinematic remediation of Picasso's painting in his film *Guernica*, Toshio Matsumoto made *Ishi no uta* (*The Song of Stone*, 1963), a 16mm short film using stop-motion animation techniques to rephotograph hundreds of still images of Japanese stonecutters in Shikuko taken by the *LIFE* magazine photographer Ernest Satow. The film's elaborate in-camera editing of photographic images impressed both Marker and historian Georges Sadoul. Yuriko Furuhata suggests that it was also most likely to have been a significant, if unacknowledged, influence on Nagisa Oshima's *Yunbogi no nikki* (*Diary of Yunbogi*, 1965), which combines documentary photographs Oshima had taken of South Korean street children in the early 1960s with a voiceover commentary drawn from the published memoir of a young Korean street boy.[31] The film crafts a strident political allegory of postwar Korea by exploiting the friction between the individual character of Yunbogi's voiceover and the collective representation of Oshima's documentary photographs. Hubert Fichte and Leonore Mau similarly used documentary photographs of daily life to create a biting critique of proletarian working conditions in postwar Germany in their photofilm *Der Tag eines unständigen Hafenarbeiters* (*A Day in the Life of a Casual Dock Worker*, 1966). An individual worker's daily routine is narrated over documentary photographs that work to consistently depersonalize it, initially through visual attention to the everyday objects in that routine and later in photographs of the working process that deny focus on any particular individual. Photographic stillness accentuates the fixity of the dockworker's living and working conditions under capitalism. The three brief interruptions of moving images in the film offer no promise of liberation, only the late-capitalist distractions of television: sports, advertising, and news reportage. In this and Oshima's film, the constitutive tension of the documentary photofilm in this period is made evident: photography provided easy and ample documentary access to the contingency of the everyday, whereas its inscription within cinematic form facilitated a modernist exploitation of the temporal differences between photography and film that would forge the film's political edge.[32]

With its painstakingly detailed semiotic reading of an infamous press photo of Jane Fonda in Hanoi, Jean Luc Godard and Jean Pierre Gorin's *Letter to Jane* (1972) is arguably the most politically didactic of the photofilms in this era, yet also the least interesting in terms of its engagement with the intermediality between photography and film. For most of the fifty-two-minute film, we contemplate the photograph in its original frame or a closely cropped detail, occasionally intercut with publicity stills from Hollywood films and Godard and Gorin's *Tout va bien* (1972), for which *Letter to Jane* served as promotional material. Godard and Gorin's dual voiceover narration is less dialogic than lecturing, frequently descending into misogynist condescension.

Offering celebration rather than critique, Varda's *Salut les Cubains* presents a vividly affirmative portrait of the youthful dynamism within post-revolutionary Cuban society in the early 1960s, which she characterizes with the phrase, "socialism and cha-cha-cha."[33] Although Varda has insisted that she wanted to make "a didactic film that was musical and pleasant to watch" rather than "an experimental film," her photofilm is nevertheless substantially essayistic in its self-reflexive concern with its own representational dynamics (9). This is immediately apparent in the credit sequence, the only part of the film that uses moving images. The film opens with interior shots of an art gallery filled with photographs of post-revolutionary Cuba as visitors circulate around the room looking at the images. A male voiceover confirms the time and place of the exhibition: "Paris, St. Germain des Prés, June 1963." The camera zooms into the musicians of an Afro-Cuban band playing in the gallery. The film's title appears over a freeze-framed close-up of the drummer. An exterior shot follows, in which the same drummer walks along the street and is joined by a member of the public tapping her hands on the drum. A wide shot reveals the band walking through the streets with a sizeable crowd watching and dancing around them. The handheld camera roams around the crowd, briefly catching Varda seemingly directing some offscreen action (Figure 1.5). The following shots of multiple cameramen filming the band imply that it is they whom she directs. Their faces are recognizable as filmmaker- and photographer-friends from the Left Bank: Resnais, Marker, Joris Ivens, Armand Gatti, William Klein, and Jacques Demy. As the camera approaches each cameraman's lens head on, the shot freezes and a credit

Figure 1.5 Agnès Varda directing in the opening credits of *Salut les Cubains* (Agnès Varda, 1963).

appears (Figure 1.6). The final shot of the credit sequence shows a hand holding up the exhibition poster in front of the band: "Cuba: Ten Years of Revolution: A Photo Exhibition."

This credit sequence frames the photofilm self-reflexively in several critical ways. First, it locates both the image-maker and her audience in Paris before the film travels to Cuba. The first few shots of the film emphatically acknowledge the French gaze upon the foreign Cuban other. That gaze extends beyond the photographs to the live musicians enthusiastically observed by both the public and the cameramen. Yet, the gallery audience moves from observation to celebratory participation as the musical performance spills out of the gallery and into the street. If this gallery audience serves as a proxy for the film's audience, then this credit sequence amplifies the dynamics of what Jane Gaines has called "political mimesis," wherein documentary film works "to make struggle visceral, to go beyond the abstractly intellectual to produce a bodily swelling."[34] Gaines emphasizes the strong role that popular music plays in such mim-icry, "often rhythmically reinforced through editing patterns, or what Eisenstein calls the 'emotive vibration' in montage" (91). The audience on screen invites the film's au-dience into such mimesis, yet simultaneously reminds the latter of the very mediation that enables their encounter with post-revolutionary Cuba. By explicitly placing her filmmaking friends within the frame, Varda also situates her film within the collec-tive commitment that Left Bank intellectuals had to post-revolutionary Cuba at the time. Ivens and Marker had made films about Cuba, Jean Paul Sartre and Simone de Beauvoir had written about their trips to witness Castro's revolution, and Henri Cartier Bresson was there on photo-assignment at the very same time as Varda.

Figure 1.6 Self-reflexive credit sequence of *Salut les Cubains* (Agnès Varda, 1963).

Moreover, given that Marker's film *Cuba Si* (1961) was still banned by the French censorship commission when Varda was completing *Salut les Cubains*, Valerie Vignaux reads the credit sequence as a necessary act of solidarity with Marker, especially since he was the one who first encouraged her to go to Cuba.[35] Marker had arranged contacts for her with the Cuban Film Institute (ICAIC), which subsequently invited her to create "a photobook that would allow other countries to better know our revolution" (147). Varda traveled to Cuba in late December 1962 with Jacques Ledoux, director of the Belgian *Cinémathèque*, who was organizing an exchange with the Cuban film archives. Taking with her two cameras (a Rolleiflex and a Leica) and a Nagra tape recorder, Varda spent one month traveling around Cuba with the intent to make a film, rather than a photobook. She returned with over 4,000 photographs, which she whittled down to 1,500 before beginning to edit the film.

Rather than structure the film around a clearly defined itinerary of her trip, she sought to group the photographs into thematic clusters. As she processed her impressions documented in the photographs, Varda wrote up a voiceover commentary alternating between two voices (which would be read by her and actor Michel Piccoli). This dialogic structure would provide one foundation for the film's editing, while music would provide the other. With its rich syncretism and diverse social functions, Cuban music not only became a key thematic concern running throughout the film, but also provided the editing structure for many of the film's sequences. Most explicitly, the revolutionary dynamism of "socialism and cha-cha-cha" is literalized in three set pieces that function like musical numbers in the film: the first shows Cuban singer Benny Moré dancing before the camera in an empty canteen while singing one of his songs; the second number presents shots of workers cutting sugar cane edited to the rhythm of a popular song; the third and final number, which concludes the film, presents filmmaker Sarita Gomez dancing the cha-cha-cha in the street with several comrades (Figures 1.7–1.9). As the song culminates, Varda reintegrates a wide variety of shots from earlier in the film: socialism literally cut to the cha-cha-cha. Varda shot these and other sequences of human movement using a Leica camera with a manual release, which created distinct spatio-temporal intervals between the shots. She was thus able to align them with the intervals between the musical notes in the songs structuring these sequences. Still images thus began to dance. Varda's repeated use of the same shots during these numbers reinforces their function less as unique photographs or even photograms, but as the visual cues *between* the moves of a dance. The occasional camera movement across photographs similarly traces either a musical movement between notes or a mental shift in Varda's attention to the image at hand (rather than an attempt to imbue the still image with the sensation of temporal duration or to better immerse the viewer).

The twenty-eight-minute film possesses a distinctively ambulatory structure. Varda explores the history of the revolution, its economic reforms, its social initiatives, and the arts in post-revolutionary Cuba through the diverse encounters she has with the Cuban people, including its political leaders, workers, artists, or simply ordinary people on the street. Exemplifying one of the key characteristics of the essay

Figures 1.7–1.9 Filmmaker Sarita Gomez dancing the cha-cha-cha in *Salut les Cubains* (Agnès Varda, 1963).

film, the shifts in theme and focus remain idiosyncratic, driven by the preoccupations of Varda's subjective perspective. As she explicitly notes in her voiceover at the beginning of the film: "I was in Cuba. I brought back jumbled images. To order them, I made this homage, this film entitled *Salut les Cubains*." Editing follows the logic of her mind as she tries to make sense of her impressions of the country. At times, her visual attention also digresses to minor, yet illuminating, observations. For instance, in a sequence on Sunday leisure, Varda notices Black girls carrying white dolls and vice versa. Piccoli's earnest voiceover is descriptive, conveying historical facts and narratives, as well as naming what Varda's camera has captured, whereas her voiceover often retorts with a playful and enthusiastic counter assertion of recognition of and solidarity with the people in the frame. For example, over a shot of two women displaying hats made from reeds, Piccoli comments, "Here, tourism in ladies' hats." An image of a militia woman holding a gun immediately follows, over which Varda responds, "Here's to Marxism-Leninism in a militia woman's beret." As Delphine Bénézet argues, such responses by Varda frequently serve as ironic feminist contestations of female spectacle or witty deflations of revolutionary machismo.[36] The rhetorical framing of such dialogic alternation between the two voices (and the shots over which they are spoken) also raises larger self-reflexive issues about the politics of representation (Video 1.2 ⏵). Piccoli's lines are frequently initiated by the constative assertion "voici" (here), which confidently articulates a cognitive mastery of the world depicted, as well as the right to consume it as image. Varda's counter-assertions are framed using the performative utterance "un salut à" (literally "a salute to" but usually translated as "here's to," "cheers to," or even "greetings to").[37] Her voiceover's direct address to the Cubans in the frame (who are frequently looking directly at the camera) treats the photographs as opportunities for encounter, recognition, and solidarity rather than just visual curiosity and consumption—photography to hail engagement with the world rather than merely put it on display for the viewer as a political tourist. Varda's photofilm demonstrated how film could provide a generative experience in which to contemplate photographs as complex social encounters between those behind the camera and those in front of it, between the self and the other.

Chris Marker's photofilms, in turn, delved even deeper into the qualities of photography by their preoccupation with the relationship between photographic temporality and the processes of human memory. Marker's *Si j'avais quatre dromadaires* shares certain formal qualities with *Salut les Cubains*—a focus on travel, a multi-voiced dialogic commentary, and a disjunctive use of editing and camera movement—but his photofilm carries the genre far further into the essayistic realm of subjective contemplation. Taking its title from a short poem in Guillaume Apollinaire's *Le Bestiaire ou Cortège d'Orphée* (1911), the film presents itself in an opening intertitle as "An amateur photographer and two of his friends comment upon a selection of photos from virtually everywhere in the world." The photographs are all drawn from the first decade of Marker's career as a photographer (1955–65), including images from China, Korea, the Soviet Union, Israel, Cuba, Greece, and Sweden. Divided into two chapters ("The Castle" and "The Garden"), the film follows no clear geographical route; its itinerary is purely conceptual.[38] *Si j'avais quatre dromadaires* opens with the photographer's own speculations on the nature of photography: the medium as a hunt for images, the photograph as the immortalization of its subject, the subject's look as the reflection of the photographer's own look (Video 1.3 ▶). Describing this "circle" as "a trap," the photographer remains self-consciously within the realm of images and his memories of taking them. At times, he and his two friends discuss images on screen as though they were directly contemplating them in a slide show ("Is this still Moscow?"); at other times, the movement of thought articulated by whoever is speaking on the voiceover seems to conjure the images that flow upon the screen ("One day I saw the poor happy … It was in Nanterre, in the slum, the first day of Algerian independence").

Marker borrows Resnais' paratactic style from *Night and Fog*, arranging images from far-flung places according to thematic categories and similarities: sunrises in different cities, human activity in public places, trains in stations. The photographer's voiceover self-consciously connects photography's embalming of time to cinema's relativity of time and space, its power to conjure imaginary simultaneities: "I can't resist the kind of film that walks you from one dawn to the next, saying things like, it is six o'clock on Earth, six o'clock at Canal Saint-Martin, six o'clock at the Göta Canal in Sweden, six o'clock in Havana." Such musing accentuates the film's abstraction in the presentational mode, confirming Jan Christopher Horak's argument that photographs in Marker's films are "themselves merely objects signifying perception, the signs of cognition, never an actual experience of the world."[39] Even the photographer's two friends, who often interject to challenge his reverie with the harsh realities of social inequality, ultimately function as qualifying counter-voices within Marker's subjectivity, for the images they conjure in support of their arguments are indeed Marker's own.

Si j'avais quatre dromadaires embodies the height of the photofilm's essayistic self-reflexivity about photography's relation to film in the 1960s. Thus, it is hardly surprising that the film would serve as an acknowledged influence on Susan Sontag's thinking about "the image-world" in her treatise *On Photography*.[40] While European and Japanese filmmakers in the late 1950s and early 1960s pursued a modernist preoccupation with the image-world and the interaction between camera and subject, North American documentarists were more concerned with how the camera could facilitate more direct and less mediated experiences of the historical world. This tension manifested most vociferously in the debates between the advocates of a European *cinema vérité*, which included Marker, and a North American direct cinema, but they also clearly shaped the differing approaches to how photographs could be incorporated into documentary film.

"A Strong Illusion of Living Continuity"

While researching in the National Archives of Canada in 1955, filmmaker Colin Low came across a remarkable collection of over two hundred photographs from the 1898

Klondike Gold Rush, which he immediately showed to his colleague, Wolf Koenig, at the National Film Board of Canada (NFB). Koenig had long been eager to make a historical documentary using still photographs. Recently discovered in an abandoned building in Dawson City in the Yukon, the original 8x10-inch glass-plate negatives taken by Wisconsin photographer Eric Hegg provided highly detailed images of both the mass migration to the Klondike and the explosive growth of the city during the gold rush. As members of Unit B in the NFB, which specialized in scientific, cultural, and animated films, Low and Koenig persuaded their boss, Tom Daly, to permit them to travel to Dawson City to shoot footage of the present-day city and collect more research for a short film based on Hegg's photographs. Webster and Stevens, an old photographic company in Seattle, provided access to several hundred more glass-plate photographs of Dawson City, including the work of the commercial photographers Per Edward Larss and Joseph Duclos, whose visual style was close to Hegg's. Once the footage and archive material had been assembled, Low and Koenig asked historian Pierre Berton to perform the voiceover commentary, which would integrate historical exposition with reflections on his own childhood spent in Dawson City.

Although some earlier historical documentaries, such as Lou Stoumen's Academy Award–winning short *The True Story of the Civil War* (1956), had already begun to use camera movement over still photographs, their techniques remained relatively crude attempts to animate static images in the creation of dramatic sequences. Low's experience in Unit B working with animator Norman McLaren led him to consider exploiting the animation stand as the means to bring life to the still photographs through aesthetically sophisticated camera movement across them. He brought in filmmaker Roman Kroitor and mathematician Brian Salt to adapt an animation stand into a camera-tracking device that could produce fluid and highly precise camera movements over still images. Daly contended that, rather than reproducing mere mechanical movement, this device generated the "pleasant accidents of natural movement," which included "natural inertia and momentum, smooth changes of direction, curved movement of any kind that the hand can draw."[41] Low and Koenig retained image resolution and tonal range by making 11x14-inch diapositives, rather than prints, from the original plates, thus permitting the camera to zoom into small details in the pictures without making the grain of the photographs or the paper fiber of a print clearly visible.

Low and Koenig were eager to create what Daly would call "a strong illusion of living continuity" in their application of photographs (4). Thus, in *City of Gold*, one can discern a number of devices that attempt to simulate the experience of live-action cinema. The camera never reveals the edge of the photographic image. To conceal the frame in this way is to disavow the double mediation of the filmic and photographic cameras, as though there were only a single camera capturing the profilmic world. It also invokes Bazin's infinitely "picturable" world beyond the edges of that single frame. Camera movement frequently follows the direction of bodies and objects in motion captured in the photograph, especially when it occurs laterally between background and foreground. This has two effects. On the one hand, the camera movement stands in for the movement that is only suggested by the static image. On the other hand, this overlaid movement also augments the illusion of depth in the image, particularly if the lateral pan is combined with a zoom. For example, in the sequence chronicling the 500-mile journey along the Yukon River to the gold fields, we encounter a photograph of several boats in the midground and background heading left and toward the photographer. Following the direction of the boats, the camera pans laterally (to the lower left) combined with a barely noticeable zoom out. A new boat comes into view in the foreground, and when it fills the frame, the camera comes to a rest. Cut to a wider shot of the river with boats heading left and away from the photographer. The camera simultaneously zooms in and pans laterally (to the upper left), once again following the direction of the boats' movement. Although these two shots fail to maintain continuity of movement between them, the voiceover commentary ("clear sailing all the way down to the gold fields") and the accompanying banjo-and-fiddle music sustain a strong sense of momentum in the sequence.

Most photographs of human subjects in the film involve their direct visual address to the camera. Rather than disrupt continuity, as it would in classical narrative cinema, this actually draws the viewer more fully into the profilmic world. Vernacular photography has so normalized such direct address to the camera that we tend to experience it as an invitation to return the gaze across the threshold of the photographic frame. In the sequence depicting the conditions at Eldorado Creek, the richest of all the gold fields, the voiceover explains that all the lucrative claims had already been staked by the "early birds" who had arrived "eighteen months before." Each shot moves closer to the miners, culminating in a photograph of a single miner taking a pause from his work and glaring aggressively into the camera lens as the voiceover notes, "For the newcomers: nothing." Combined with the miner's antagonistic look at the camera, this line of commentary implicates us, the film's viewers, as the newcomers who have arrived too late. Berton further binds the viewer into the past through subsequent shifts between third and second person when describing the challenges faced by the prospectors in the Eldorado Creek, "Only a few got claims. These came to realize that you couldn't just scoop up the gold by the shovelful. You had to burn your way down through the permafrost." Although he maintains the past tense throughout, his pronoun shift nevertheless implicates the viewer in the historical moment on screen.

Moreover, Berton's voiceover commentary plays a critical role in suturing the viewer into the nineteenth century. The film and Berton's voiceover begin with a complex imbrication of past and present. The film title appears over an extreme longshot of the Klondike landscape. Text appears over the shot: "There are moments and places in history that stir men's imaginations. In this film, Pierre Berton tells of one such moment and place—the famous town where he was raised." Although this text refers to the singularity of "one such moment," Berton's voiceover commentary in fact invokes three historical moments of human imagination: his own present contemplation of his hometown as he recalls his childhood there, his childhood play that imaginatively engaged with the town's fabled past, and the historical moment of the gold rush which inspired tens of thousands of men to make their way to the Klondike seeking fortune. The landscape shot similarly invokes multiple temporalities. After the text disappears, the camera tilts down into the valley, revealing Dawson City. It is initially unclear whether we are observing a photograph or film footage—careful contemplation of the foreground will reveal the slight movement of a few pine trees in the breeze. Moreover, no apparent markers of twentieth-century modernity are visible from this distance. Is this the town today or in the past? Cut to a closer aerial shot of several blocks of the town. The prevalence of empty lots in almost every street suggests bygone glory. The film cuts again to a largely static shot at street level with 1950s-era parked cars. The only movement in the shot comes from gently wafting smoke from a chimney in the background and an old man who slowly walks across the foreground from left to right as the camera follows him. The present and the moving image are clearly confirmed visually in this third shot, but they are haunted by the remains of the past. Berton initiates his voiceover by signaling both past and present, "This was my hometown and my father's town before me. It's a quiet place: a few stores, a restaurant, 300 maybe 400 people." The camera records the old men who sit on the hotel porch chatting and the town's children playing baseball. Berton's voiceover uses both the young and the elderly to lead the viewer into the past, to his childhood past playing in the ruins of the town, and to the glorious past of the gold rush itself through the old men reminiscing "the good old days."

Gradually human figures disappear from the present-day footage of Dawson City as the camera lingers on the abandoned ruins of houses, shops, locomotives, and steamboats, while Berton frames each set of ruins in relation to his childhood and the gold rush. These shots are all highly photographic, evoking the modernist visual style of Walker Evans in terms of composition, abstraction, and reduction of depth. The only movement in the frame comes from gently swaying grass and fireweed seeds drifting through the air (Figure 1.10). Berton notes the seasonality of their presence, "Every summer when the seeds of the fireweed drifted across the valley of the Yukon River, we kids used to roam through these decaying buildings." These wispy seeds thus both confirm the presence of the moving image and intimate the presence of multiple pasts. Eventually this sequence concludes in the cemetery on an ambivalent note as Berton reflects, "Most of the men are gone with the steamboats. Of the tens of thousands who came here, only a handful found the gold they were seeking. And yet very few, I think, regretted the journey to Dawson City for the Great Stampede was the highpoint of their life." Daly felt that this progression from living people to ruins to graves prepared for the transition to the still photographs that would be introduced in the following sequence, which depicts the infamous trek across Chilkoot Pass: "You know they are dead. So even the unconscious expectation of their moving is already ruled out by the order of the images up to this point in the picture. The next time you see these people they are appropriately still, forming a line wending its way into the Yukon" (4).

Still photographs then remain exclusively on screen until almost the end of the film, when the images transition back to present-day moving images. These transitional sequences involve a fundamental ambivalence between movement and stasis;

Figure 1.10 Landscape shots reminiscent of Walker Evans's photographs in *City of Gold* (Wolf Koenig and Colin Low, 1957).

whereas *Night and Fog* deploys intermedial ambiguity to draw the viewer's attention to questions of representation, here it facilitates the smooth transport between present and past. Like the opening shot of the film, it is hard to discern if the first three static landscape shots of the mountains around Chilkoot Pass are photographs or contemporary film footage. As the camera tilts down a snowy mountain in the third shot, a carefully masked dissolve introduces a new shot that continues to tilt down until a static line of human figures appears in the frame, finally confirming the photographic status of the image. The camera shifts direction as it pans right and zooms out, following the line of prospectors up the mountain's incline in the midground. Along the way, the camera catches sight of a single man standing in the foreground, apart from the line as he looks at its progression (Figure 1.11). Here we see not just a sophisticated movement across the image that traces a viewer's likely cognitive attention to the original photograph, but also a figure of perceptual identification within the frame whose line of vision we join as the camera pans past him. Camera movement over photographs in *City of Gold* frequently permits these two lines of visual attention to intersect—that of the viewer of the photograph and that of its subject(s)—which augments the viewer's immersion into the profilmic world of the photographs.

The final sequence of photographs in the film, which concerns the festivities in 1899 combining Dominion Day and the Fourth of July, begins with a conventional

Figure 1.11 The Chilkoot Pass in *City of Gold* (Wolf Koenig and Colin Low, 1957).

alternation between wide shots of the crowd and close-up details of individual faces. It culminates with an unusual pan across a large crowd photo that visually embodies the structure of feeling Berton describes in his voiceover commentary. He asks, "What were they celebrating really?" So far from home and so patently unsuccessful in their pursuit of gold and wealth, most of these men, argues Berton, "found themselves seized by a curious mixture of feelings, not the least of which was a strange elation." It was in the adventure itself that "they had already found what they were seeking." At first, we see a wide shot of a crowd of men standing in front of a stage. The film then cuts to a closer shot of a contemplative man in the crowd looking to the right. The camera slowly pans left until it finds another man lost in thought as he gazes to the right. After a pause, the camera continues to pan left until it finds a third man, who is also reflectively looking off into the distance to the right (Figures 1.12–1.15). Although the men's faces remain enigmatic, the camera movement running explicitly counter to the direction of the men's visual attention offers a poignant articulation of their "curious mixture of feelings."

The sequence culminates in close-ups of individual faces staring directly into the camera, with the final shot zooming out to reveal a group of men all contemplatively returning the camera's gaze (Video 1.4 ⏵). The next two shots offer conceptual continuity with the previous shots through images of collectivity: a pile of pickaxes and a pile of spades. It is only by the third shot, an old lantern in front of a broken window,

Figures 1.12–1.15 Festivities in 1899 combining Dominion Day and the Fourth of July in *City of Gold* (Wolf Koenig and Colin Low, 1957).

that we might realize we are back in the present and back to moving images, with a cobweb swaying gently in the corner of the window frame. A subsequent shot of a woman's shoe covered in gently moving cobwebs consolidates the image of the past's ruin. Eventually, Berton's voiceover returns as he contemplates his own unknowing childhood play amid such ruins. The subtle visual play here between stasis and movement seamlessly transitions back to the present that is inscribed fully in film and that will frame the remainder of the documentary. Unlike the dialectical juxtaposition of past and present in *Night and Fog*, *City of Gold* constructs a carefully charted gradual progression from the present into the past and back again. Intermedial ambiguity between still and moving images facilitates smooth immersion into the past rather than cognitive uncertainty about the representational nature of the images at hand. The use of camera movement in *City of Gold* plays a key role in such immersion into the self-contained world of the Klondike Gold Rush, aligning the film firmly with the ideological orientation of the Board's Unit B. David Jones argues that the unit's films were characterized by "an idea of *wholeness*," one that sought to articulate universal themes through the integrity of the films' particular worlds rather than any explicit connection to a wider world.[42]

The pursuit of the universal theme within archival material shaped the development of the historical documentary in US television as it entered the 1960s, most notably in the Project XX series of compilation documentaries produced by NBC following the critical and popular success of its landmark series, *Victory at Sea* (1952–3). Television scholar William Bluem identified this new mode as the "theme documentary," which "relies upon the active effort to create 'worlds of imagination'—to design and execute some larger statement reflecting universal truths which are inherent within the documents of life."[43] As Project XX producer Donald Hyatt turned from twentieth- to nineteenth-century history, with documentaries such as *Meet Mr. Lincoln* (1959) and *Mark Twain's America* (1960), the series applied the "still-in-motion" techniques developed by Low and Koenig to a much larger photographic archive.[44]

Often considered his most accomplished documentary of the series, Hyatt's *The Real West* (1961) drew from visual research in an unprecedented number of archives and personal collections across the country. The program imitates *City of Gold* in its opening credits with film footage of weeds blowing through a Western ghost town. Initiating what would become a common convention of the history program in later decades, the documentary's narrator (Gary Cooper) acts as a charismatic presenter, addressing the camera directly on a set made to resemble a Western frontier town. The program's use of still-in-motion techniques is less well-crafted and less precise than *City of Gold*, as it marshals together a wide variety of archival images, including some non-photographic still images, such as paintings and prints. Panning shots are strung together with dissolves to loosely convey the momentum and scale of the Western Trail; conflicts are evoked through editing structured around a simple left/right contrast between opposing forces. Hyatt's innovation in using photographs lay in the combination of photographic portraits and first-person testimony in the voiceover. Hyatt recognized that the stillness of the photographic portrait could exceed the moving image in its capacity to convey a particular emotion: "An expression on a man's face … is gone in an instant, and with it the emphasis, the emotion, and the mood of that instant. Because this technique is less mobile it is often more effective."[45] In one of the most effective sequences of the program, Hyatt presents a diverse series of Edward Curtis portraits of Native Americans, each accompanied with Cooper's voiceover quoting a succinct expression of Indigenous resistance to settler colonialism. This verbal supplement allows the viewer to recognize the sitter's resistant stare back at the camera's gaze. In his later program specifically focused on the Native American history of dispossession, *The End of the Trail* (1969), Hyatt further elaborates this technique with individual voice actors reading settler and Indigenous testimonies arranged in dialectical opposition. Hyatt's innovative voicing of photographs would be adopted and further refined two decades later by Ken Burns in his blockbuster PBS series *The Civil War* (1990).

"Abstract Visual Equivalence Between Pictures"

When Apple was developing its new photographic application iPhoto in 2002, Steve Jobs approached Burns to request permission to use his name on a new function, the "Ken Burns effect," which would allow users to incorporate zooms, pans, and dissolves into their digital slide shows.[46] The release of iPhoto may have been the moment when the phrase entered popular culture, but Burns had been associated with such still-in-motion techniques since the original television broadcast of *The Civil War*, a series that had made him a household name.[47] Burns has repeatedly acknowledged that he did not invent these techniques. He credits both *City of Gold* and his Hampshire College mentor, the photographer Jerome Liebling, as the main influences on his techniques for animating photographs.[48] Yet Burns has also frequently resisted the reduction of his documentary aesthetic to a single formal strategy: "My thing is the combination of at least eight elements: four visual; four oral; photographs, newsreels, interviews and live cinematography, and then first-person narration, third person narration, music and sound effects. And their interplay."[49] Burns scholar Gary R. Edgerton similarly argues that Burns's reputation from *The Civil War* onward rests not only on "the formal complexity of his still-in-motion filming," but, moreover, on his capacity to incorporate "an even greater number of technical elements than had ever been attempted or even envisioned before him."[50] Although all the major elements of Burns's documentary style were already present in his first PBS documentary, *Brooklyn Bridge* (1982), they achieved full maturity in *The Civil War*.

Burns's formal innovations in using sound effects, voiceover, and live-action landscape cinematography, in combination with still photographs, elaborated and expanded the techniques originally developed by Low and Koenig in *City of Gold*, and Hyatt in his *Project XX* documentaries. Whereas Hyatt repeatedly used the same sound effect (cicadas) to imbue exterior photographs with a generalized sense of temporality and presence in *End of the Trail*, Burns developed a richer and more nuanced set of sound effects to accompany photographs in *The Civil War*. Some sounds were introduced to match visual elements, such as a horse-drawn carriage or a church bell tower, while others created a sense of space beyond the frame by introducing sounds, such as artillery fire, which could not be tied to any visual elements within the frame. We see this latter strategy in the very first photograph to appear in the series: Wilmer McLean's farmhouse near Manassas, Virginia, which was involved in the First Battle of Bull Run in 1861. As the camera zooms in to highlight three human figures seated in front of a house idyllically surrounded by trees and meadow, we hear both the muffled sounds of artillery and the series narrator (David McCullough) elaborating how the battle raged across McLean's farmland. The series consistently presents photographs with a combination of sound effects and music or voiceover narration (and often all three together). Placed higher on the sound hierarchy of the documentary, music and voiceover provide a continuity between diverse still images that benefit from quite different sound effects to render them livelier. Sound effects thus recede to the aural background, where they augment the illusion of depth in the images they accompany. They also provide an impression of an ongoing temporal present that contrasts with the past tense narration of McCullough's voiceover (Video 1.5 ▶).

Burns's use of diverse voiceovers in the series expanded Hyatt's strategy of having Gary Cooper's voiceover quote multiple sources in *The Real West*. Burns hired renowned actors to read out letters, diaries, speeches, and essays of the key figures in his narrative of the war, including Sam Waterston as Abraham Lincoln, Jason Robards as Ulysses S. Grant, Morgan Freeman as Frederick Douglass, and Julie Harris as Mary Chestnut. When played over their photographic portraits, these differentiated and identifiable voices enhance the visual impression of intimacy and presence in the photographs. Moreover, the verbal performance of these literary texts' direct address resonates with the visual direct address of the photographic portrait. Yet after almost every spoken performance, the voice actor names the source of the quotation, which has the effect of bracketing its direct address to the audience. Each voiceover thus acknowledges its status as a documented quotation, a historical remnant from the past. However, with only a few exceptions throughout the series, Burns does not draw his audience's attention to the fact that the thousands of photographs he incorporates are also historical remnants. These images remain for Burns illustrative visual evidence, transparent portals for immersing his audience into the past.

Interweaving stasis and motion, the live-action landscape shots of historical sites in *The Civil War* resonate with the tension between historical past and living present that structures the arrangement of the other elements in the series. Burns chose to film the sites as close as possible to the days on the calendar on which the battles took place.[51] They were mostly shot in the interstitial periods of daybreak or dusk, without any camera movement and only the faintest hint of movement within the frame, such as mist drifting slowly across still water. Burns instructed his cinematographers to shoot such scenes "in the manner of taking still photographs."[52] Whereas Hyatt brought his on-screen presenter Walter Brennan to the present-day site of the Battle of the Little Bighorn in the concluding scene of *The End of the Trail*, Burns excludes human presence from his live-action shots of the war's historical sites. Although many shots include historical buildings, the age of such structures is minimized by the exclusion of any modern-day element that would serve to locate the image in the historical time of the present. Viewers are aware that they are watching footage shot in the contemporary present: the crisp, color moving image contrasts with the monochrome still photographs, while the landscape footage shares the same visual quality of 16mm film talking-head interviews. Indeed, just as the charismatic talking heads of Shelby Foote and other historians resonate with the captivating personalities of the war narrative presented through portrait photographs, so too do the live-action landscape shots parallel the overwhelming abundance of landscape photography from the war and its immediate aftermath.

Due to the long exposure time and complicated technical procedure required by photography in the 1860s, the medium was incapable of capturing the immediacy and motion of battle, which came to be documented by sketch artists on the scene. The most skilled photographers of the Civil War recognized the limited and specific capacities of the relatively new medium. As art historian Anthony W. Lee notes of Alexander Gardner, one of the most important photographers of the war, "the camera pictured not events but instead only the sites and remains of events already passed; it registered, mostly by implication and imaginative reconstruction (and through the services of the letterpress), the marks of history; and it everywhere betrayed its own belatedness."[53] In this context, we can see how Burns's documentary series fits into the long history of the war's visual representation extending back to Gardner's seminal American photobook, *A Photographic Sketch Book of the War*, published in 1866. Each of the one hundred photographs in Gardner's book was accompanied by a letterpress text on the opposite page, which alternated between specific historical explication of the image's content and anecdotal digression. Similar to the voiceover narration heard over both the historical photographs and the color landscape footage in Burns's series, the photographs of Gardner's book required a textual supplement to generate the "implication and imaginative reconstruction" that could allow the "marks of history" to register in the reader's mind.[54] Although *The Civil War* lacks the ambulatory contingency of Gardner's book, Burns was deeply invested in creating what he called "emotional chapters," which would have "an ability to float between episodes."[55] Such episodes bring together first-person testimony from diaries and correspondence with the photographic documentation of life in wartime (often Gardner's photographs) in order to convey what Burns sees as central to his documentary filmmaking: "the very powerful emotional resonances that seem to emanate from the collision of individuals and events and moments in American history" (1032). Many historians have taken issue with this heavy reliance on personal discourse, arguing that without adequate historical contextualization, it merely produces "the illusion of social history" and a view of "history as nothing more than collective biography."[56]

The sharpest, most succinct moments of such emotional resonance occur for Burns within the brief scenes he calls "telegrams," which are "short bursts that also have a certain potential to move but are more or less tied to a specific moment or a specific time" (1037). As Edgerton notes, these scenes tend to revolve around private reactions to specific historical moments or events documented in personal writings, which Burns then structures around single archival photographs (11–12). A prime example of this type of scene appears in episode six after the narrative exposition of the Battle of Cold Harbor and its decimation of Grant's Union army. A photograph shows a dead soldier lying in front of a pile of wood in a field. As the camera zooms into the young man's face, with his wide-open eyes and gaping mouth clearly visible, McCullough narrates, "After the battle, the diary of a young Massachusetts volunteer was found spattered with blood. Its last entry read, 'June 3, 1864, Cold Harbor, Virginia: I was killed'" (Figures 1.16–1.17). The photograph in this scene was taken by Timothy O'Sullivan after the Battle of Spotsylvania, which occurred almost two weeks before Cold Harbor, and the dead soldier is from the Confederate rather than the Union Army. The photograph's historical referent matters less for Burns than its capacity to visualize the horror and doom articulated by the Union soldier in his last diary entry. Photographs here serve to visually illustrate the affect articulated in other forms of historical documentation.

Historical referentiality was not the only aspect of the archival photographs subject to creative treatment by Burns. His aesthetic manipulation of the images frequently demonstrates "an almost ruthless disregard for their original state," according to John C. Tibbetts.[57] By selecting details for our attention, through either camera movement across the image or cutting to cropped areas of it, Burns performs a kind of recomposition, creating what Tibbetts sees as "new raw materials" that suggest "a sense of what Kracauer calls 'endlessness,' i.e. the sense of a world going on in all directions beyond the edges" (126). In fact, Burns often speaks of his engagement with photography in three dimensional terms: "To merely acknowledge its plasticity, to not just see its two-dimensionality but to go into its world and to trust that that world had a past and a present. And to activate it."[58] Burns treats the photographic image as though it were profilmic space subject to analytical editing. Whereas Tibbetts and Edgerton read such treatment of the archival photographs as critical to Burns's ability to emotionally engage his viewers with the historical events, rhetoric scholar Judith Lancioni argues that his analytical editing actually encourages viewers to "recognize that the photographs are versions of the past that can be evaluated for the ideological implications of their composition."[59] Mobile framing, she argues, prolongs our viewing of the image, thus extending the time provided for deciphering what we see. If Tibbetts sees a potential identification with the mobile camera *into* the represented three-dimensional space captured by the image, then Lancioni treats such identification with camera movement as occurring *across* the surface of the two-dimensional image of the photograph. The "act of purposeful discovery" in such identification is epistemological rather than narrative, self-reflexive rather than immersive (402). Similarly, she regards the generation of new shots by cropping portions of a single

Figures 1.16–1.17 Photograph of young Confederate soldier killed at the Battle of Spotsylvania, 1864, in *The Civil War* (Ken Burns, 1990), episode 6.

photograph—what she calls "reframing"—as an opportunity for viewers to recognize the archival photograph as a particular interpretation of reality, rather than its mere reproduction. The reframed image can thus propose an alternative interpretation, such as calling out the ideological dynamics of marginalization or erasure occurring within the original image. Yet for such a self-reflexive critical process to occur, the documentary would actually need to explicitly acknowledge the original act of photographic framing, something that the series consistently resists.

Only in the brief "telegram" scene about Matthew Brady's 1862 exhibition "The Dead of Antietam" in episode three does this 11½-hour series actually visualize the photographic frame by matting the images presented on screen.[60] Following an introductory shot of a photographic workshop producing stereoscopic images, four photographs of dead soldiers are presented, each through a rapid fade-in and fade-out from black (Figures 1.18–1.19).[61] The first three images appear with a black matte that disappears as the camera zooms into center of the image; the final image opens on a close-up detail, and the black matte appears after a zoom-out reveals the complete photograph. However, this unique presentation of the photographs serves more to accentuate the rhetorical eloquence of the elegiac voiceover (a *New York Times* review of the exhibition) than to elaborate how photographs came to frame the war for the American public at the time.[62] Consistently fading out to black, the photographs encourage us to read them as mental images conjured in the mind's eye, thus resonating with the voiceover's invocation of dreams: "The dead of the battlefield come up to us very rarely, even in dreams."[63] Although the newspaper reviewer praises Brady for bringing home "the terrible reality and earnestness

Figures 1.18 Stereograph production (French photograph taken in 1860 that Burns uses to illustrate Mathew Brady's stereograph production) in *The Civil War* (Ken Burns, 1990), episode 3.

Figures 1.19 Photograph of Union dead at the Battle of Antietam, 1862, by Mathew Brady, in *The Civil War* (Ken Burns, 1990), episode 3.

of the war," Alan Trachtenberg has argued that the Northern public were just as prone to reading such images within the framework of martyrdom and patriotic sacrifice, especially within the context of their newspaper circulation as engraved illustrations.[64]

Although the vast majority of still images incorporated into the series are photographs, Burns does include engravings, drawings, and paintings to visualize events that cameras were unable to capture, such as battle scenes and the execution of John Brown. Produced well after the end of the war, many of these battle paintings depict the historical events of the war through the explicitly romanticizing lens of late-nineteenth-century popular memory. *The Civil War* makes no formal distinction between its presentation of photographs and these types of hand-rendered images.[65] All equally subject to Burns's formal techniques of cinematic dynamization, these still images engender the kind of "*abstract visual equivalence* between pictures" that Allan Sekula associates with the institution of the archive.[66] In his seminal essay on reading the photographic archive, Sekula argues that to place photographs in an archive liberates them from the contingencies in which they have been put to use. Yet that liberation ultimately constitutes "an *abstraction* from the complexity and richness of use, a loss of context" (154, emphasis in original). For Burns to be able to treat the thousands of photographs and other still images included in the series as "new raw material" available for sophisticated cinematic rendering, he needed to maintain the abstract visual equivalence produced by their archivization.

At the beginning of the final episode of the series, McCullough briefly acknowledges the scale of photographic practice during the war by mentioning that more than a million photographs were made during the four-year conflict. Yet rather than historically contextualize the photography displayed in the series, this telegram scene serves merely to set up a broader point about how fast the war fell into oblivion. McCullough describes the disintegrating interest in war photographs, noting that surviving glass negatives were often sold for their glass rather than their images: "In the years following Appomattox, the sun slowly burned the image of war from thousands of greenhouse glass panes." The details of photographic history serve here merely as an allegory of national forgetting in relation to the war. Indeed, Burns shows little interest in photography in its own right, especially in relation to its own history. It functions for him as a raw material in historical documentary's audio-visual representation of a past made imaginatively accessible to viewers.

Digital Augmentation

Now that it is a ubiquitous special effect in editing software that can be automatically applied to any set of digital images, the Ken Burns effect facilitates the abstract visual equivalence between pictures with far greater ease than the assiduous analog labor needed to produce his series *The Civil War*. Moreover, the digitalization of film editing has facilitated new means to animate still photographs, most popularly with the so-called 2½D parallax effects pioneered by editor Jun Diaz in *The Kid Stays in the Picture* (Brett Morgen and Natalie Burstein, 2002), a documentary biopic based on Hollywood producer Robert Evans's eponymous memoir. Restricted by Evans's reluctance to be interviewed on camera for the film, Morgen and Burstein sought ways to dynamize the large collection of still photographs and archival footage that Evans made accessible to them. Diaz began to experiment with the stills, using Photoshop to separate elements on different depth layers in the image and then using AfterEffects to create animation between the separated elements. The resulting parallax effect bears a resemblance to stereoscopic photography as the static planes of foreground and background appear to diverge through subtle movements imitating the effect of eye movement in parallax vision. Diaz integrates this novel effect into an array of devices that maintained a continual sense of dynamic movement to the image-track, including the more conventional use of camera movement across photographs, incessant dissolves between still and moving archival images, and rudimentary stop-motion sequences created from different stills during publicity shoots. In many sequences, Diaz pushes the parallax effect to excess, mixing color with monochrome in a single image, simulating emphatic rack focus between different planes in a photograph, and manipulating the scale of human figures such that spatial relations become expressive rather than realistic (Figures 1.20–1.21) (Video 1.6 ▶).

Figures 1.20–1.21 Jun Diaz's 2½D parallax effect makes spatial relations expressive in *The Kid Stays in the Picture* (Nanette Burstein and Brett Morgen, 2002).

The opening shots of the film establish the excess of these effects in terms of visually characterizing Evans's interiority as a flamboyant, outsized Hollywood personality: a Steadicam graciously roams the sumptuously lit grounds and interior of Evans's Beverly Hills home as snippets of sound related to Evans's career come in and out of audibility. The camera settles on a table of framed photographs depicting cherished moments in Evans's personal and professional life. Since the filmmakers envisioned Evans's home as "a wonderful metaphor for his internal landscape," this shot of his photo table sets up the subsequent still photographs in the film as subjective images, visual manifestations of the memories that Evans recounts on the voiceover, which thus need not maintain the indexical quality of photographic evidence.[67]

Although commentators on the film read the visual excess of the 2½D parallax effects as a specific visualization of the Hollywood mogul's aggrandizing self-perception, the effect itself was widely lauded as a promising new tool for documentary filmmakers and was subsequently imitated in a variety of documentaries using still photographs, assisted by numerous how-to articles in professional magazines and online publications.[68] The effect has become a standard component of documentary television's digitally enabled visual style (what John Caldwell calls "televisuality") and, like the Ken Burns effect, a near-ubiquitous technique that frequently descends into visual cliché.[69] In the search for new means to animate still photographs and immerse audiences in their worlds, documentary filmmakers have turned to digitally animated simulations based on archival photographs and film footage. Seán Ó Cualáin's *Men at Lunch* (2012) is a prime example of such efforts. The Irish television documentary investigates the enduring power and appeal of the iconic, but unattributed, 1932 photograph of eleven ironworkers nonchalantly having lunch while perched atop a girder high above the street during the construction of the Rockefeller Center. Like other documentaries focused solely on a single iconic photograph, *Men at Lunch* faces the challenge of how to visually present that image repeatedly while sustaining viewer engagement with it.[70] Ó Cualáin responds to the task through three principal means: a) applying diverse forms of visual treatment to the photograph, including full-frame presentation, the Ken Burns effect, and the 2½D parallax effect; b) editing the photograph together with related photographs and footage, both archival and simulated, that situate it in a specific place and historical moment; and c) locating the physical photograph as an object in the material spaces that have given it meaning and value, including the archives of the Rockefeller Center and Corbis (which owns the intellectual property of the image), the homes of individuals who claim relatives in the picture, and the New York tourist shops that sell postcards of the image.

While the film devotes considerable screen time to the photograph as material object, Ó Cualáin shows little interest in the actual history of the photograph's circulation and the question of precisely how it became iconic. Its iconicity is a given to be explained by an array of (largely Irish American) cultural commentators who consistently resort to highly mythologized narratives of immigration and national identity: "This is why I love this photograph. In seventy years, they've gone from the gutters of South Street to the towers of Manhattan" (Peter Quinn).[71] The focus on the material photograph primarily serves the film's investigative narratives that seek to discover who took the photograph, who is actually in the picture, and whether the photograph was faked. Only the final question is significantly answered with Corbis archivist Ken Johnston symbolically piecing together the fragments of the archive's broken glass negative as he declares its authenticity as the original untampered negative. Despite considerable screen time devoted to the unsubstantiated claims of two Irish American cousins that their fathers were in the photograph, the identities of the picture's subjects (as well as its photographer) remain unproven by the end of the film.[72] However, the general failure of the film's investigative narratives only serves to bolster its contextualizing narrative about the picture's iconic power: the mystery and anonymity of the image enhances the capacity for its viewers to project their own immigrant identities and family histories onto it.

The application of the 2½D parallax effect to the photograph lends visceral support to such identificatory projection. It not only enhances the viewer's immersion into the space of the photograph, but also bolsters the dimensional perception of the vast space between these heroic men and Manhattan far below them. Much of the power of the original photograph lies in its impression of precarious suspension, augmented by the presence of a cable in the foreground and the absence of the structures holding up the girder on which the men sit. Several shots in the film even emphasize the cable through the simulation of negative parallax—the cable, rendered out of focus, appears to dangle in front of the image itself (Figure 1.22).[73] For all its spatial differentiation of elements in the picture, the 2½D parallax effect cannot escape the fact that each element remains two-dimensional. Like the perceptual paradoxes that accompany 3D cinema, the spatial separation of elements within the photograph potentially draws attention to the very flatness of the elements themselves.

The film's boldest attempt to viscerally convey the men's heroic labor comes in its use of digitally simulated archival footage of an aerial shot of midtown Manhattan. In black-and-white footage with emphatic, digitally added scratches, a camera appears to hurtle through the sky above Manhattan toward the construction site at Rockefeller Center. The camera comes to a halt right before a girder at the top of the construction, on which a row of eleven ironworkers sit with their backs to the camera (Figure 1.23) (Video 1.7 ▶). For all its visceral thrill of movement through historical space and the

Figure 1.22 The depth illusion of the 2½D parallax effect in *Men at Lunch* (Seán Ó Cualáin, 2012).

Figure 1.23 Simulated archival film footage from "behind" the iconic photograph in *Men at Lunch* (Seán Ó Cualáin, 2012).

promise of access to "the other side" of the iconic photograph, this aerial shot engenders a paradoxical impression of both realism and artifice. It is a digitally created reenactment crudely masquerading as archival footage. Moreover, it provides access to a perspective and visual mastery of space that was clearly historically impossible in the early 1930s. Digital special effects designed to enhance viewer immersion into the historical world depicted in the photograph ultimately risk producing the very opposite effect. In a manner similar to the tensions within 3D cinema spectatorship, viewers become self-consciously aware of the photograph as image and the visual manipulation to which it has been subjected. A device for greater spectatorial immersion into the world depicted in the photographic image ironically becomes a perceptual obstacle that calls attention to, and questions, the representational status of the image.

As we have seen across the chapter, the incorporation of photographic images into documentary film through cinematography and editing techniques has generated divergent tendencies to either foreground or obscure the status of the photograph as representation. The tendency initiated by Resnais' *Night and Fog* pursues an essayistic interrogation of photography's representational claims to truth, whereas the tendency within mainstream historical documentary that was established by Low and Koenig's *City of Gold* works to occlude the representational mechanics of photographs in the service of spectatorial immersion into a historical world that appears accessible precisely through the medium's seeming transparency. Nowhere is this opposition clearer than in the two films' use of intermedial ambiguity between film and photograph. If *City of Gold* muddles the perceptual distinction between the two precisely at moments when the documentary seeks to seamlessly transmit the viewer between present and past, then *Night and Fog* blurs the two media through the subtle interplay of stillness and almost imperceptible movement to disturb the viewer's epistemological assumptions about the possible truths produced by the images before them. Whether functioning as uncanny tension or integrative transition, intermedial ambiguity provides documentary film with a richly generative device for incorporating photography.

Beyond this essayistic tradition of incorporating photographs as an encounter between viewer and image, rather than an immersion of viewer into image, lies another sort of encounter—with the photographic object itself. In the next chapter, I explore how photographs function as elements of documentary mise-en-scène. Not merely images, photographs are also objects with rich material histories and uses that documentary film can enable us to see differently.

2
Filming the Photographic Object

Although the Ken Burns effect has become one of the most heavily used techniques in historical documentaries, an alternative approach to the use of historical photographs has also emerged since the early 1960s, one that fully recognizes that the photograph is not only an image of the past, but also a material object with its own history. This approach treats the photograph as an element of the film's mise-en-scène rather than merely as raw visual material available to the animating treatment of cinematography and editing or as a representational image subject to self-conscious analytical interrogation through these two compositional elements of film. By framing photographs as material objects, documentary filmmakers can thus raise some of the fundamental questions about photography as a social practice, rather than just a medium: What do people do with photographs? What are the sources of their value and meaning within social and political actions? How does the significance of these visual objects change as they move from one context to another? Moreover, to emphasize the photograph as mise-en-scène not only recognizes the material history of the picture, but also explicitly situates the photograph within the present historical moment, which the Ken Burns effect obviates through its disavowal of the photograph's frame. To present the photograph in this manner confronts the film's audience not just with an image that means, but with an object that matters. In this chapter, I examine a range of documentaries from the 1960s to the present that engage histories of political violence and conflict in a diversity of ways through the materiality of photographs. Unlike conventional photojournalism, it is not the particular visual content of the photographic *images* in these films that directly and singularly bears witness to such violence, but the ways in which photographic *objects* have been deployed within specific forms of social and political action. I borrow the term "photographic object" from Geoffrey Batchen's influential essay "Vernacular Photographies," in which he elucidates the significance of ordinary photographs' non-photographic materiality (e.g., frames, albums, pendants, painted prints) to our multi-sensory experience of them within social action. Even the creases, tears, stains, and annotations on a family snapshot can contribute to how it comes to matter to us as a photographic object.[1]

The chapter begins by analyzing three documentaries about photographic albums produced in relation to atrocities perpetrated by Nazi officers and German Wehrmacht soldiers during World War Two: Jerzy Ziarnik's *Powszedni dzień gestapowca Schmidta* (*A Working Day of Gestapo Man Schmidt,* 1963), Irina Gedrovich's *Fotoliubitel* (*Amateur Photographer,* 2004), and Erik Nelson's *Scrapbooks from Hell: The Auschwitz Albums* (2008). The albums in these films are found objects that pose profound questions about amateur photography as historical evidence. Given

A Medium Seen Otherwise. Roger Hallas, Oxford University Press. © Oxford University Press 2023.
DOI: 10.1093/oso/9780190057763.003.0003

how heavily amateur photographs rely on spoken or written narrativization and exposition for their meanings to be communicated, the films closely examine the physical arrangement of images and textual inscriptions in each album for clues to comprehend both their personal meanings for their makers and their historical value for our contemporary understanding of German acts of genocide and atrocity during World War Two. These films also demonstrate a visual fascination with the physical state of the albums as rare visual remnants of historical trauma that have miraculously survived into the present.

The second section of this chapter shifts focus from documentaries about specific photographic objects to those that pay close attention to the physical relations between human bodies and photographic objects, particularly in the diverse gestures of handling photographs. To touch a photograph is to express an affective relation to it, but such gestures are more than merely individualized personal behavior. Particularly in contexts of political violence, they articulate affect toward the photographic object that is profoundly social and political in significance. Performing the act of physically holding a photograph before an audience, whether live or mediated, became a powerful strategy for mobilizing political affect in the late twentieth century, epitomized by the Argentine mothers of the disappeared in the late 1970s, who publicly wore portraits of their missing children on their bodies and later carried placards and banners bearing enlargements of these photographs. Filmmakers have not only documented these strategies, but also come to recognize the possibilities for critical self-reflexivity in filming their own physical handling of photographs related to political violence and atrocity. I analyze two documentaries from different political contexts that engage in such strategies: Sylvia Stevens and David Fox's *Picturing Derry* (1985), about the photographic representation of the divided city in Northern Ireland, and Sebastian Moreno's *La Ciudad de los Fotógrafos* (*City of Photographers*, 2006), about photojournalists during the Pinochet regime in Chile. While *Picturing Derry* concentrates on how its social actors handle photographs in order to reveal the destabilized distinction between public and private in Northern Ireland, *City of Photographers* documents how holding photographs has functioned in Chile as a political tactic, first to challenge the political violence of the dictatorship, and then to sustain the memory of it in the post-Pinochet era.

The chapter concludes by turning to the materiality of the digital image. Through close readings of Errol Morris's feature documentary *Standard Operating Procedure* (2008) and Forensic Architecture's documentary short *Rafah: Black Friday* (2015), this final section examines how the virtual mise-en-scène afforded by digital cinema provides a visual space in which digital photographs produced in the context of political violence and conflict can be deployed in ways that generate more material evidence than merely their visual content. Since metadata is a constitutive component of digital photographs' materiality, they can be precisely located in time and place, and therefore also in relation to one another. This mathematically calculable relationality of media objects is indeed a vital characteristic of digital culture.[2] The documentaries delve into what such metadata and the temporal and spatial relationality between photographs revealed by it can permit us to know about the events in Abu Ghraib prison in 2003 and in Rafah during the 2014 Israel/Gaza conflict. Although both documentaries place the photographs in visual spaces that shift between the two-dimensional and the three-dimensional, their visual strategies pursue differing ends. Whereas Morris is most concerned with using the relations between multiple images to complicate prevailing conceptions of what truths the digital photographs from Abu Ghraib can actually reveal, the Forensic Architecture documentary works to build what Eyal Weizman calls an "architectural-image complex," in which digital photographs are embedded, through their metadata, in a 3D architectural model that can generate new forensic evidence of potential war crimes perpetrated during the conflict.[3]

Like other fields in the humanities, photography studies have undertaken a materialist turn over the past several decades. This shift from prioritizing the photograph as visual image to approaching it also as material object drew from a number of intellectual developments, including the general historicist reorientation of the humanities that followed the ascendency of critical theory in the 1980s, the gradual expansion of photography studies from the hermeneutic discipline of art history to the interdisciplinary field of visual studies, and the growing interest in the material dimensions of the analog photograph in light of the proclaimed immateriality of the digital image. Anthropologists, in particular, recognized how photographs—as three-dimensional physical objects, not just two-dimensional images—facilitate significant forms of social and cultural interaction. Photographic meanings are negotiated not only through visual apprehension of the image, argues Elizabeth Edwards, but also through "(t)he stories told with and around photographs, the image held in the hand, features delineated through the touch of the finger, an object passed around, a digital image printed and put in a frame and carefully placed, dusted and cared for."[4] Moreover, as Edwards's quotation attests, our experience of photography is multisensory, incorporating hearing and touch, as well as vision.[5] Paradoxically, it has been photography's material foundation as a physical trace of the world, its indexical quality, that has focused the ontological debate about the medium on questions of the transparency, authenticity, and truth of the photographic image more than on the actual material qualities of photographic objects themselves and our phenomenological experiences of them. Geoffrey Batchen contends that, even in the most sophisticated discussions about photography, there is a tendency to "look through" the photograph (as a two-dimensional portal onto the world) rather than to "look right at" it (as a three-dimensional object in the world).[6] Photographs are indeed "tactile, sensory things" generated by social relations in time and space.[7]

The materiality of photography matters because it is never merely "a neutral support for images."[8] As Edwards and Janice Hart contend in the introduction to *Photographs, Objects, Histories*, photographic materiality can be understood on two significant and interrelated levels: on the one hand, there is "the plastic materiality of the image itself," that is to say, its photochemistry, the surface on which it is printed, or any physical embellishments applied to it; and on the other hand, there are "its presentational forms," such as *cartes de visites*, albums, and frames, as well as the numerous manifestations of its non-photochemical reproduction in publications ranging from tabloid newspapers to luxury art books. This material diversity to photography is critical to its capacity to traverse differing contexts and, in the process, transform its meanings: "negatives become prints, prints become lantern slides or postcards, ID photographs become family treasures, private photographs become archives, analog objects become electronic digital code, private images become public property, and photographs of scientific production are reclaimed as cultural heritage."[9]

The capacity for digital photographs to traverse multiple formats and platforms is far greater than analog images because of the power of the computer, according to Lev Manovich, to function as a universal "media machine," which derives its ability to "transcode" across formats from the particular qualities of digital new media: its numeric coding, modular organization, automation, and variability.[10] In the early years of digital studies, this ease of transcoding was often tied to the idea that, unlike analog media, new digital media were fundamentally immaterial in nature, existing as states rather than as matter, or as Nicholas Negroponte put it in 1995, bits rather than atoms.[11] But more recent scholarship has challenged these assumptions by elaborating the diverse materiality of digital media.[12] For example, Matthew G. Kirschenbaum differentiates between two types of materiality: forensic and formal.[13] Forensic materiality refers to the unique, individualized physical traces produced by digital media, such as the micron-size inscriptions on a magnetic drive, the heat from processing a large digital file, or the blue light from an electronic screen that can cause digital eye strain. On a larger scale, the seemingly weightless and ubiquitous digital clouds of the networked era rely on vast data centers that consume enormous amounts of energy. Whether large or small, visible, or hidden, the hardware required to maintain our contemporary networked culture is immense, substantially challenging the concept of digital media's utopian immateriality. Defined primarily in relation to software, formal materiality acknowledges that file formats do not only create the modular capacities of digital objects to function within multiple software environments, but also impose constraints on the ultimate mutability of data.[14] For example, once a JPEG image file has been compressed in size, certain data is irretrievably lost, which may subsequently constrain its functionality in different software programs. On the other hand, digital images also contain more than visual information. This metadata—including information about where, when, and how the photograph was taken—can be mobilized by software programs to generate valuable new meanings and information that exceed the individual photograph and its visual content as an image. Software allows this relationality between digital images to be mapped within 3D virtual environments for the purposes of measuring data, calculating new information, and also communicating it to an audience. Such new virtual mise-en-scène for presenting digital images, as we see in *Standard Operating Procedure* and *Rafah: Black Friday*, marks a significant shift in filming the photographic object in documentary: from a relationality between analog photographic objects and the people who do things with them to a relationality between the digital photographic objects themselves.

Leafing Through Rediscovered Albums

Although photographic objects occasionally made an appearance in the mise-en-scène of midcentury documentaries, they generally served as straightforward rhetorical tropes. In Humphrey Jennings's *Listen to Britain* (1942), for instance, an eyeline match connects a middle-aged woman at home looking longingly at a framed photograph of a uniformed young man, succinctly conveying ideas of family, service, and sacrifice. Jennings opened and closed *Family Portrait* (1950), his documentary about postwar Britain, with shots of pages from a photo album, clearly emphasizing the film's analogy of nation as family. Photo albums construct meaning in ways that are at once typical and atypical, public and private, collective and individual. This fundamental "idea of the album," as Martha Langford calls it, becomes a central pre-occupation for documentaries about German soldiers' photo albums as they seek to understand what meaning and value such narrativized visual objects held for those who made them, and also for those into whose hands they subsequently fell, including Holocaust survivors, allied soldiers, prosecutors, and historians.[15]

Amid the emergent discourse of the Holocaust in the early Sixties, two Polish filmmakers, Janusz Majewski and Jerzy Ziarnik, turned to personal photo albums made by German soldiers in World War Two as the subject for short documentaries. Interest in such albums reflected the increasing attention paid to the mentality of the perpetrator after Adolf Eichmann's trial in 1961. Majewski's *Album Fleischera* (*Fleischer's Album*, 1962) focuses on a collection of over two thousand photographs taken by a German soldier from Görlitz, which the director discovered through a chance conversation with a taxi driver, while Ziarnik's *A Working Day of Gestapo Man Schmidt* focuses on the album of a Gestapo officer in Kutno, which was held in the archives of the Central Committee for the Investigation of Nazi Crimes in Poland.[16] Although both filmmakers use voiceover, camera movement, and editing to reframe these perpetrator images, only Ziarnik treats Schmidt's album explicitly as an element of mise-en-scène.

A Working Day of Gestapo Man Schmidt opens with an exterior shot of the Justice Ministry in Warsaw followed by an interior shot of the Committee's office door. A safe is opened and a photo album removed and placed on a table. After the title appears across the image of the album, an anonymous hand opens it (Figure 2.1). At the end of the film, these shots are repeated in reverse as the album is returned to the safe. Such narrative bookending is rich with competing meanings. On the one hand, it implies the authenticity of the visual evidence on display—valuable documents locked away in the offices of the state—but, on the other hand, its circular structure and the visual trope of un/locking also suggest that we are being invited into the self-contained world of Schmidt's mentality. The sparse information offered by Ziarnik's voiceover commentary presents the album as a found object, an enigma in need of interpretation

Figure 2.1 An anonymous hand opens the album in *A Working Day of Gestapo Man Schmidt* (Jerzy Ziarnik, 1963).

by the viewer: "We know that his name was Schmidt. He worked in the Gestapo. We don't know if he tormented the arrested people in person, or only gave commands. In January 1945, in his hurriedly abandoned flat, this album was found, featuring photos which he mostly made himself and signed with his own comments."[17] The voiceover then shifts to simply translating Schmidt's clinically matter-of-fact captions and annotations in the album. Ziarnik consistently moves the camera across the borders of the photographs to the accompanying captions to simulate the viewer's search to understand the logic of the images in the album, which alternate between brutal persecution (of Jews and Polish partisans) and quotidian banality (in Schmidt's military life). The film accentuates such normalization of atrocity not merely through dialectical editing, but also in the attention given to Schmidt's material arrangement and exposition of his photographs in the album, revealing a fastidious personal documentation of the political violence in which he participated. For instance, Schmidt depicts a Gestapo manhunt for resistance fighters in central Poland through the iconography of the road trip: pictures of himself proudly standing in front of his vehicle, a hand-drawn map of his itinerary and statistics of the distances traveled (as well as the number of men captured) (Video 2.1 ▶) (Figures 2.2–2.3). Ziarnik also makes effective use of erratic camera movement across seemingly innocuous travel photographs of roads and streets to evoke the relentless hunt for hidden resisters.

Figures 2.2–2.3 Schmidt documents his manhunt for resistance fighters through a mix of bureaucratic data and iconography of the road trip in *A Working Day of Gestapo Man Schmidt* (Jerzy Ziarnik, 1963).

Mikolaj Jazdon notes that Ziarnik repeatedly frames Schmidt as a hunter pursuing trophies, yet we should be careful not to read this as merely the filmmaker crafting an analogy, for it also foregrounds how German soldiers were encouraged by the Nazi state to record and document their war experiences through the prevailing norms of amateur photography.[18] At the end of the film, Ziarnik's commentary returns to relocate Schmidt's self-portraits firmly in the present moment, to reframe them as wanted posters. He speculates on whether Schmidt survived the war, asking us to look closely at Schmidt's face. Returning to the photo of Schmidt standing proudly in front of his car, Ziarnik's voiceover intones, "Maybe someday, you'll see him abroad driving a Volkswagen or a Mercedes. Before we close this album, look at this man!" By directly addressing the audience with the present-day existence of the album, Ziarnik imbues it with a new prospective value, for it enables a call to bring Nazi perpetrators like Schmidt to justice.

Interest in German soldiers' amateur photography during World War Two continued to grow in the subsequent decades, culminating in the national debate that erupted in Germany in the late 1990s over the Hamburg Institute for Social Research's traveling exhibition *Verbrechen der Wehrmacht: Dimensionen des Vernichtungskrieges, 1941–1944 (Crimes of the German Wehrmacht: Dimensions of a War of Annihilation)*, which sought to demythologize the national narrative that the regular German army (Wehrmacht) did not participate in atrocities on the Eastern Front. Controversies over the historical accuracy of labeling and attribution of visual evidence led to the withdrawal and then revision of the exhibition in 2001, which reduced the numbers of photographs displayed and increased the supporting documentation that accompanied the remaining images.[19] *Amateur Photographer*, Irina Gedrovich's short documentary about the diary and photo album of an ordinary Wehrmacht soldier on the Eastern Front, explicitly addresses this relationship between soldiers' amateur photography and the discursive contexts in which it produces meaning. Like Ziarnik, Gedrovich begins and ends her film with the emphatic display of material objects before the film camera. After a credit sequence focused on shots of an old Zeiss-Ikon enlarger, *Amateur Photographer* presents a series of close-up shots of Gerhard M.'s wartime diary and photo album as an unseen hand slowly turns their pages.[20] The film concludes with shots of documents from M.'s trial at a Soviet Military Tribunal in 1952, including the hand-written trial record, his mugshots, and the sentencing document. Gedrovich uses M.'s war diary and his trial records as a kind of parallax frame to contextualize and explicate his photographs. The film follows M.'s wartime career on the Eastern Front, focusing primarily on the years 1941 and 1942. Like Schmidt's images from Poland, M.'s photographs alternate between the everyday banalities of military life on the front and atrocities committed against civilians and enemy soldiers in the Soviet Union. Gedrovich's editing masterfully illuminates the imbrication of banality and atrocity within both types of images. In one sequence, for instance, playful shots of German soldiers fishing on a river cut to a close-up of a soldier strenuously plunging a knife into the head of a fish, an image suggestively masking the violence perpetrated against humans that remains outside of the frame (Video 2.2 ▶).

When the subsequent photograph introduces a soldier carrying a stick with a large fish impaled on it, Gedrovich's camera moves to gradually reveal the human atrocity in the background of the photograph, where a village is being torched by Wehrmacht soldiers. Banality and atrocity are here revealed to be co-present within a single image. After M. is wounded in 1943, the film rapidly covers his promotion to lieutenant, his iron cross, and his surrender to the Americans at the end of the war. M. moves to East Berlin, becomes a citizen of the GDR, and joins both the Communist Party and the Soviet-German Friendship Society in 1951. His photo album and diary found during a search of his apartment lead to his arrest, trial, and conviction (of crimes undisclosed by the film). He is executed in Moscow in 1953.

Although Gedrovich makes effective use of Ken Burns's combined techniques for animating photographs—sound effects, musical counterpoint, and camera movement (especially an erratic set of movements to evoke the chaos of the battlefield)—she gradually draws our attention to the material qualities of the photographs and that which surrounds them. A third of the way into the film, we encounter a photographic negative showing a German soldier searching a civilian. Clearly noticeable are two pieces of tape holding the negative to a page, and in the lower right-hand corner of the frame are the words "Foto-Negativ" written across the edge of the image. After the film inverts the negative into a positive image, a cut brings us to background details of the image as the camera scans the faces of men anxiously staring back. The camera zooms out to show the photographic print on a yellowing page with its negative taped below and M's signed explanatory caption written across its corner in German (Figure 2.4). Below it, we see a Russian translation of M's words (Figure 2.5). On the

Figure 2.4 M's description (in German) is written over the print and negative in *Amateur Photographer* (Irina Gedrovich, 2004).

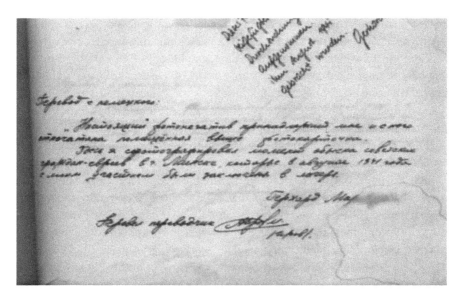

Figure 2.5 The Russian translation of M's description below the photographs in the trial record in *Amateur Photographer* (Irina Gedrovich, 2004).

voiceover, we learn that M's text identifies the photograph as the capture and internment of Soviet Jews, in which he participated. The voiceover's double narration of M's words throughout the film—first in German and then in English translation (Russian in the film's original release)—becomes immediately clear in this shot. It reproduces the discursive process of M's trial and the lack of subtitles draws our attention more fully to the handwritten captions and translations inscribed across the images on the page. This is the first of many photographs in the film that are taken from M's trial documents rather than from his original photo album. The film subsequently moves back and forth in a parallax manner between the present-tense narration of M's wartime diary and the retrospective voice of his testimony during the military investigation of his war crimes.

This auditory and visual parallax structure to the film achieves several things. First, it acknowledges how the meaning and value of such amateur photographs rely more heavily on external frameworks than most other types of war photography. Second, it traces how those meanings change profoundly as the photographs are resituated in different material and discursive contexts (from the private expression of identity in the diary and the album to the public testimony in legal prosecution). And finally, the parallax structure facilitates a critical distance for the film's viewer to closely examine the perpetrator's visual and mental perspectives without necessarily being ethically compromised by them. We may thus gain deeper insight into the objectification of the other that pervaded photographs by German soldiers (including ethnographic curiosity, antisemitism, and military or political enmity), while minimizing further potential objectification caused by our own historical gaze on these images. Gedrovich concludes the film with more recent images of Russian soldiers in Chechnya reflected on the lens of a SLR camera, intimating a contemporary resonance within a Russian context for these photographic objects from World War Two that have been plucked from the obscure reaches of a Russian military archive. In this contemporary coda, *Amateur Photographer* warns Russian audiences against national complacency, for Germany has not been alone in a dangerous collective amnesia and denial around wartime atrocity committed by ordinary soldiers. The film's final image thus urges Russians to reflect upon the perpetration of atrocity in their own more recent conflicts.

If Gedrovich worked to resist reobjectifying the victims of Nazi atrocity primarily through her complex arrangement of the perpetrator's voice framing the images, other filmmakers have chosen to counterpoint the victim's testimonial voice against the perpetrator's photograph, to allow the survivor to speak back to the image. For instance, in his 1984 documentary *Auschwitz, l'album, la mémoire* (*Auschwitz, the Album, the Memory*), Alain Jaubert frames the images from the Lily Jacob Album (a unique photographic documentation by two SS officers of Hungarian Jews being processed on the ramp at Auschwitz in 1944) with a montage of voices that includes quotations from Holocaust writers and four women survivors of Auschwitz, who comment upon the photographs, discussing what the camera has occluded and noticing small details that spur their memories. Jaubert further contests the capacity of the photographs to bear witness to the Holocaust through his philosophical commentary in the voiceover, the increasing abstraction of his extreme close-ups, and his visual attention to the photographs' margins (Figure 2.6).[21]

Polish filmmaker Dariuz Jablonski brought the survivor explicitly into the film frame to contest the perpetrator's image in *Fotoamator* (*Photographer*, 1998), his documentary about the color slide collection of Walter Genewein, the Nazis' chief accountant in the Lodz ghetto. Jablonski adapts Ziarnik's archival framing device in *A Working Day of Gestapo Man Schmidt*, but instead of the photographs being retrieved from the archive, the last surviving witness of the Lodz ghetto, Dr. Arnold Mostowicz, is shown making his way through the shadowy aisles of the archive before sitting in front of an antique slide projector showing Genewein's photographs. These carefully staged shots frame his emotionally charged and richly evocative testimony of the atrocities he witnessed as a direct and contemporary contestation of the cold objectifying gaze of Genewein's bureaucratic and sanitized visualization of the ghetto. Mostowicz revisualizes with words precisely what Genewein occluded through his images.[22]

We once again see a human figure entering the mysterious space of the archive in the opening pre-credit shots of Erik Nelson's *Scrapbooks from Hell: The Auschwitz Albums*, but this time it is not the survivor who penetrates the obscure space of the institution, but the archivist. Arriving in the darkness of the night, she puts on her white lab coat and floods the room with light before retrieving an archival preservation box from locked storage. She removes a file containing a single page from a photo album and begins to carefully clean the photograph of two SS officers on the

Figure 2.6 Close-ups of photographic edges in *Auschwitz, the Album, the Memory* (Alain Jaubert, 1984).

page (Figure 2.7). A close-up of the handwritten caption reveals the album's context: "Auschwitz 21.6.1944." As its title unabashedly suggests, *Scrapbooks from Hell* is a television documentary, made for the National Geographic Channel by one of the industry's most prolific and successful producers of "forensic history."[23] After the United States Holocaust Memorial Museum announced that an anonymous donor had gifted the museum the remains of a personal photo album belonging to Karl Höcker (the adjutant to Richard Baer, the commandant of Auschwitz I), Nelson began research for a program about this important historical discovery. Discussions with museum archivist Rebecca Erbelding revealed significant parallels between the Höcker Album and the Lily Jacob Album, despite their starkly different subject matter—the Höcker Album depicted the social life of Nazi commanders of the camp, whereas the Jacob Album meticulously documented the genocidal processing of victims in the camp. The only surviving photographs from inside the Auschwitz complex (save the four *Sonderkommando* photos), the Jacob and Höcker Albums contained images shot during roughly the same period in the summer of 1944, and they were both miraculously rediscovered by accident at the end of the war. *Scrapbooks from Hell* analyzes the albums in relation to one another in order to furnish new evidence beyond what each album is able to generate on its own.

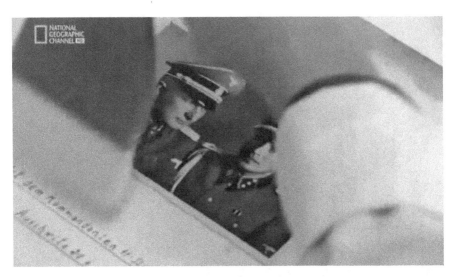

Figure 2.7 An archivist cleans a photograph from the Karl Höcker album in *Scrapbooks from Hell: The Auschwitz Albums* (Erik Nelson, 2008).

Containing photographs of Höcker's family life and leisure time with his fellow German officers in the camp, Höcker's album was rediscovered in an abandoned apartment in Frankfurt in June 1945 by an American army officer who had requisitioned the space as accommodation during his stay. Elsewhere, as American forces were liberating the Dora-Mittelbau concentration camp in April 1945, Lily Jacob, a young Hungarian Jew sick with typhoid, stumbled across a different photo album in the camp infirmary as she was searching for a blanket. On looking closely at the album, she was astounded to see that it systematically documented the very transport that had brought her and her family to Auschwitz in May 1944. She saw photos of her rabbi, her family members, and even herself on the arrival ramp. Although historians have established that the photographs were likely taken by Ernst Hofmann and Bernhard Walter, SS photographers in the camp, the actual purpose of the album has never been fully established, especially in light of the strict prohibition against photography in the camps. Given that its meticulously labeled images document the camp's processing of Hungarian Jews from arrival to just before they were taken to gas chambers, it may have been prepared as an official reference for higher authorities in Berlin or for Baer, who had only recently been appointed the camp commandant. Images from the album were used as evidence in the Frankfurt Auschwitz trials, and in 1980 Jacob donated the album to Yad Vashem, Israel's Holocaust Museum.

Scrapbooks from Hell devotes considerable attention to the compelling material histories of these albums, presenting both as unique and invaluable objects that now require the highest levels of museological care. Like the Höcker Album in the pre-credit sequence, the Jacob Album is at one point presented to the camera as it sits in a preservation box while an archivist turns its opening pages; in other shots, we see the album in its regular location on permanent display in Yad Vashem. Despite this visual emphasis on the materiality of the albums, the program also subjects the photographs at various moments to special effects techniques that accentuate their virtual qualities as still images animated by the motion of digital video. For instance, the program does not just use the television documentary convention of green-screening a photograph behind the speaker in talking-head interviews: it also first introduces these speakers through a digital fade-in over the photograph, which has the effect of dematerializing both the photograph and the interview subject (Figure 2.8). Elsewhere in the program, Nelson applies a parallax 2½D effect to group shots from the Höcker Album. As the camera appears to zoom into a photograph, foreground figures appear as though stereoscopically on a separate plane from those in the mid-ground. Although, as I have discussed in the previous chapter, this technique is most often used in contemporary documentaries to enhance the immersive qualities of camera movement in relation to photographs, it can, like 3D cinema, also easily undercut the realism of the image with the separated planes appearing like paper cut-outs. Nelson does not apply this effect to any photographs from the Jacob Album, and for good reason. Since the program culminates in a forensic analysis of one of the photographs from that album, any application of digital special effects would potentially undermine the indexical truth of the physical coordinates captured in such photographs. Nelson gathers on screen a team of forensic analysts to determine if an officer seen facing away from the camera in a photograph from the Jacob Album of the arrival ramp at Auschwitz was indeed Karl Höcker (Video 2.3 ▶). Since Höcker's prosecutors in Frankfurt were never able to provide sufficient legal proof that he had been present during the selection process at Auschwitz, he only received a sentence of seven years. By matching anthropometric

Figure 2.8 The dematerializing effect of green-screen and fade-outs in *Scrapbooks from Hell: The Auschwitz Albums* (Erik Nelson, 2008).

measurements taken from a photograph in Höcker's album with the officer pictured on the ramp, the forensic analysts ultimately declare the high probability that Höcker is indeed in the photograph from the Jacob Album (Figures 2.9–2.10). The transposition of fragments of the original photographs into 3D virtual environments translates indexical images into the material data needed for measurement, but in doing so, it paradoxically abstracts the images from not only their historical referents but also their own materiality as historical objects, which *Scrapbooks from Hell* foregrounds so emphatically elsewhere in the documentary.

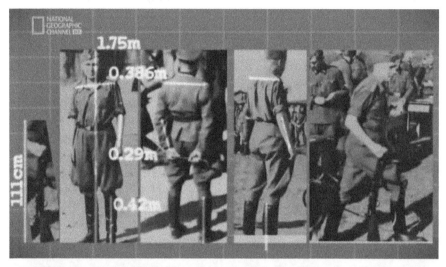

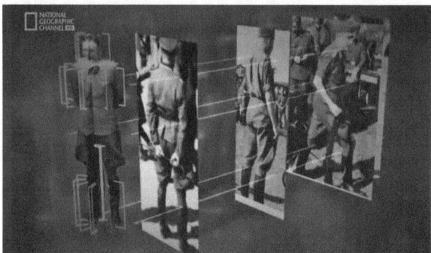

Figures 2.9–2.10 Forensic analysis of the photographs from the Jacob and Höcker albums confirm Höcker's presence on the arrival ramp at Auschwitz in *Scrapbooks from Hell: The Auschwitz Albums* (Erik Nelson, 2008).

Documentaries about Nazi photo albums focus so much attention on the mate-riality of these photographic objects because they embody a paradox. On the one hand, they constitute unique, and often extremely rare, photographic evidence of atrocity and genocide, yet on the other hand, their material form as an album occludes as much as it reveals since the meaning and value of photo albums are only fully realized through the acts of oral narration around them. The emphatic found-ness of these albums, often by sheer accident, amplifies the paradox: their miracu-lous survival produces their auratic value, yet the irrevocable severance from their original contexts of circulation and narration augments their opacity and enigma as historical evidence. Through its alternation between contemplating the photo-graphic object and scrutinizing the photographic image, documentary film illumi-nates this paradox.

The Social Gesture of Handling Photographs

Although brief in length, Harun Farocki's engagement with the Jacob Album in his film *Bilder der Welt und Inschrift des Krieges* (*Images of the World and the Inscription of War*, 1989) has undoubtedly generated more critical discussion than any other film using those images. In this essay film on the visuality of technological mo-dernity, Farocki turns to one particular photograph from the album—a long shot of the selection process on the ramp with a young Jewish woman walking across the foreground as she looks back—in order to illustrate one of the core ideas of the film, namely that preservation and destruction are intertwined components of modern visuality.[24] In several shots we see Farocki himself leafing through Serge Klarsfeld's published reproduction of the album. In one of them, when he comes to the page with the photograph of the Jewish woman on the ramp, he places his hand across her figure, shielding it from his own camera. While the voiceover com-mentary during this shot emphasizes the camera as part of the equipment of the camp, Farocki's hand gestures an ethical refusal to reproduce the objectification of the original photograph (Figure 2.11).[25] This shot contrasts sharply with one of the film's most widely used, and highly ambiguous, publicity stills (an image not in the actual film), in which Farocki's hands form a frame around the woman's head and shoulders, potentially signaling both Farocki's imposition upon the photograph and his imbrication in the original photographer's gaze. Farocki's literal handling of the archival images in *Images of the World* visually articulates his ongoing interrogative relationship to them. It is not only the photographs that become an element of mise-en-scène, but also the hands that touch them, thus rendering visible the filmmaker's work *with* images, rather than merely *through* them (as in the Ken Burns effect). This visual trope of handling the photograph was part of a larger Brechtian praxis that Farocki shared with his early collaborator Hartmut Bitomsky. Both filmmak-ers not only filmed themselves browsing through photographs and leafing through photobooks, but also found ways to foreground the process of working with archival

Figure 2.11 Harun Farocki's hand gestures an ethical refusal to reproduce the objectification of the original photograph from the Lily Jacob Album in *Images of the World and the Inscription of War* (Harun Farocki, 1989).

moving images, such as filming themselves watching television screens or viewing footage on an editing machine.[26]

To visually thematize the handling of photographs in the process of making films about images was not unique to Farocki and Bitomsky during this period of increasing documentary self-reflexivity, especially given the dual influence of materialist thinking about photography and Brechtian aesthetics on European documentary during the 1970s and the early 1980s. Sylvia Stevens and David Fox's *Picturing Derry* provides an innovative, if critically overlooked, example of this kind of documentary, which emerged out of the new opportunities for independent and experimental television in Britain. The television program rejects the then-emergent conventions of television documentaries about photography, which included observational footage of photographers shooting, camera movement over still photographs, and interpretative commentary on individual pictures by experts or the photographer. Instead, *Picturing Derry* places far greater visual emphasis on the materiality of the photograph—on how and where photographs are displayed, on how people handle them, and on how the filmmakers themselves work with such images. In its interviews with local and international photojournalists, amateur photographers, visual artists, police photographers, and members of a local photo workshop, *Picturing Derry* emphatically foregrounds the materiality of the photographic object over the full-frame presentation of photographic images. We watch them handling a range of photographic objects (prints, magazines, newspapers, albums) in carefully staged settings filled with photographs. Challenging hierarchies of photographic value, the program blurs the boundaries between professional and amateur and between public and private through its profilmic placement of documentary subjects in relation to physical photographs.

Three significant contexts provided the conditions of possibility for *Picturing Derry* and its innovative documentary strategies. First, the political situation in Northern Ireland intensified during the early Thatcher years, following her hardline response to the Republican Hunger Strikers in 1981. Bobby Sands had proven the political efficacy of an electoral strategy for Sinn Féin, while the provisional IRA stepped up its bombing campaign in mainland Britain. Both developments prompted the further pathologization of Republican political violence by the British press and increased levels of state surveillance of Republican communities in the North. Second, leftist photographic culture in Britain increasingly shifted away from the ethos of working-class empowerment and autonomy in the community photography movement of the 1970s to a more theoretical critique of representation arising from the emergent field of cultural studies in the early 1980s.[27] Established in 1982 with funding from the Gulbenkian Foundation, Derry Camerawork stood at the crossroads of this historical transformation, for it combined community-based photography with an ideological critique of dominant representation. Its work in photographic education with local Derry youth would provide the foundational material for *Picturing Derry*. Third, the establishment in 1982 of Channel Four, Britain's third public-service television channel, provided significant new opportunities for documentary filmmakers. The channel's public remit included a commitment to commission and buy programming from independent producers as well as to serve the broadcasting needs of unrepresented communities. Under the founding leadership of Jeremy Isaacs, Channel Four built a strong reputation for both arts programming and experimentation in television aesthetics.

Picturing Derry begins with long takes that pan across the contemporary urban landscape of the Bogside neighborhood in Derry, catching sight of children sledding down a snowy slope. However, the banality of the shots' content is undermined by a discordant jazz score, which renders the camera movement ominous and unsettling. These landscape shots are not conventional location B-roll, for they both raise our skepticism about the transparency of images of Derry and foreshadow the issue of state surveillance of the local community, which is given substantial coverage later in the program. Fox and Stevens locate and stage the interviews with photojournalists very precisely, in order to situate each photographer in relation to their class and geographical origin. All take place in living rooms rather than the professional settings normally chosen to bolster the authority of the speaker in such interviews. The English photojournalists sit comfortably in spacious bourgeois homes, while the local photographers are tightly framed in their cramped working-class living rooms. Moreover, camera movement within the interviews further encourages comparison between photographers from inside and outside Derry. When Derry photojournalist Willie Carson discusses the co-presence of everyday family life and political violence or its imminent threat, the camera pans away from his talking head and toward his mantelpiece on which are arranged a number of his photographs that illustrate the dichotomy of life in Derry that he describes. On the contrary, when Fleet Street photographer Clive Limpkin talks about the professional privilege of being able to leave the site of violence, the camera pans from his family photo table to the sofa on which he sits with his professional photographs stacked on the coffee table. This ability to separate political violence from family life is unavailable for those living in Derry. As Trisha Ziff, the founding organizer of Derry Camerawork, has noted about the social and political conditions of photography in Northern Ireland, "The notion of 'the family' becomes more collective and is extended to the community in conflict with the British state. The boundaries between 'the personal' and 'the public' disintegrate. While the home is no longer the private domain, events on the street in turn become personalised."[28]

Picturing Derry borrows the strategy of interviewing photographers with a stack of their photographs or publications in front of them from *Master Photographers* (1983), Peter Adam's popular six-part series for the BBC, in which the art historian led a conversation about photographic aesthetics with a modernist master as the latter leafed through one of his books or perused his prints.[29] However, Fox and Stevens replace Adam's aesthetic preoccupation with a focus on the political, economic, and social conditions determining the production and reception of the photographs under discussion. How each interviewee physically handles the photographs indicates much about their relationship to the images they discuss, and the camera carefully observes this non-verbal behavior. The anonymous police photographer holds a pencil that he uses to point to specific details in his forensic photographs, signaling the professional distance he wishes to maintain from the photographic subject (Figure 2.12). The nonchalant manner in which international photojournalist Terry Fincher pulls out one of his own photographs from the messy pile on his desk intimates a casual sense of his own cosmopolitan mastery of the world that he captures through his camera. During a group interview with members of Derry Camerawork, a young woman, who raises ethical concerns about photojournalism's reliance on decontextualized sensation, opens up a copy of *Life* magazine to a double-page photograph of a mother in hijab grieving the death of her four young children. Hardly touching the edge of the magazine, the young woman's outstretched palm lays bare her moral indignation at the spectacle of photojournalism. After amateur photographer Eileen Robson turns each page of her photo album, which documents the overlapping worlds of family and political

Figure 2.12 An anonymous police officer points to a forensic photograph in *Picturing Derry* (David Fox and Sylvia Stevens, 1985).

events, she tenderly lays the fingertips of her hand on the page in a gesture of such care and respect for the lives and deaths recorded on each page (Figure 2.13).

The deliberate framing of photography as mise-en-scène becomes most visible in the six scenes of metacommentary interspersed throughout the program. In a bird's-eye shot, we see a man and a woman (Fox and Stevens) standing around a large table as they place a variety of photographic materials on it and begin to discuss the issues raised by them (Video 2.4 ▶). Sometimes dialectical, sometimes complementary, the conversation alternates between the voices of Fox and Stevens, who raise more questions than conclusions in their visualized process of working with images. At each return to this defamiliarized abstract space, the photographs discussed by the interviewees in the previous scenes are added to the growing mass of pictures on the table (Figure 2.14). The filmmakers' contemplative handling of the photographs, books, and illustrated magazines is always framed by a closer shot, but with a canted angle that abruptly violates the photograph's original framing. This is a defamiliarizing technique clearly borrowed from a famous scene in John Berger's series *Ways of Seeing* (1972), in which Berger, laterally framed, leafs back and forth through the pages of the *Sunday Times* magazine to analyze the "incomprehensible" contrast on its pages between the commodity fetishism of

Figure 2.13 Eileen Robson's photo album combines Belfast family life and political history in *Picturing Derry* (David Fox and Sylvia Stevens, 1985).

advertisements and the suffering of news photographs. In their original treatment for the program, Fox and Stevens made clear their intent to use Derry Camerawork's studio space as "a place where the products of different photographic practices collide" and become "a stage where ideas, questions and insights coming out of investigation of the many representations of Derry, can develop in front of the camera."[30] Indeed, the work of *Picturing Derry* was facilitated precisely by the critical pedagogy of Derry Camerawork. Yet the highly staged abstract space of the metacommentary scenes, unrecognizable as any real place in Derry, ultimately detaches the political project from its local place. The treatment of photographic materiality in *Picturing Derry* points in two different directions that would be taken up by other documentary filmmakers during the 1980s and beyond. Political documentaries like Susana Muñoz and Lourdes Portillo's *Las Madres: The Mothers of Plaza de Mayo* (1985) would record the ways in which Latin American activists deployed the social gesture of handling photographs in their performative politics, whereas other performative documentaries made for Channel Four, like Prathibha Parmar's *Memory Pictures* (1988) and Isaac Julien's *Looking for Langston* (1989), would stage elaborate tableaux in which presenters and actors would engage with photographic objects through touch as well as sight.[31]

Figure 2.14 Co-directors Sylvia Stevens and David Fox discuss the politics of photography in *Picturing Derry* (1985).

Made in the same year as *Picturing Derry*, *Las Madres: The Mothers of the Plaza de Mayo* illuminates how Argentine mothers and grandmothers of the disappeared explicitly deployed the holding and wearing of portrait photographs in their political struggle against the state. The shifting presence of photographs in the film participates in what Patricia Zimmermann reads to be its narrative arc—from individual loss to collective political action.[32] Across the film, the significance of photographs is gradually framed less in relation to their indexical bind to specific individuals than to their broader iconic capacity to represent the collective entirety of the disappeared.[33] As the women march around the plaza in the opening scene of the film, the camera repeatedly isolates individual women in the frame and draws our close attention to the photographs of their missing children and grandchildren that hang around their necks like devotional scapulars (Figure 2.15). By wearing the photograph, the mothers align the physical bond between mother and child with the indexical bind between the photograph and its referent.[34] By performing this in the plaza, they politicize it as a public act of *habeas corpus*. When photographs subsequently appear in the documentary's interviews with individual women in their homes, they are no longer mere family photographs. For instance, Aida Suarez is interviewed in her kitchen as a placard with an enlarged photograph of her son rests against a wall at the edge of the frame, signifying not only his disappearance, but also her embodied activism against

Figure 2.15 Mothers of the Disappeared wear the photographs of the missing during their protests in Buenos Aires in *Las Madres: The Mothers of the Plaza de Mayo* (Susana Muñoz and Lourdes Portillo, 1985).

it. The mothers are increasingly shown in relation to multiple portraits, whether it be the photo collage at their community center or the banners they carried on political marches as the movement grew. *Las Madres* visualizes the subsequent intergenerational passing down of the mothers' activism through the tactile metaphor of young Argentines wheat-pasting posters of the disappeared on the streets of Buenos Aires (Figure 2.16).

In her analysis of the intergenerational transmission of such performative activism with photographs, Diana Taylor draws on a genetic analogy, "Like DNA, images and strategies conveyed through these performances build on prior material, replicating and transforming the received 'codes.'"[35] This occurs on an intermedial level in Sebastián Moreno's documentary *La Ciudad de los Fotógrafos* (*City of Photographers*, 2006), in which the filmmaker retraces the work of the Asociación de Fotógrafos Independientes (AFI) (Independent Photographers Association) during the Pinochet regime in Chile. Moreno's film draws on the legacies of both his father José Moreno, who was one of the co-founders of the association, and Patricio Guzmán, his elder in Chilean political filmmaking. Guzman's *Memoria Obstinada* (*Chile, Obstinate Memory*, 1997) clearly influenced the young filmmaker with its dual strategy of retracing the people featured in his documentary masterpiece *La Batalla de Chile*

Figure 2.16 The photo-based activism of the Mothers of the Disappeared is taken up by the next generation in *Las Madres: The Mothers of the Plaza de Mayo* (Susana Muñoz and Lourdes Portillo, 1985).

(*The Battle of Chile*, 1975–9) and confronting contemporary Chilean audiences with its images for the first time. At the beginning of *City of Photographers*, José shows us around the association's dusty, and now-defunct, darkroom. Opening a drawer, he pulls out a large print by AFI photographer Luis Navarro and declares, "here's the non-official story of this archive," as he holds it up for the camera. Considered one of the first "denouncement photos" against the Pinochet dictatorship, Navarro's nationally disseminated photograph shows a large crowd standing before the entrance to a mine in Lonquén (outside Santiago) in 1978, where the remains of fifteen disappeared local men had just been discovered. Navarro is shown returning to the site today with his camera in one hand and the photograph in the other. All that remains of the mine entrance are ruins, complicating Navarro's attempt to relocate the precise spot where he took the photograph. As he holds the photograph, Navarro recalls recognizing one of the victims from his shirt pattern since he'd originally reported on them as missing persons in 1973. At the end of the Lonquén sequence, Navarro finally finds the spot where he took the original photograph. The camera assumes his point-of-view of the ruins, and then his hand gradually raises the photographic print until it fills the entire frame (Figures 2.17–2.18). Each time Navarro is here seen holding the photograph, this haptic trope functions differently—first as an orienting tool in the

Figures 2.17–2.18 Luis Navarro locates exactly where he photographed the discovery of fifteen bodies in Lonquén in 1978 from *City of Photographers* (Sebastian Moreno, 2006).

present, second as an *aide mémoire* to recall a detail of the past, and third as a witness standing against oblivion.

Throughout *City of Photographers*, Sebastian Moreno works to replicate and transform the received codes for staging photographs in the service of political activism against the authoritarian state, yet he does so not through photography itself, but rather through film. This is more than an accomplished cinematographer honoring the legacy of his photographer father (and colleagues) through his own medium. With its capacity to engender a continuous unfolding of time in the present tense, the moving image proves itself to be an apt medium to observe how the pluperfect tense of the photograph (what Barthes calls its "that-has-been" quality) actually functions in the historical moment in which the material picture is held up for display by a human witness.[36] In *City of Photographers*, with its second-generation witnessing of the disappeared, these scenes inevitably generate highly complex temporalities. When Moreno visits Helena Maureira, whose four sons were among the disappeared of Lonquén, he first films her, like the women in *Las Madres*, among the variety of photographs—posters, placards, laminated cards, and painted canvases—that fill her private shrines at home. She speaks of her comfort at having them present, of being able to imagine speaking with them directly. The following shots show her looking through Navarro's photographs of the crowds at the mine entrance when the bodies were discovered; Navarro's voiceover establishes that event as a turning point in the dictatorship: "Since the first moment this was discovered, Chile becomes aware of the horror. . . . the disappearance of civilians becomes a fact." Moreno visually affirms the significance of both Maureira and Navarro to this critical moment in Chilean history in a single shot: looking directly at the camera, Maureira holds up a book of Navarro's photographs that is open to a page showing a photograph of her wearing her sons' portraits on her coat during Mass (Figure 2.19). The double inscription of Maureira holding photographs to her chest multiples the affective capacity of this gesture. In front of Moreno's camera, she holds tight to personal memory (through her own image), to the event now recognized as history (in the publication she holds) and

Figure 2.19 Helena Maureira holds a photobook with a picture of her holding her son's photograph in *City of Photographers* (Sebastian Moreno, 2006).

to the solidarity she shares with Navarro (as different kinds of public witness to the events at Lonquén).

Navarro reappears again near the end of the film outside La Moneda, the presidential palace in Santiago, as he recounts his arrest in 1981 when he tried to photograph Pinochet entering the palace. The film suddenly returns Navarro to Lonquén as if to remind us of the state's retributive motive for persecuting the photographer who helped establish the fact of the disappeared in 1978. Navarro recounts how the regime tried to destroy his credibility by falsely claiming he had always been a state collaborator. Moreno then hands him a photograph to examine and asks him to explain it. Visibly fraught, Navarro holds it up for the camera to see (Video 2.5 ▶) (Figure 2.20). It shows an old man in visible distress, holding his head in his hands. Navarro reveals that after being released from prison, his father insisted that he tell him what had happened there: "Once I told him, this was his expression." Navarro makes no mention of torture, but there is no need. His father's silent gesture amply bears witness to its ultimate inexpressibility. If Navarro's photograph of his father radically remakes the notion of photographic portrait as witness (by picturing the listener, not the witness-survivor himself), then Moreno's filming of Navarro in this scene works equally to reconfigure this politicized act of holding a photograph that has been so central to activism around the disappeared in Latin America. Navarro's bodily expression in this scene is as significant as his father's; rather than grasp the image of a missing loved one, he holds tight to the loved one who enabled him to externalize his own unspeakable trauma. Moreno concludes his film by once more visualizing the witness to the witness. The aging members of the AFI walk the streets of contemporary Santiago wearing placards with their own photographs as they had

Figure 2.20 Luis Navarro holds a picture of his father's reaction to hearing his son's account of imprisonment in *City of Photographers* (Sebastian Moreno, 2006).

once done in the 1980s to avoid state censorship in the press, yet now they so in the name of sustaining collective memory of the dictatorship. Moreno's camera lingers on the complete absorption of the young people who have caught sight of these photographs on the street.

From the image of Iranian student Neda Agha-Soltan killed in the Green Revolution to the notorious Abu Ghraib pictures, vernacular photographs and video stills continue to be deployed in public protests as visual objects to be held, carried, and worn. Yet their qualities as digital images also demand attention to a newer form of photographic materiality and how documentary films have come to frame it.

Material Relations Between Digital Photographs

Standard Operating Procedure, Errol Morris's documentary about the notorious Abu Ghraib photographs, divided film critics and scholars. As Kris Fallon notes, the negative and positive responses to the film tended to align with how the film's rhetorical project was understood.[37] Scholars such as Bill Nichols, who read the film to be about the events themselves at Abu Ghraib, criticized it for its aestheticization of trauma, its failure to explicitly indict the US military high command, and its singular focus on the perspective of the perpetrator.[38] On the other hand, scholars like Linda Williams interpreted the film's project to be an investigation of the images produced in Abu Ghraib and how they framed our understanding of the events: "It asks us to interpret the interpretation, to witness the witnesses. But it does so not only by citing the photos that so 'forcibly' framed these acts of inhumanity but also by reframing and contextualizing them, showing us how very delimited these frames were."[39] All of the scholars taking this latter representational approach invoke digital elements—from digitally added frames to high-definition video and database aesthetics—as central to their arguments.[40] In fact, *Standard Operating Procedure* arguably represents one of the most sustained examinations within contemporary documentary film of the digital photograph and its implications for bearing witness to political violence and conflict. With the collaboration of acclaimed title-sequence designer Kyle Cooper, Morris developed specific visual strategies to interrogate the Abu Ghraib images through their material qualities as digital media objects. Only very rarely do we see any of these images fill the entire frame. Rather, the Abu Ghraib images appear as photographic objects on a black background, which fluctuates between the impression of two-dimensional flatness and three-dimensional depth. Morris presents the photographic objects in two principal ways, depending upon whether they are individual or multiple images.

Centered in the frame, the individual images are positioned upon a dominating black background that occupies more screen space than the photograph itself. The digitally added white border around each image accentuates our attention to the act of framing performed by the photograph. For Williams, these white frames are critical to the film's ideological work, in that "they call attention to the work of presentation that the film performs in framing them and invite us to consider what kind of witnessing they constitute."[41] Although Williams treats them as marks of digital mediation, I would argue that their visual impact derives from their capacity to simultaneously evoke both the ephemeral, virtual presence of the electronic image and the material solidity of the printed snapshot. Many of the photographs appear and disappear from the screen through fades from and to black, a process that ultimately foregrounds the white frame as the first and last visual trace on the screen. Whereas fading a photograph to black in full frame evokes impressions of memory or the passing of time related to the content of the image, applying a fade to black to a photograph on a black background suggests the evanescence of the photographic object itself.[42] However, the persistent use of the white frame around the photographs also recalls mid-century amateur snapshots, which were frequently printed commercially with white borders, or even the Polaroid, the quintessential late-twentieth-century vernacular form of photography. Although the Abu Ghraib photographs were circulated around the prison electronically (mostly through CDs), this visual reference to vernacular photography's analog past situates them in the same historical tradition of soldiers' amateur photography that Gedrovich's *Amateur Photographer* investigates.[43] It is precisely these complex amateur motivations shaping their production and initial circulation that most interest Morris in the film.

When the film presents multiple photographs on screen, they are almost always seen in motion, beginning with the title credits, in which a random stream of Abu Ghraib photographs slowly float away from the camera into a black void. The slow movement and shrinkage of these discrete electronic objects generate an impression of three-dimensional, but infinite, space. Kris Fallon reads this image and others as visualizations of the database structure, which Lev Manovich argues to be the dominant symbolic form and operative structure of digital new media.[44] Fallon elucidates how Morris presents the database quality of digital photography as key to understanding the fundamental ambiguity of the Abu Ghraib photographs. Computers store image files as numerically organized data that can be rearranged through software in whatever order or form suits the user. Through an extensive interview with Army investigator Brent Pack and visualizations of his forensic analysis, the film traces the military's attempt to reconfigure the largely random cluster of images derived from three cameras into a coherent narrative of the events documented in the photographs (Video 2.6 ⊙). The investigative processes to determine the time and location of each image are illustrated in 3D digital animation through the synchronization of specific images on multiple moving timelines and the embedding of images into 3D architectural models of the prison (Figures 2.21–2.22). The ultimate responsibility of Pack's investigation for the Army lay in determining if any of the photographs constituted evidence of criminal acts. Morris illustrates this process, which is narrated by Pack, through a stylized reenactment that shows an anonymous hand stamping photographic prints of the Abu Ghraib images with either the words "Criminal Act" or the acronym "S.O.P." (Standard Operating Procedure). This return to the emphatic materiality of photographic prints and their physical handling

Figure 2.21 Photographs embedded within a 3D architectural model of the Abu Ghraib prison in *Standard Operating Procedure* (Errol Morris, 2008).

Figure 2.22 Photographs placed chronologically within moving timelines in *Standard Operating Procedure* (Errol Morris, 2008).

provides a striking visual trope for the bureaucratic arbitrariness that characterized the process of determining the photographs' legal status as evidence.

In contrast to this single appearance of photographic prints in the film, *Standard Operating Procedure* references, in several different ways, one of the key phenomenological transformations of digital photography: we now view most photographs as digital objects on an electronic screen rather than as printed images. In arguably one of the most remarkable moments of the talking head interviews in the film, Morris asks Military Intelligence Specialist Roman Krol to examine a photograph of himself and several other soldiers abusing detainees with water and Nerf balls. Because Morris is filming with his Interrotron apparatus, Krol has to lean in and peer directly into the camera/screen in order to scrutinize the photograph that Morris is showing him.[45] This singular moment in the film becomes an emblem of the complex inescapable layers of mediation involved in any engagement with the Abu Ghraib images. Benson-Allott writes, "Krol's scrutinizing gaze ... reminds the viewer that his interview is both an image and an engagement with images."[46] Morris's recourse to image flows rendered in 3D digital animation also acknowledges the multifarious, dispersed, and transient nature of digital photographs and our everyday engagement with them. We experience them—paradoxically for photographs—as objects imbued with duration and movement: "They have a kind of mobility as we scroll across them, clicking one or another in and out of the foreground of the screen's shallow's space."[47] In a move that gestures to the diverse remobilizations of the Abu Ghraib images within public culture, the film's animation at times imitates the ways in which digital objects in screen interfaces respond to the haptic commands from a mouse, trackpad, or touchscreen by expanding, contracting, sliding, and disappearing. Several sequences also mimic the durational quality of a digital slide show, in which the automated transmission between images of the soldiers' aimless leisure time and their abuse of prisoners highlights the seamless integration of banality and brutality in Abu Ghraib.

Arguably the most significant aspect of the shift to viewing photographs on electronic screens has been the fact that they are now instantaneously available to see on the very apparatus that has taken the shot, transforming our relationship to the images we create.[48] Morris illustrates this phenomenon at two crucial moments of the film: when it addresses the most infamous image from Abu Ghraib, the hooded prisoner on the box, and the pictures taken by Sabrina Harmon of prisoner Mandadel al-Jamadi, who had been tortured to death during CIA interrogation. The film's reenactments of these events each include close-ups of the camera's LCD screen at the moment the photographs were taken, thus implicating our gaze within the soldier's visual perspective in taking a photograph and immediately inspecting it (Figure 2.23). These self-conscious shots intensify the question of what motivated the soldiers to taken them, but the film resists any definitive answer and suggests differing and contradictory sets of motivations in each case. By including a rarely seen photograph taken by Harmon that shows Staff Sergeant Ivan Frederick at the edge of the frame looking at the LCD screen of his own camera while the hooded prisoner stands behind him on the box, Morris implicitly lends support to the argument that

Figure 2.23 Reenactment of Sabrina Harmon viewing the photograph she took of Mandadel al-Jamadi in *Standard Operating Procedure* (Errol Morris, 2008).

this specific spectacle of abuse was staged precisely for the camera (Figure 2.24). By contrast, the forensic-looking photographs that Harmon took of al-Jamadi's corpse are initially framed by her testimony to suggest that she wanted to document the crime of his death, but the film's subsequent display of the notorious shot of Harmon smiling with her thumbs up in front of the corpse immediately undermines her claim. She responds by explaining that she simply reacted with her automatic re-sponse when she finds herself in front of a camera. In both cases, Morris visualizes the soldiers' instantaneous contemplation of their own digital photographs on the devices that took them, in order to foreground the paradoxical dynamics of digital vernacular photography in our understanding of the Abu Ghraib images—to pre-serve a moment for its instantaneous consumption.

Standard Operating Procedure combines the virtual mise-en-scène created from the photographs' metadata with the physical mise-en-scène of the reenactments, which are based on perpetrator testimony, not to establish an affirmative, verifiable truth claim about what happened in Abu Ghraib through the indexicality of the pho-tographs, but to raise questions about the ambivalent function of the camera within the prison. By doing so, it frames Abu Ghraib as a site of exception in the juridical sense rather than a specific exception to standard operating procedure (the "bad apples" trope consistently invoked by the US state).

With the development of the smartphone and its ever-expanding technical cap-acities as a digital camera, vernacular photography not only enjoys a vast ubiquitous presence at sites of conflict and political violence, but also generates ever more infor-mation, both visual and non-visual, for forensic investigation. The research agency Forensic Architecture makes considerable use of vernacular digital photography in its investigations of contemporary conflicts within urban environments. It not only plays a key role in its forensic methodologies but also feature prominently in the short documentary films that are central to the public communication of their findings. Founded in 2011 by Eyal Weizman with the fiscal support of the European Research Council and based at Goldsmiths, University of London, Forensic Architecture

Figure 2.24 Ivan Frederick viewing the photograph he took of the hooded man in *Standard Operating Procedure* (Errol Morris, 2008).

carries out architectural and media research on behalf of human-rights organizations, political-justice groups, and international prosecutors, in relation to specific
cases of human-rights violations. Generated from the collaboration of architects,
filmmakers, programmers, lawyers, and scientists, it also seeks to forge a new interdisciplinary field that uses architectural evidence to address systematic violations
of human rights.[49] The increasing urbanization and mediatization of war generate a
huge amount of visual evidence about conflicts, which is captured by diverse sources,
including military forces, journalists, civilians on the ground, and commercial sat-
ellites. Mostly available in real time or during ongoing conflict, this proliferation
of images has been transforming the legal and political processes of international
human rights, which have long been grounded in witness testimonies collected after
conflicts have ended. Moreover, as visual evidence of conflict proliferates in both
quantity and form, its capacity to produce historical or legal truth claims becomes
ever more contested. Forensic Architecture thus draws on the etymological origins of
the term forensics—the Latin *forensis*, meaning pertaining to the forum—to situate
its work in two sites: "the *field* is the site of investigation and the *forum* is the place
where the results of an investigation are presented and contested."[50]

Given that the history of modern forensics has largely entailed procedures that
permit the state to police its subjects, Forensic Architecture aims to forge a counter-
hegemonic practice by applying forensic methods to the analysis of state violence,
thus reversing the forensic gaze between the state and its subjects.[51] Cognizant of
the deployment of "forensic warfare," in which the state marshals selective evidence
to justify war and destroys or denies evidence of its own human-rights violations,
Weizman frames the work of Forensic Architecture as "both the production of evidence and the querying of the practices of evidence making."[52] Although the agency
has presented its research in many legal proceedings, including the genocide trail of
two former Guatemalan dictators (Luca Garcia and Rios Montt), a Palestinian village's petition against the West Bank Wall in the Israeli High Court, and the murder
trial of a German neo-Nazi gang, Forensic Architecture does not limit its public communication to the courtroom. Adopting a strategic and multiscalar approach to producing public truth, its individual projects circulate through art galleries, the web, the
press, academic venues, and on-site public meetings, as well as legal forums.

The critical methods of Forensic Architecture respond to the various challenges of
multiplicity facing human-rights movements. First of all, single incidents, or events,
such as the Abu Ghraib scandal, are often dismissed as the actions of individual "bad
actors" breaking "standard operating procedure." Patterns of gross and systematic
violations must be proven if governments or military leaders are to be held legally
accountable.[53] Second, the analysis of visual evidence in both critical scholarship and
political activism has focused primarily on singular images which clearly capture
the perpetrator's violation of the victim. The vast remainder of the images generated
in relation to an event are deemed too partial, fragmentary, or decontextualized to
prove a case. Finally, the digital era has produced a shift for human-rights work from
grappling with information scarcity around violations to managing the proliferating

abundance of visual evidence: "As the stack of hay is getting higher we're no longer looking for needles but at the disposition of the stack."[54] Architecture provides the means to perceive relationality within such abundance, replacing the notion of the archive with that of the architectural-image complex. Digital three-dimensional models can facilitate "an assemblage of evidence" in which the time-space relationships between individual pieces of evidence are made visible through an architectural environment.[55] In this context, architecture becomes "useful not only as primary evidence, the object of analysis, but rather as an optical device, and as a way of seeing."[56] Moreover, such digital modeling permits the synthesis of diverse sources of evidence, from witness testimonies and sound recordings to films and photographs. Truth claims thus emerge not autonomously from individual evidentiary objects, but from the information produced by their spatio-temporal alignment into an architecturally arranged assemblage that reveals more than the sum of its parts.

The short documentaries produced by Forensic Architecture not only present these assemblages of evidence, but also detail, in a scientific mode of methodological self-reflexivity, precisely how they have been generated. They generally enunciate a matter-of-fact rhetorical tone and display a modular structure. Both these qualities enable sections of the documentary to be incorporated into other media produced by collaborating partners, which often deploy a more deliberate tone of advocacy. Forensic Architecture's collaboration with Amnesty International on a project about the deadliest days in the 2014 Israel/Gaza conflict produced a nine-minute documentary, *Rafah: Black Friday* (2015), which exemplifies the agency's use of vernacular digital photography in its methodology and presentation of research. While the complete documentary has mostly been seen either in the context of Forensic Architecture's website and in its gallery exhibitions, Amnesty International inserted modular segments from it into two quite different products of the collaboration: the online version of their official seventy-two-page report on "Black Friday" and the advocacy videos used in their social media campaigns.[57] Whereas Forensic Architecture's documentary employs an analytical discourse reminiscent of Harun Farocki's essay films and focuses on the specific evidence that could be generated by its methodologies, Amnesty's campaign videos rely on the conventional means of political documentary, including the multimodal narratization of events (through voiceover, talking heads, on-screen text, and time codes), diverse sources of visual evidence (news reports, crowdsourced vernacular images, drone footage, and interviews) and the explicit articulation of a political truth claim (that Israel perpetrated the war crimes of disproportionate, indiscriminate, and retributive attacks on civilian populations).[58]

On August 1, 2014, Israel and Hamas agreed on a seventy-two-hour humanitarian ceasefire, which was immediately broken in a firefight near Rafah, in which an Israeli officer, Lieutenant Hadar Goldin, was captured by Hamas fighters. Israeli military forces responded by invoking the controversial "Hannibal Command," which unleashes enormous firepower in the vicinity of the capture in order to foil it, even if it leads to the death of civilians or the captured soldier. Israel launched over two thousand bombs, missiles, and shells on Rafah that day, and after the four days of bombardment ended, scores of Palestinian civilians had been killed.[59] The joint investigation by the two organizations collected over seven thousand digital photographs and videos from civilians, journalists, and Israeli soldiers (through the veterans' group Breaking the Silence), along with numerous eye-witness testimonies, in order to assess if Israeli forces had committed disproportionate or indiscriminate attacks on densely populated civilian areas, which constitute war crimes. The geopolitical stakes of any such investigation were heightened since the Palestinian Authority had recently joined the International Criminal Court (ICC) by ratifying the Rome Statute in April 2014.[60] Moreover, Palestinian civilians took great risks in recording the attacks—Israeli open-fire regulations allow killing anyone aiming a camera at soldiers. The Palestinians knew that the images they recorded on their cameras or cellphones could provide valuable evidence, not just for international media reporting, but also any future case brought to the ICC.[61]

Rafah: Black Friday opens with a video clip of the Israeli bombing of the Al Tannur neighborhood in Rafah, which the documentary later closely analyzes for information about the ordinance deployed in the attack. Occupying less than half the total area of the frame, the clip is surrounded by a white background that remains in place throughout the documentary. In contrast to the depthless black background behind the digital images in *Standard Operating Procedure*, the white background here evokes the clinical look of a laboratory or the blank space of a photographer's lightbox, continuously signaling that the digital videos and photographs presented to us are media objects (Video 2.7 ▶). Their frames are always visible; never does an image fill the entire frame of the documentary. Upon this constant experimental white space, a series of visual analyses are performed that gradually shift from two dimensions to three. Through a progression of visual devices, including the grid, the split screen, the image stack, the timeline, and the 3D architectural model, the archive becomes architectural-image complex.

As the female voiceover describes the range of visual evidence collected, a grid of fifty-six images appears, randomly mixing digital video and photographs shot by "witnesses who experienced the events firsthand." The documentary makes no ontological distinction between digital video and photography in this initial presentation of the evidential archive; it will later both freeze moving images and animate a series of photographs in the service of measurement, synchronization, and geospatial alignment. Three pieces of video footage depicting the bombing of Al Tannur are selected from the grid. While the other images fade from view, the three clips enlarge and align along a horizontal axis. Similar to *Standard Operating Procedure*, such movement of the clips within the frame reinforces the visual impression of a graphical user interface on which digital media objects are arranged and manipulated by a user, in contrast to the more conventional presentation of the profilmic world in documentary film. Comparing the smoke plumes from the bombs in each clip permits the temporal synchronization of the footage since plumes and clouds have unique, if perpetually morphing, forms. After the footage freezes at the moment when the plumes match in all three clips, their digitally traced outline is carried over from image to image to demonstrate the match. As extracted photograms, the images are now available for spatial mapping to determine the exact location of their camera and the bombing itself. One of the three photograms is placed alongside a satellite photograph of the area in a kind of split-screen arrangement, as structures are identified, located, and measured in each image. While the photogram remains static, the satellite image is subject to numerous zooms and pans, which follow the lines of measurement that ultimately lead to the locations of the camera and the bombing. The split-screen presentation visually illustrates how the relationality between images is key to their capacity to reveal critical spatiotemporal information about the bombing under investigation (Figure 2.25). The value of these photographic images therefore lies less in how their iconic representation depicts an event and more in the spatio-temporal data to be gleaned from the comparative measurement of visual elements within them, especially when the images' metadata is missing, corrupted, or incorrect. Moreover, when the documentary overlays one photograph of a bomb plume over another in an overlapping image stack, creating the animating effect of a flipbook (with the assistance of an electronic page-flipping sound), it is not to render the evidence more realistic to the viewer, but to verify that the photographs have been accurately synchronized in time (Figure 2.26). To visually summarize the temporal synchronization of all the image sources in relation to one another, a two-dimensional horizontal timeline subsequently appears across the screen, with thumbnail images aligned at specific time codes.

The architectural-image complex is realized in the final stage of visualizing the event, in which the two-dimensional still and moving images are vertically positioned

Figure 2.25 Split-screen presentation illustrates how Forensic Architecture was able to calculate information from the relationship between images in *Rafah: Black Friday* (Forensic Architecture, 2015)

METADATA: 23:43:21

Figure 2.26 Overlaid image-stacks create the animated impression of a flipbook in *Rafah: Black Friday* (Forensic Architecture, 2015).

Figure 2.27 Still photographs and moving images are integrated into a 3D architectural model of Rafah in *Rafah: Black Friday* (Forensic Architecture, 2015).

within a 3D architectural model of Rafah (Figure 2.27). Simulated camera movement around the model enhances the illusion of three-dimensional space, while the fourth dimension, time, retains a Vertovian relativity: time moves forward and backward, progresses in slow and fast motion, and freezes at various moments of analysis.[62] Applying photographs and photograms to an abstract architectural model, combined with this temporal elasticity, reinforces our perception of them as discrete media objects subjected primarily to mathematical analysis, despite their photographic realism. The evidentiary payoff of this complex visual mapping becomes clear when the video footage originally seen at the beginning of the documentary is reversed and frozen, revealing the actual bombs before impact. Since the photograms are embedded in the architectural model, they can be accurately measured and identified (as US-made, 1-metic ton Mk84 ordinance) (Figure 2.28).

Rafah: Black Friday concludes by rhetorically ceding forensics to the power of testimony. The camera flies over the architectural model to the site of the apartment building destroyed by the Mk84 bombs. Time is reversed to the moment before the bombs' impact as we hear survivor-witness Inam Ouda Ayed bin Hammad describe the trauma of being caught on the street just as the bombs landed. Her testimony not only provides critical on-the-ground information about the bombing, but also bears witness to the human magnitude of what is at stake in the preceding forensic analysis. The screen fades to white, and the female voiceover narrates that she fell unconscious and sixteen people died in the bombing, including her five-year-old son. His name and photographic portrait appear in silence on screen, followed by the names of the other fifteen victims (only some with accompanying photographs). Several of the photographs are creased and dog-eared, highlighting their material substance as auratic, affectively charged objects, the precise opposite of the data-mined digital images that have preceded them.[63] Like all of Forensic Architecture's documentaries, *Rafah: Black Friday* treats digital photographs and photograms as media objects with formal materiality (in Kirschenbaum's sense) whose evidentiary value derives most from their relationality, from the data released by visual comparative analysis and

Figure 2.28   3D visual mapping facilitates the identification of the missile used in the attack in *Rafah: Black Friday* (Forensic Architecture, 2015).

measurement performed through the virtual mise-en-scène of 3D architectural modeling. Although that three-dimensional space is abstract and virtual, it nevertheless provides the ground upon which the materiality of war can be measured and potentially transformed into legally actionable evidence. But, as the documentary's conclusion confirms, Forensic Architecture insists on the integral, rather than oppositional, relationship between the forensic and the testimonial. For Weizman, both matter and witness are different, but complexly interrelated, sensors that record conflict and they are most productively configured within the three-dimensional digital space of an architectural image complex.[64] If *Rafah: Black Friday* constructs architectural image complexes in order to generate new forms of forensic evidence that derive from calculations enabled by digital materiality rather than from the visible appearance of an indexical trace inscribed in the image, then *Standard Operating Procedure* employs the architectural image complex less to produce new forensic evidence than to raise critical questions about what kind of the truths can be established from what is visible in the frame.

As this chapter has elaborated across diverse historical contexts, vernacular photography has played an enduring role in the cultural mediation of war and political violence. From the scarcity and accidental recovery of Nazi perpetrators' photo albums through the embodied haptic engagement with photographic objects by political activists to the promiscuous plenitude of digital photographs in the network age, a constant dynamic remains. As material objects, vernacular photographs circulate through public and private spheres, shifting meaning, value, and even form as they cross the diverse thresholds between the two. The films and television programs that I have discussed in this chapter not only document the political and historical value of these material relocations of photographs, but also enact them. As elements of documentary mise-en-scène, such photographic objects come to be seen, and understood, otherwise by their placement elsewhere than their original circuits of exchange and display. Rather than merely present photographs as indexically authenticated visible evidence, documentary films demonstrate what can be done with photographic objects, either through profilmic observation (*Las Madres* or *City of Photographers*) or the construction of abstract cinematic space (*Amateur Photographer* or *Rafah: Black Friday*).

3
Filming the Photographer

Roger Kahane's French television documentary *Henri Cartier-Bresson: The Modern Adventure* (1962) illustrates a fundamental challenge for documentaries about living photographers: how do you film the creative act of taking a photograph when the latter medium is predominantly constructed around the instantaneous apprehension of time? Even the most static of photographic genres, such as landscapes and portraits, involve an exposure that still normally measures just a fracture of a second. Central to the field of photojournalism, in which Cartier-Bresson holds legendary status, has been the idea of capturing of a fleeting instant from the complex flows of an unfolding event or the intricate dynamics of a social world. Indeed, Cartier-Bresson's concept of photography's "decisive moment" has become one of the shibboleths of the medium. In the essay for his seminal 1952 photobook *Images à la sauvette/The Decisive Moment*, Cartier-Bresson extols a philosophy of photography that emphasizes its ephemeral nature; photographers, he argues, "deal in things that are continually vanishing."[1] Photography meets the dynamic ephemerality of the world with "a new kind of plasticity," which arises from the photographer's capture of the momentary equilibrium of the lines of movement and arrangement produced by the subject of the photograph (32). But Cartier-Bresson's concern for the geometry of forms and the photographer's intuitive ability to recognize them in the decisive moment captured in a successful photograph was never a pure formalism. His seminal definition of the decisive moment balances form with meaning: "To me, photography is the simultaneous recognition, in a fraction of a second, of the significance of an event as well as of a precise organization of forms which give that event its proper expression" (42). If photographers work "at the speed of a reflex action," how then can filmmakers record their creative process? In documentaries about other static visual media, such as drawing, painting, and sculpture, the temporal process of the artwork's creation is at least visually available for the film camera to record. Early art documentaries even used special set-ups to provide a better view of the creative process; for example, Paul Haesaerts' *Visit to Picasso* (1949) films the artist's swifts brush strokes through a glass pane on which he is painting.[2]

Cartier-Bresson proves to be a particularly allusive subject for Kahane's camera as the photographer moves through Parisian streets with his Leica in hand. All we get to see is a tall man dart through crowds, occasionally whipping out his camera to grab a shot, but he is mostly too swift for Kahane's cameraman to subsequently record what had caught the photographer's eye. The most revealing shots in these scenes are close-ups that focus on the gestural details of Cartier-Bresson's body in motion: how he holds his camera in between shots or how he stands momentarily on tiptoe to catch the decisive moment (Figures 3.1–3.2). In his essay for *The Decisive*

A Medium Seen Otherwise. Roger Hallas, Oxford University Press. © Oxford University Press 2023.
DOI: 10.1093/oso/9780190057763.003.0004

Figures 3.1–3.2 Capturing Henri Cartier-Bresson's bodily gestures as he seeks out the "decisive moment" in *Henri Cartier-Bresson: The Modern Adventure* (Roger Kahane, 1962).

Moment, Cartier-Bresson writes explicitly of the need to have a "velvet hand, a hawk's eye," that is to say, to approach subjects unobtrusively, "on tiptoe," but also to be vigorously alert and nimble as to where to capture the decisive moment (28).[3] Kahane uses these scenes sparingly in his thirty-minute documentary, aware that they could easily become repetitive and unengaging. Most of the documentary is devoted to a conversation about photography that Kahane conducts with Cartier-Bresson and two Parisian intellectuals, Jean Bardin and Bernard Hubrenne. Staged at multiple sites (cafes, parks, streets, and Cartier-Bresson's darkroom) for both rhetorical purpose and visual variety, the conversation constitutes a format that emphasizes photography as a discourse of the public sphere, and not just a professional or artistic practice.[4]

If the durational medium of film struggled to adequately capture the creative process of photography, a largely instantaneous medium, then one solution for documentary filmmakers was to create moving images that imitated the visual style and perspective of the photographer. Such aesthetic mimicry promised viewers the capacity to see the world as the photographer does. It is already clearly visible in the first documentary about a photographer: Willard Van Dyke's *The Photographer* (1948), featuring his mentor, Edward Weston. Beginning with Van Dyke's short film, this chapter examines how documentaries about living photographers have deployed aesthetic mimicry in various ways and to different ends, depending on the photographic genre under consideration, the visual technologies available, and the historical contexts in which the photographers worked. Although aesthetic mimicry has often been put in the service of discourses of artistic intent and stature, such as in the genre of the "great artist" documentary, its deployment can nevertheless also create opportunities to explore the political and ethical dimensions of the photographic medium, sometimes in ways that the filmmaker had not necessarily intended or anticipated. Aesthetic mimicry therefore paradoxically enables a capacity to see photography otherwise rather than just similarly to the photographer. Although mimicry has a long history within the aesthetic pedagogy of apprenticeship, contemporary critical theory has also recognized its broader capacity for subverting, often unknowingly, the authority of that which is being imitated.[5]

In analyzing two documentaries about photojournalists, *War Photographer* (Christian Frei, 2000) and the series *Witness* (David Frankham, 2012), I draw on Ariella Azoulay's reconceptualization of photography as civil contract to explain how documentary film can enhance our understanding of the political relations connecting the photographer, the subjects of the photograph, and its viewers.[6] In both these documentaries, shifts between different visual perspectives generate a potential space of critical awareness for their viewers, who can begin, in Azoulay's words, "to watch" photography, to trace the claims made by its various "citizens." A specially designed microcam attached to James Nachtwey's camera in *War Photographer* produces shots that exude immediacy and mediation at once, but also draw a sharp aesthetic contrast with Nachtwey's own monochrome photographs and the carefully framed Betacam shots that imitate the photographer's visual style. *Witness*, by turn, exploits the newly available digital SLR cameras that take both high-definition still and moving images, forging an aesthetic mimicry that has more to do with treating photographs like film and vice versa, than with impersonating a photographer's particular visual style.

Shifting to a slower, more static photographic genre, *Manufactured Landscapes* (2006), Jennifer Baichwal's documentary about landscape photographer Edward Burtynsky, forges another kind of aesthetic mimicry as it seeks cinematic equivalents to Burtynsky's photographic modernism. As it adopts camera movement and the durational aspect of the long take to visualize the industrial sublime, the film does not just achieve aesthetic equivalence to Burtynsky's photography. Baichwal also delivers a complementary extension of it, addressing an absence often leveled by critics about his photography, namely, actual lived human experience within the industrially transformed landscapes he documents. Turning to another contemporary landscape photographer, Andreas Gursky, the chapter concludes by considering what happens when aesthetic mimicry is taken to its logical, if absurd, extreme. If it gives us the capacity to see the world as particular acclaimed photographers do, what is to stop us from making such pictures ourselves? In *Gursky World* (2002), British filmmaker and art critic Ben Lewis wryly lampoons the pretensions of the global art world by attempting to make his own "Gurskys" and then asking the photographer himself for critical feedback. Aesthetic mimicry ultimately devolves into postmodern farce.

Seeing Through the Photographer's Eyes

Although US wartime propaganda films occasionally addressed the importance of photography to the war effort, Willard Van Dyke's *The Photographer* would be the first documentary film to specifically focus on the practice of a particular photographer.[7] Commissioned by the Division of International Motion Pictures at the US State Department and produced by Affiliated Films, which Van Dyke co-founded in 1946, the documentary about Edward Weston was part of a planned series on American artists, including Martha Graham, Georgia O'Keeffe, and Frank Lloyd Wright.[8] Weston's photographic practice and lifestyle served the ideological needs of the State Department well at the beginning of the Cold War as it attempted to frame the aesthetic innovations of modernism in distinctively American terms.[9] The unique landscape and natural objects of California had been the principal subject of Weston's modernist photography since his return from Mexico in 1927. Moreover, his very modest lifestyle in a small cottage on the Northern Californian coast near Carmel lent a Waldenesque air of rugged individualism to his public image as an artist. The simplicity of his technique, which involved a view camera and contact printing from 8x10-inch negatives, could also be celebrated as an aesthetic articulation of straightforward American ingenuity.

Aside from Van Dyke's personal connection to Weston, he seemed the appropriate choice of subject for the first documentary about the art of photography due to his philosophy of the medium and the aesthetic influence he held over other midcentury

American photographers. After rejecting the Pictorialism that grounded his early career, Weston became the most influential champion of "straight" or "pure" photography, the idea that photographers should pursue the specificity of the medium rather than attempt to imitate the aesthetics of other media (particularly painting, which had been the aim of the Pictorialist movement). In 1932, Weston joined with Van Dyke and five other Californian photographers, including Ansel Adams and Imogen Cunningham, to form Group f.64, a short-lived, but ultimately influential, group, which show-cased their commitment to "pure photography" in a traveling group show. Its accompanying manifesto argued that photography must develop as an art form according to the "actualities and limitations" of its own medium and that it should not possess any of the "qualities of technic, composition or idea, derivative of any other art form."[10] Weston was the guiding figure of the group and his stature as the leading photographer of a medium-specific modernism was consolidated in 1946 when the Museum of Modern Art in New York exhibited a retrospective of his work.

Eager to pay homage to his photographic mentor, Van Dyke chose to shoot the film himself.[11] Although Weston had largely abandoned his photographic practice by 1947, due to his increased debilitation from Parkinson's Disease, the promise of the film shoot excited him, and he would later write to Van Dyke expressing satisfaction at the photographs he took during the filming of the documentary.[12] The State Department insisted on a highly didactic voiceover (written by Irving Jacoby), which Van Dyke felt compromised the aesthetic achievement of his cinematography and Alexander Hammid's editing. The voiceover consistently hammers home the ideological imperatives of individualism ("the integrity to search for what pleases him, not for what he thinks will please others") and nation ("an American artist who can reveal his country's beauty in a language all men can understand"). Distributed internationally in 1948 and domestically in 1951 through museums, universities, and film societies, *The Photographer* received critical acclaim in the United States for its illumination of distinctively American modern art and its own genuinely documentary film aesthetics.[13]

The narrative structure of the film is straightforward: Weston and his unnamed female assistant are introduced in Los Angeles; they travel to various California landscapes seeking subjects to photograph; they take photographs in different locations; they develop a print in the darkroom; and, finally, they sit around Weston's fireplace with his friends who are perusing books of photographic history (which permits the voiceover to locate Weston's position within the photographic canon). As was the norm for mid-century US documentary film, Weston reenacts his work practices specifically for the camera in carefully staged scenes. Although the role of the assistant (performed by an actress hired by Van Dyke) reflects Weston's biographical history of working with young female assistants, her principal purpose for Van Dyke was a rhetorical one, allowing him to stage scenes in which the assistant becomes the film viewer's on-screen proxy as Weston explains his techniques with the camera and in the darkroom.[14] The voiceover narration reinforces this visual alignment with uses of the first-person plural and generalizable assertions, such as, "To study photography with Edward Weston is an opportunity to learn about art itself." To first establish the viewer's alignment with the assistant, she is introduced in the film's opening scene as an amateur photographer taking a snapshot of two fishermen at the seashore in an attempt, according to the voiceover, to "capture the moment" for memory. The voiceover swiftly contrasts the amateur's approach to photography to the artist's, which recognizes that the photograph can be "an experience in itself." The young woman is immediately recast as an apprentice to the great master artist as they prepare for their car journey through the Californian landscape—aesthetic mimicry functions here as mode of artistic pedagogy both for the assistant, Van Dyke, and the film's viewer. Rejecting the glamour and technological modernity of Los Angeles (figured through Hollywood Boulevard and an automated carwash), Weston and his assistant head for the Sierra Nevada. The alternation between shots of Weston looking out of the car windows and eye-line matches of his supposed views align the film viewer with "the pleasure of looking" that Weston takes in seeking out the right image: "his most important tool is not his camera, but his eye" (Figures 3.3–3.4). The car window serves as a material analogy for the cognitive act of framing a view into a picture; such shots would become a common visual trope for later documentaries to suggest the photographer's oscillation between observing and framing the world.

In the first scene depicting Weston's process of taking a photograph, Van Dyke gradually positions his own camera ever closer to Weston's, first behind the tripod as Weston selects his angle, then with Weston under the cloth of his view camera as he makes final adjustments (Figure 3.5), and finally in the place of Weston's own lens as the image comes into focus. This third shot constitutes an impossible view, given that Van Dyke's movie camera cannot simultaneously inhabit the same position as Weston's photographic camera.[15] Yet the largely static nature of landscape photography and the shared technological basis of film and photography in the camera lens permit this visual sleight of hand. Although later scenes will occasionally repeat this visual trick to demonstrate different technical aspects of photography, such as comparing the focal lengths of various lenses, the film's principal device for allowing the viewer to see like Weston centers on Van Dyke's cinematography broadly imitating the visual aesthetic of Weston's photographs, including their specific subject matter, sharpness, composition, and tonal range. As if to confirm Van Dyke's stylistic imitation, the first of these sequences is immediately followed by a series of Weston's photographs presented with white mattes. The sequences of aesthetic mimicry begin with an extreme close-up shot of Weston's face as his eyes scan off-screen space (Figure 3.6). Although the first shot to follow might be regarded as an immediate eyeline match, the subsequent shots depict diverse subjects that could not be seen from a single location. It is in these moments that Van Dyke's movie camera performs an aesthetic mimicry of Weston's photographic style—he films the natural world as though with his mentor's aesthetic eye (Video 3.1 ▶). If the camera moves, it only comes to rest once a Weston-like composition has been found

Figures 3.3–3.4 A POV shot aligns the viewer with Edward Weston's aesthetic framing of the world in *The Photographer* (Willard van Dyke, 1948).

Figure 3.5 Aligning the viewer with Edward Weston's gaze under the camera cloth in *The Photographer* (Willard van Dyke, 1948).

Figure 3.6 Sequences of aesthetic mimicry begin with a shot of Edward Weston looking offscreen in *The Photographer* (Willard van Dyke, 1948).

(Figures 3.7–3.8). Reinforced by the voiceover's seamless alternation between third person references to "the artist" and "Weston" and first-person invocations of "we" and "us" during such shots, this aesthetic mimicry offers the viewer the modernist promise to perceive the world anew, to see it as Weston does. Yet, in line with the film's ideological function as Cold War soft propaganda, its voiceover continually empties the radicality of modernist vision by stressing art as the pursuit of pleasure, emotion, and meaning in highly individualistic terms. In a scene depicting the assistant's own search for images among the ruins of a former mining town, the voiceover implores, "That is the hardest part of an apprenticeship in art—to open the gates around our hearts so that we can feel freely, to clean up the clutter of our mind so that we can think clearly."

Although the film recasts modernist perception as an individual responsibility on the part of liberal subjects to feel and think for themselves, *The Photographer* did establish a set of documentary conventions for filming the practice of photography, in which the film viewer is given access to multiple subject positions, including that of the photographer, the photographic camera, the profilmic observer (in this case, Weston's assistant), and the observational stance of the film camera itself. Moreover, aesthetic mimicry of the photographer's visual style by the documentary's cinematography has become a particularly popular device in documentaries about photographers. For example, Reiner Holzemer's documentary *William Eggleston: Photographer* (2008) follows Eggleston as he meanders the outskirts of Memphis in search of images. Holzemer embraces Eggleston's idiosyncratic eye for surreal detail in shots of the location during moments when the film camera is not trained on the photographer. Holzemer's use of the device suggests the idea of Eggleston implicitly teaching the filmmaker how to see like him by letting him witness his working practice—Holzemer becomes Eggleston's de facto apprentice. Documentary filmmakers have also used aesthetic mimicry in staged scenes to convey the aesthetic perspective of photographers no longer living to partially compensate for the lack of filmed footage observing them at work. For example, Brenda Longfellow's documentary about Tina Modotti, *Tina in Mexico* (2003), presents reenacted scenes from Modotti's life in beautifully rendered chiaroscuro monochrome that imitates the photographer's visual style.[16]

Weston remained a significant subject for documentaries about photography in the succeeding decades, including Lou Stoumen's Academy Award–nominated *The Naked Eye* (1956) and Robert Katz's *Edward Weston: Day Books* (1965), a two-part public television program. Stoumen's film has an odd and uneven structure. The first thirty minutes cover a range of topics from vernacular photography to the history of photographic technologies (including cinema) to the photojournalists Weegee and Alfred Eisenstaedt; the remaining forty-five minutes are devoted to Weston's life and photography. Stoumen restages some scenes from *The Photographer* (with Brett Weston taking the place of his father), recycles some actual footage from Van Dyke's film, and concludes *The Naked Eye* with color shots of Point Lobos, California, in aesthetic mimicry of Weston's late commercial color work for Kodak at that coastal location. Focusing more heavily on a biographical narrative, *The Naked Eye* also alternates

Figures 3.7–3.8 The camera moves until it rests upon a Weston-like composition in *The Photographer* (Willard van Dyke, 1948).

in its deployment of Weston's photographs, at times examining them as examples of photographic art and at other times putting them in the service of illustrating his life narrative, including some hackneyed metaphorical shots, such as crashing waves to evoke the turmoil of his marriage break-up. This alternation between interpreting photographs and using them for biographical illustration would become a standard convention of the photographer documentary in the decades to follow.

Much shorter than the section on Weston, the nine-minute sequence devoted to Weegee makes no effort to imitate his aesthetic in its filmed footage. It merely follows him as he wanders the streets of New York in what is presented as a typical day for the photojournalist.[17] The temporal contingency involved in the photojournalist's capture of the "decisive moment" makes it difficult for the filmmaker to simply imitate Weegee's street photography in his filming of those social worlds. Stoumen resorts to other visual strategies to reveal the essence of Weegee's photographic practice (Video 3.2 ▶). In a scene on the Bowery, Weegee is filmed photographing a man drinking from a milk carton. Stoumen immediately cuts to a pair of hands holding the photograph that Weegee has taken of the man. The hands flip the photograph over to its verso, revealing Weegee's distinctive professional stamp, the mark of his photographic brand (Figures 3.9–3.11). Although Stoumen only uses this device once in the film, it would become one of the most common conventions of the photographer documentary: shoot the photographer in the act of taking a picture, then immediately insert the finished photograph to reaffirm the visual mastery of the photographer, as well as the "genius" of the photographic medium in its ability to snatch an instant from the flow of time.[18]

Although Stoumen does not use cinematography to mimic Weegee's photographic style, the film's editing imitates a visual strategy straight from Weegee's photobook *The Naked City* (1945), which provides most of his photographs used in *The Naked Eye*.[19] In the book, Weegee frequently places images on facing pages that appear to imply that subjects in one photograph are looking at those in the image across the page-spread. Arguably the most notorious example of this occurs on pages 86 and 87, where Weegee's photograph "At an Eastside Murder" (a group of children excitedly looking beyond the frame) is paired with an image of a bloodied murder victim on the street. The film uses shot-reverse-shot between such photographs to produce a similar effect of gazes across images. Moreover, he also resorts to rapid cuts, zooms, and pans within individual photographs to accentuate the looks among subjects within a single frame. Stoumen here draws our attention to Weegee's depiction of *The Naked City* as "a city of spectators," continually preoccupied with acts of looking, often across the thresholds of life and death, rich and poor, performer and audience.[20] Whereas *City of Gold* (discussed in chapter 1) uses cinematography and editing to immerse the viewer into the world depicted in the photographs, *The Naked Eye* employs them to self-consciously highlight the relations among the photograph's subjects, the photographer, the camera, and the photograph's viewer. Stoumen's film neither sutures its viewer to the gaze of Weegee's camera, nor attempts to imitate the photographer's visual style in the service of enhancing viewer identification. Rather,

Figures 3.9–3.11 Cutting from Weegee's act of photographing on the Bowery to the printed photograph in *The Naked Eye* (Lou Stoumen, 1956).

The Naked Eye observes the dynamics of looking in and around Weegee's photography, initiating what would become another significant component of documentaries about photographers.

Watching Photography

As *The Naked Eye* illuminates, film permits us to see photography's relations of looking which lie beyond the camera's singular gaze. Although lacking any substantive discussion of film and other moving image media, Ariella Azoulay's reconceptualization of photography in her book *The Civil Contract of Photography* provides a valuable framework for figuring out how documentary film can reorient the ways in which we see, and thus comprehend, these relations among photographic subjects, photographers, cameras, and viewers. In her move to repoliticize photographic theory by shifting it away from its long-standing preoccupation with affect (in particular, empathy, pity, shame, and compassion), Azoulay adopts the term "watching" to describe her reconceptualization of the medium:

> Photography is much more than what is printed on photographic paper. The photograph bears the seal of the photographic event and reconstructing this event requires more than just identifying what is shown in the photograph. One needs to stop looking at the photograph and instead start watching it. The verb "to watch" is usually used for regarding phenomena or moving pictures. It entails dimensions of time and movement that need to be reinscribed in the interpretation of the still photographic image.[21]

To "watch" photography is to enact "an ethics of the spectator" rather than "an ethics of seeing or viewing" (130). In other words, she rejects the now-pervasive argument in photographic theory, following Sontag and others, that the camera's gaze—its socially constructed visual perspective—posits the photograph's viewer as an ideologically and ethically implicated "passive addressee."[22] Moreover, Azoulay complicates the Barthesian "noeme" of photography, the idea of photograph's ontology as a "that-has-been."[23] Rather than mere evidence of what is visible in front of the camera in that moment, "the photograph is evidence of the social relations which made it possible" (127). Those relations ultimately involve not only the photographer and photographed, but also the viewer of the photograph, as well as the camera itself.[24] For Azoulay, no single party in the event of photography has full control over its meaning. As "a *mass* instrument for the *mass* production of images" (113), photography needs to be understood, she argues, as "a space of political relations" (20), in which new forms of political action are possible. This "civil contract" renders all the human parties involved in the photographic event—the photographer, the photographed, and the viewer—as citizens of photography, whom the camera recognizes, regardless of their legal status.[25]

To watch a photograph is thus to self-consciously examine the "montage of the heterogeneous viewpoints" of all the parties involved in the photographic act (384). This montage of various and conflictual viewpoints is preserved as a set of visual traces within a single frame, "a rectangular, steady, frozen field of vision," requiring careful reading by the viewer, who thus plays an active civic role in the creation of a photograph's meaning (384). The viewer who watches also recognizes her own viewpoint as participating in this perspectival montage that constitutes the event of photography. Azoulay decenters the photograph from the event of photography, contending that the relations that facilitate the photograph are in fact the core of photography, not the photograph itself. Nowhere is this more apparent than in her claim that the event of photography can occur even when no photograph is taken: "I think of the photographic event as an effect of the potential penetration of a camera, accompanied by the possibility that a photograph will be produced within its field of vision."[26]

Documentary films about living photographers at work enhance our capacity to watch photographs in that they can document much more of the relations between the parties in the event of photography than is visually captured within a photograph, or even all the photographs taken in a particular photographic encounter. They illuminate the dynamics among photographer, photographed, and camera, recording the interaction of the differing viewpoints of the parties involved, often even including viewers of the photographs as they look at them on walls, pages, or screens. The capacity of film editing to suture diverse times and spaces thus lends film as a medium to the task of explicating the event of photography in Azoulay's sense. By filming the event of photography, documentaries foreground the ethical and political dynamics among the different viewpoints that constitute it. They also urge us to consider the contingency of such an event rather than the visual and temporal fixity of the photograph. Moreover, the frequent use of hand-held cinematography in such scenes reinforces our contemplation of contingency through the impression of embodied presence that it generates. For example, Reiner Holzemer's *Magnum Photos: The Changing of a Myth* (1999) follows four contemporary members of the fabled agency, including British photographer Martin Parr as he meanders the streets of Bristol and Bath in search of the eccentric and the surreal in everyday life. Holzemer's camera observes him negotiating consent to photograph his subjects through spontaneous and fleeting conversations with people on the street, a contingency that is reflected in the aesthetic of Parr's photographs.

Christian Frei's Oscar-nominated documentary about American photojournalist James Nachtwey, *War Photographer* (2001), extensively illustrates this capacity of film to augment our understanding of the relations constituting the event of photography. Not only does Frei's film observe the photographer in the field over extended periods of time, but its cinematography and editing also visually separate and differentiate the perspectives that generate the event of photography. Although *War Photographer* functions on the surface as a celebratory portrait of Nachtwey as great artist and "concerned photographer," its novel use of a digital microcam attached to Nachtwey's SLR camera—one of several types of aesthetic mimicry in the film—actually fractures the film's visual perspective rather than tightens its alignment with Nachtwey.[27] It thus opens up a critical space within this apparent panegyric, a space for the film's viewer to "watch" Nachtwey's photography and therein begin to discern the competing viewpoints that constitute the event of photography in his pictures.[28]

Nachtwey ranks as one of the most acclaimed photojournalists of his generation, but like his contemporary, Sebastião Salgado, his work has often been cited in the critical debate over the "terrible beauty" and "beautiful suffering" of contemporary photography's aesthetic framing of war, disaster, and atrocity.[29] His photographs consistently foreground the vulnerability of the human body. Filled with injured, emaciated, lifeless, and decaying bodies, his highly visceral images frequently make for disturbing and upsetting viewing. Carefully framed visual ambiguity exacerbates the difficulty of his images. As critic Sarah Boxer notes in her *New York Times* review of his 400-page, 11-pound photobook, *Inferno*, "In Mr. Nachtwey's photographs, the boundary between living and dead is slim.... Some of the dead are tossed together in postures too intimate for the living. When you see legs dangling, the first response is a shudder. What is the status of the bodies they belong to?"[30] In her critical defense of Nachtwey's photographic practice, Susie Linfield instead sees his photographs as "visual oxymorons," which function through "an odd, compelling combination of misery and serenity, of edginess and supreme control, of horrible content and stylized form."[31] Whereas Linfield views Nachtwey's formalism as a process of "distilling, structuring, cohering the conditions" of his subjects' lives and deaths, other critics seriously question the ethical position of his aesthetics. In his *New Yorker* review of *Inferno*, Henry Allen contended that the compositions were built on "the nerve-damaged flatness of postmodern aesthetics."[32] Much of the criticism leveled at Nachtwey's formalism emphasizes how his books and exhibitions separate the photographs from contextualizing information. For instance, *Inferno* offers only an introductory paragraph of historical background for each section of the book and pushes all the photographs' captions to the end of the book. Even Linfield must admit, "By segregating text and pictures, Nachtwey undermines his self-proclaimed intention to promote understanding and inspire action" (2).

Although the film's generic title suggests a portrait of Nachtwey as representative of his profession, *War Photographer* goes to great lengths to prove the exceptional quality of Nachtwey and his work. The panegyric mobilizes the dominant conventions of the documentary portrait of a photographer to frame him in contrast to the popular stereotype of the war photographer as a hardened, fast-living, risk-taking adventurer.[33] Interviews with friends and colleagues (including magazine editors Hans-Hermann Klare and Christiane Breustedt, journalist Christiane Amanpour, cameraman Des Wright, and screenwriter Denis O'Neill) testify to Nachtwey's courage, compassion, dedication, patience, and self-sufficiency. Frei also follows him on assignment in Kosovo, Indonesia, and Palestine, observing the care and patience he brings to the photographic encounters with his subjects. Calm and soft-spoken in conversations on the scene, he remains quiet and methodical while he shoots, occasionally holding up a light meter to verify his camera settings amid a conflict zone. In addition, the camera lingers on Nachtwey's endurance when he is shooting in difficult and dangerous situations, such as the noxious sulfur mines in Indonesia or the streets of Ramallah filled with tear gas and bullets. Interviews and voiceovers with Nachtwey himself provide insight into his philosophy of photography as well as his working methods. For instance, he explains how he tries to remain as respectfully unobtrusive as possible to his subjects: "I want to feel open in my heart towards them. And I want them to be aware of that. And people sense it, with very few words and sometimes with no words at all." The final avowal implies a troubling conception of intuited consent—he does not need to ask his subjects for their consent to be photographed for they can feel his respect intuitively. The documentary also includes multiple scenes of Nachtwey's technical care as he methodically works with his photographs, examining a contact sheet, editing a sequence of prints, checking book proofs, instructing his printer on multiple adjustments to the development of a print, or supervising the installation of his work for an exhibition at the International Center of Photography in New York.

War Photographer explicitly contrasts the integrity of Nachtwey's creative process with the cynical expediency of the photo editors who use his images in their publications. Frei's editing directly connects Nachtwey's work in the field with that of the editors at the German illustrated magazine *Stern* in the sequence following the opening credits, which cuts from Nachtwey taking a picture in war-ravaged Kosovo to a laser printer in the magazine's Hamburg office as it churns out a page-spread galley that includes the very photograph Nachtwey had taken in the previous shot (Figures 3.12–3.14). In the office, foreign editor Klare reviews a draft feature spread of Nachtwey's photographs. As he scans the double-pages tacked to the wall, Klare laments, "It seems too graphic and unemotional. I would prefer those grieving people." His colleague responds by highlighting a "super" shot of "a sad figure walking through the streets of destruction." That we have just witnessed the context in which Nachtwey took that particular photograph in the previous scene accentuates the aesthetic abstraction and decontextualization of the editors' deliberations. Later, Klare is shown revising the copy for the feature as one of his colleagues looks over his shoulder. Both their faces reveal a certain blasé dissatisfaction with the generic prose Klare is writing. These scenes implicitly defend Nachtwey's professional integrity against the charge that his photographs are exploitative in their unsettling combination of viscerality and formalism. The problem lies not with Nachtwey, the scene suggests, but with the spectacle-driven mass media that publishes his work.

Arguably the most insightful, and controversial, strategy of the film is its use of microcam cinematography. Both the marketing and reviews of the film stressed the unique and illuminating effect of attaching a digital microcam to the side of Nachtwey's 35mm camera, thus providing a visual perspective very close to Nachtwey's own viewfinder. Robert Koehler's *Variety* review dubs it "Frei's masterstroke" that is "more than a mere device, it's a completely fresh way of capturing a photographer going about his work."[34] Other critics have nevertheless pointed out how the technical device exposes Nachtwey's photographic practice to ethical

Figures 3.12–3.14 A cut sutures two moments of framing: James Nachtwey shooting in the field and editors in the offices of Stern magazine in *War Photographer* (Christian Frei, 2001).

interrogation. John Anderson remarks, "Being able to watch so closely as the photographer relentlessly shoots a group of grieving Kosovo women is certainly educational. But it can hardly be the lesson Frei, or Nachtwey, intended."[35] The real significance of the microcam cinematography, however, lies less in the presumed access it gives to Nachtwey's specific visual perspective than in its capacity to open up the viewer's understanding of the event of photography and the multiple looks that constitute it.

Nachtwey initially refused Frei's request to make a documentary about him, but it was Frei's proposal to use microcam cinematography that finally convinced the solitary photographer, who saw the technology as less disruptive of his shooting than a full camera crew.[36] With the technology firm Swiss Effects, Frei developed two microcam devices to attach to Nachtwey's camera. The first microcam was fitted tightly against the body of the camera pointing upwards to a 45-degree angled mirror, which captured the top right-hand side of the camera, Nachtwey's index finger on the shutter, and the view in front of the camera (Figure 3.13). The second microcam was affixed to a flexible arm pointing back at the camera body and lens, providing a counter-angle of the photographer and his camera. Frei assured Nachtwey that his cinematographer, Peter Indergand, would remain at a certain distance as he shot Betacam footage of the photographer at work. Frei was himself even farther away, remotely controlling the microphones on both the microcam and the Betacam. Frei wanted the three pictorial elements of the film—the microcam, the Betacam, and Nachtwey's photographs—to retain their visual distinctiveness. He thus instructed Indergand to shoot as steadily as possible so as not to compete with the rough, immediate quality of the microcam images. However, the microcam shots possess within them an overriding tension between their sense of immediacy and a certain distancing effect, which A. O. Scott notes in his *New York Times* review: "This startling effect of immediacy is necessarily accompanied by a sense of detachment, not only from the people and objects Mr. Nachtwey sees, but from the man himself."[37] The fixed presence of the camera body in the lower section of the image continually reminds the viewer of the representational mediation in play, not just of the photographs that Nachtwey takes, but also the moving images. Moreover, the fixed position of Nachtwey's camera in the frame produces jump cuts between the microcam shots since the foreground remains constant while the background changes, ultimately undermining the microcam's effect of immediacy and proximity.

An ethical queasiness lies at the heart of this tension between immediacy and detachment. As *War Photographer* reminds us in its opening epigraph, Nachtwey follows Robert Capa's dictum that, "If your pictures aren't good enough, you're not close enough." We witness this commitment to proximity throughout the scenes of Nachtwey shooting. Two scenes of grieving women in Kosovo are particularly striking in this regard. In the first, families return to their burnt-out homes (Video 3.3 ▶). As women step off a truck, Nachtwey follows one of them closely as she walks through the wreckage of her home in solitary grief. In the second scene, we witness the exhumation of a shallow grave as relatives look on anxiously. Once a body is retrieved, attention turns to several women of the family who begin wailing inconsolably. In a long shot of the grieving women, we barely notice two important figures: Nachtwey, who is kneeling right in front of the women, and a woman in the group who holds up a portrait photo of the person being grieved (in an act of *habeas corpus* reminiscent of the Argentine mothers of the disappeared) (Figure 3.15). While we may be struck by how physically close Nachtwey gets to his subjects, the woman's act of holding a photograph suggests that these Kosovans acknowledge the necessary publicity of their grief as an act of witness. A moment later, a few subtle gestures further confirm this self-awareness of the Kosovans' relationship to the international media and their right to claim a role within the civil contract of photography. A young man moves to comfort the most distraught of the women, inadvertently blocking Nachtwey's view of the woman, who proceeds to use the interruption to check his light meter. Another family member gently moves the young man to the side, politely gesturing to Nachtwey's camera. Yet these subtle acknowledgements of the tacit consent for the photographer's presence do not mitigate the visceral unease produced by the micro-cam shots, which embody both Nachtwey's extreme physical proximity to his subjects and the simultaneous physical separation from them that his camera creates.

At times, Indergand's cinematography digresses from observing Nachtwey and turns to the people and their environment directly. Especially in the Kosovo scenes, these Betacam shots often imitate Nachtwey's aesthetic of stark geometry and emphatic use of the frame's margin, as well as his thematic preoccupation with brutalized bodies (Figures 3.16–3.17). Given that the microcam shots already provide a better physical approximation of the photographer's actual perspective, this additional variety of aesthetic mimicry may seem superfluous. Yet, regardless of Frei's intent, their inclusion amplifies the viewer's perception of the multiple looks at play whenever a

Figure 3.15 As James Nachtwey shoots a grieving Kosovan woman, another woman holds a photo portrait as an act of witness in *War Photographer* (Christian Frei, 2001).

Figures 3.16–3.17 Cinematographer Peter Indergand imitates James Nachtwey's aesthetic of stark geometry and emphatic use of the frame's margin in *War Photographer* (Christian Frei, 2001).

photograph is taken. Although the photographic subject's look is never acknowledged directly by Nachtwey nor Frei (either through direct visual address to the camera or embodying the subject's visual perspective), the fracture of the film's visual field into multiple perspectives encourages the film viewer's self-conscious consideration of all the looks that structure the event of photography, including photographer, subject, camera, and viewer. Frei may have set out to produce a panegyric for Nachtwey as the great artist and inspiring citizen of the world, yet the documentary's elaborate configuration of diverse visual perspectives opens up a space in which the relations between them become more visible. Despite its emphasis on the photographer and his photographs, *War Photographer* ultimately offers partial room for its viewer to start watching Nachtwey's photographs and thus begin the work of reconstructing the event of photography that has produced them.

Produced over a decade after *War Photographer*, David Frankham's four-part HBO documentary series *Witness* (2012) exploits a more recent technological development in the service of watching the event of conflict photography: single-lens-reflex (SLR) digital cameras that produce both professional-grade still and moving images. Frustrated with what he perceived to be the distanced and remote coverage of global conflict zones by television news, Frankham approached a number of photojournalists working in these zones with the idea of producing a series that would intimately capture the experience of being a conflict photographer.[38] In the service of seeing through the eyes of a photographer, Frankham insisted on hiring a photographer rather than a television or film professional to shoot the documentary. In fact, photographers Jared Moossy and Eros Hoagland began shooting material for the series pilot in Juárez, Mexico, without actually deciding who would serve as the cinematographer and who would act as the photographer-subject. Despite no prior experience shooting video, Moossy went on to become the series cinematographer, filming over a period of two and a half years in Mexico, Libya, Brazil, and South Sudan. He shot everything on a Canon EOS 5D Mk II, an SLR digital camera that has been widely adopted by both photojournalists and independent filmmakers due to its compact size, light weight, and image quality (in both still and moving images).[39] Aesthetic mimicry here extends to the technical apparatus itself. Moossy shoots with very similar (and in some cases the same) equipment as the photographer whom he is filming. The photographs and video footage in *Witness* thus share very similar visual qualities of resolution, lighting, and color, unlike *War Photographer* with its stark formal distinction between different types of images. Photographs become more fluidly integrated into the flow of moving images in *Witness*, shifting emphasis away from the photographs themselves to the conditions and relations of the event of photography. Although *Witness* retains a deep respect for the photographers it documents, the series fosters no aura of sanctity around either the photograph or the photographer.

The third episode of the series follows French photographer Véronique de Viguerie as she returns to South Sudan to continue documenting the Arrow Boys, locally organized militias established to protect villages from the terror of Joseph Kony's Lord's Resistance Army (LRA). De Viguerie accompanies both the Arrow Boys and the Ugandan Army as they pursue the LRA in the jungle on the border between South Sudan and the Central African Republic. The episode literalizes the photojournalist's hunt for images by embedding her in the physically demanding and dangerous pursuit of the LRA rebels in the bush. Yet the documentary repeatedly reinforces de Viguerie's position as an outsider. She is interviewed early in the episode in Paris and is then seen in a traveling montage that takes her to remote villages in South Sudan. Moreover, Moossy repeatedly captures her taking photographs through dirty or misted car windows, a multiplex photographic analogy that evokes the frame, lens, and filter (Figure 3.18). Late in the episode, de Viguerie substantiates the analogy when she comments in voiceover, "In some situations, it is helpful to look through the camera to make it more bearable, to have this filter between you and what you're photographing."

Witness elaborates de Viguerie's position in the event of photography through both the content of the footage selected and its formal properties. While greater attention is paid to her interactions with her subjects beyond the moment when she is photographing them, the documentary's framing of her working methods further emphasizes the relations between her and her photographic subjects. Although the episode provides little historical and political background to the LRA's insurgency in South Sudan, it does insist on marking the specificity of this situation by naming each location visited as well as each person interviewed and photographed by de Viguerie. Since she is returning to places she has already visited on a previous assignment for the French magazine *L'Optimum*, de Viguerie brings multiple copies of the magazine, as well as stacks of prints from the previous assignment, to show and distribute to her subjects and their communities.[40] These scenes highlight the photographer's sense of responsibility to share with her subjects how they have been represented within international media as well as honoring their right to their own image. The photographic object here serves as a gift, representing a concrete act of civil recognition by the photographer toward her subject.

A scene with a former LRA abductee, Seba, illustrates well how de Viguerie strives to respect those rights in multiple ways. At the beginning of the scene, de Viguerie shows Moossy's camera a photographic portrait she took of Seba and her baby on the previous assignment while she summarizes Seba's story of abduction, forced

Figure 3.18 Cinematographer Jarod Moossy frequently captures Véronique de Viguerie photographing through car windows in *Witness* (David Frankham, 2012).

marriage, rape, and pregnancy. Immediately on reuniting with Seba, de Viguerie hands the photograph to her as a gift. A sit-down interview is then interwoven with footage of de Viguerie photographing Seba in her hut. At the end of the sequence, the photographer shows her subject the pictures she has just taken on the camera's viewing screen (Figure 3.19). As de Viguerie uses the moment to share with Seba that she is herself pregnant, Moossy captures this intimate connection between the two women first as video footage and then as a photograph. Exemplifying Azoulay's conception of the photograph as "a trace of a space of human relations," this scene consistently deemphasizes the photograph in favor of the relations that produce it.[41] When de Viguerie's photographs appear in the scene, they are granted the same visual status as the video footage that precedes and follows them—as raw "footage" to be edited into an assemblage. Furthermore, the photographs and their making engender opportunities to build and augment those human relations rather than just visually registering them. Many other scenes in the film also prioritize what de Viguerie does before and after she gets out her camera. In the Makpandu refugee camp, she speaks with another victim of LRA atrocity, Bienvenue Anili, first in a conversation with a group of men about the failures of military intervention and then alone with Anili as he describes to her the slaughter of a large part of his family, including the decapitation of one of his daughters. Coupling these two scenes together positions Anili as a participant in the collective struggle against the LRA and not just an individual grieving victim of it. In the searing testimonial encounter between Anili and de Viguerie, Moossy's camera alternates equally between witness and listener. When the scene culminates with de Viguerie picking up her camera and taking a portrait of Anili, it

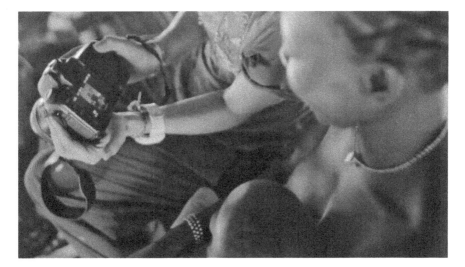

Figure 3.19 Véronique de Viguerie shows her subject, Seba, what she has just photographed in *Witness* (David Frankham, 2012).

appears as an act of respect toward the witness-survivor, mutually performed rather than simply captured by the talent of the photographer.

Notably, this scene between Anili and de Viguerie opens with a video shot of Anili that aesthetically mimics her photograph of him that culminates the scene (Figure 3.20). Throughout the documentary, Moossy's video footage often imitates de Viguerie's photographic style, with its low camera angles, midground positioning of subjects, and visual emphasis on location (Video 3.4 ▶). Whereas Frei uses aesthetic mimicry in *War Photographer* to reveal to viewers how Nachtwey's aesthetic framing of the world generates such compelling photographs, Frankham puts it in the service of centering the event of photography rather than its product. Editing in the scenes of de Viguerie at work alternates between the viewing positions of Moossy's and de Viguerie's cameras. Since their Canon EOS cameras capture still and moving images, video footage is occasionally replaced by still photographs. Despite the minor variance in color tone and lighting between the still and moving images, these photographs are not privileged over the video footage. They remain on screen only momentarily, not long enough for viewers to contemplate them as aesthetically autonomous individual photographs. In a climactic scene, when one of the Arrow Boys has been shot during a nighttime search, four photographs of the injured man are flashed on the screen in quick succession, interspersed by black frames to generate a strobe effect. In all such scenes, the photographs retain the same status as the adjacent video shots—elements of the image flow created by the film's editing. Unlike *War Photographer*, with its consistent attention to Nachtwey's patient and painstaking labor to capture the decisive moment with his camera, *Witness* situates de Viguerie's acts of photographing,

Figure 3.20 Jared Moossy's opening shot mimics this photograph that Véronique de Viguerie takes of Anili, a survivor of LRA atrocity, in *Witness* (David Frankham, 2012).

and the pictures that arise from them, within the relationships she builds with her subjects. Her photographic practice also differs substantially from her male peers in series.

The episode only touches upon gender explicitly in two brief moments when de Viguerie discusses her decision to continue working while pregnant and her strategic use of femininity in difficult situations. Yet the episode's sustained emphasis on her relationship building with her subjects creates a gendered contrast with Eros Hoagland and Michael Christopher Brown, who featured in the other episodes. Both men discuss their relationships with other male photojournalists who have served significant paternal roles for them professionally, namely Hoagland's father John, who was killed in El Salvador in 1984, and Tim Hetherington, who was killed in an attack in Misrata, Libya, in 2011, in which Brown was also injured. Moreover, Hoagland and Brown also spend substantial time on conventional masculinist themes of the profession, such as the pursuit of the most striking images, the dangers they face in the field, and the mysterious allure of the profession. Although they each grapple with the ethical challenges of their profession, their conclusions remain focused on the perspective of the photographer, not their relation to the other participants in the event of photography. For example, the opening credit sequence of the Juarez episode concludes with Hoagland's strident assertion, "I am not there to tell you what is happening. I am there to show you what I saw, what happened to me, and you can come upon your own conclusion." Brown is less certain, but still internally focused, when he notes, "The most important piece of equipment is what you have inside, your sense, your conscience. My own sense of right and wrong, and then it caught me." By contrast, the South Sudan episode concludes with de Viguerie's reflections on the ethics of intervention after we have just seen her actively participate in life-saving treatment of a wounded Arrow Boy in the bush: "I am a human first, and then I am photographer." Although *Witness* underplays gender as an issue within photographic practice, the contrast between de Viguerie on one hand and Hoagland and Brown on the other is undeniable, permitting the episode to subtly foreground a feminist conception of photojournalism that emphasizes the relationality among photographer, camera, and subject over and above the conventional masculinist emphasis on the trials of getting the picture.[42]

Aesthetic mimicry in *Witness* does not aim to provide the viewer with access to the photographer's own distinctive aesthetic vision of the world. Its foundation in a shared camera apparatus contributes not only to seamless integration of still and moving images, but also to a fluid mutability of positions between those of the photographer and the cameraperson observing the photographer. At times, it even becomes ambiguous as to who is holding the camera, de Viguerie or Moossy. Ultimately, it matters little that some of the photographs seen in the episode were taken by Moossy rather than de Viguerie. The viewer attends not to the photographer's aesthetic choices but to the positions and relations that constitute the event of photography. Even more than in *War Photographer*, the viewer of *Witness: South*

Sudan can watch photography closely, to discern the political claims of citizenship made by its various actors and to recognize the new forms of relation that could be realized if such claims are observed.

From Aesthetic Mimicry to Complementarity

If the photojournalism of Nachtwey and de Viguerie relies on the possibility of physical proximity to their human subjects, then the landscape photography of Edward Burtynsky requires the opposite, a distance that can reveal the scale at which modern human civilization has transformed the natural world in the Anthropocene. Burtynsky's large-format photographs of quarries, mines, refineries, factories, waste sites, and other industrially produced landscapes have garnered both high acclaim and rigorous criticism. His modernist techniques of abstraction and defamiliarization are read contrastingly as either the source of the work's political import or the very means by which his photography depoliticizes the ecological degradation it depicts or implies.[43] Burtynsky acknowledges that his motivation to work with Canadian filmmaker Jennifer Baichwal on a documentary film about his work stemmed not only from the desire to broaden the audience for his photography, but also from an intention to provide "the extended context of where these images were coming from."[44] He recognized that a documentary film about his photography could furnish what critics charged was a crucial omission from the images themselves, namely the social contexts of those living and working in such manufactured landscapes. Unlike her previous documentary, *The True Meaning of Pictures: Shelby Adams' Appalachia* (2002), Baichwal's documentary about Burtynsky, *Manufactured Landscapes*, avoids explicit discussion of the contentious critical debate about the photographer and instead finds cinematic form to complement and extend the work accomplished by his photography. This mode of aesthetic mimicry does more than just generate cinematic equivalents to Burtynsky's photographic aesthetics; more importantly, it constitutes an expansive complementarity, an intermedial means to multiply the meaning and significance of the work. Burtynsky was so pleased with this collaboration that he sought to work on a second film with Baichwal, but this time as a co-director, embracing filmmaking as fully part of his own visual practice. The resulting documentary, *Watermark*, constitutes the film component of his 2013 multiplatform project on our contemporary relationship to water, which included a traveling exhibition and a photobook published by Steidl, the world's most prestigious photobook publisher.

Burtynsky's oeuvre builds upon the legacy of *New Topographics*, the landmark 1975 exhibition and photobook, in which the photography of Robert Adams, Lewis Baltz, Bernd and Hilla Becher, and others demystified the natural landscape by documenting the banal surfaces of late capitalist environments of industry and commerce.[45] Burtynsky developed an aesthetic that combined the flat abstraction of New Topographics with elements of the Romantic sublime, which the original practitioners of the movement so actively resisted in their 1970s work. Following the typological tendency championed by the Bechers, Burtynsky's projects in the 1980s and 1990s were organized around specific types of industrial landscapes found around the world, including mines, railcuts, quarries, and tailings. By mid-career, his projects expanded in both conceptual scope and geographical scale, including a study of China's rapid industrialization and urbanization (2005), as well as wide-ranging thematic explorations of the culture of oil (2009) and global water resources (2013). In 2018, he collaborated with Baichwal and Nicholas de Pencier on *The Anthropocene Project*, which combined a documentary film, VR short films, an exhibition, and a book. [46]

Aesthetic ambiguities pervade Burtynsky's photographs, created by a set of techniques that he characterizes as "the democratic distribution of light and space across the whole field," which aim to equalize the formal qualities of everything in the frame so that the viewer "will fall into the surface and read the detail."[47] This latter phrase highlights the perceptual gap between two and three dimensions that his photographs mine for richly generative ambiguity. Drawing on nineteenth-century landscape photographers like Francis Frith and Carleton Watkins, Burtynsky adopts an elevated perspective in most of his photographs, so that the foreground begins at a perceived distance from the viewer. The sense of mastery and the transcendent perspective normally assumed from such a "hovering" position above and outside of the landscape are destabilized by the pictures' various techniques of depth-flattening abstraction. Burtynsky shoots at dusk, at dawn, or during overcast days to minimize contrast and the depth effect from shadows. His framing frequently eliminates the horizon or pushes it to the top of the picture, minimizing perspectival vision. Aperture and exposure are set to create the highest possible depth of field, in order for every minute detail in the picture to remain sharp and potentially noticeable to the viewer. The dense visual detail of Burtynsky's pictures remains central to the critical interpretation of his work. Mark Kingwell argues that the "structuring power of the detail," especially the striking singular detail of a lone figure or a colorful object, binds the photographs into an oscillation between "pure aesthetic formalism and the informing realistic ends of photojournalism."[48] For other critics, the detail of a singular human figure pulled from the visual density of Burtynsky's pictures reinforces their invocation of the Romantic sublime. The human detail both reassures and terrifies us, but it is no longer nature producing the effect of sublimity, but the industrial processes that have transformed the natural landscape.[49]

The tension between the elevated view and the abstracted aspects of Burtynsky's pictures creates multiple ambiguities: What is actually depicted in the photograph? What is its scale? Where is the camera located? David Campany reminds us that locating the point of view is crucial to a medium built around distances and perspectives: "An unorthodox vantage point may render abstract even the most optically clear photograph. Likewise, an apparently abstract photograph may cohere once we know its point of view."[50] Campany situates Burtynsky's formal ambiguities within a modernist politics of abstraction and defamiliarization shared by other contemporary landscape photographers like Adams, Richard Misrach, and Andreas Gursky. It is a risky strategy, as Campany notes, that is open to the charge of empty postmodern formalism or, even worse, the aestheticization of disaster.[51] For example, Marnin Young contends that, "It seems only a step away from a covert neo-liberal apology for the exploitation of the natural environment ('even an environmental holocaust doesn't look bad!') or, even worse, mere post-modernist irony ('good thing we know better than to take beauty too seriously!')."[52] Despite his collaborative engagement with NGOs and educational projects about climate change, environmental protection, and sustainable economies, Burtynsky remains adamant in his aesthetic resistance to any form of didacticism in his photographs. As he explains in voiceover at the end of *Manufactured Landscapes*, "If I said this is a terrible thing we're doing to the planet then people will either agree or disagree. By not saying what you should see, that may allow them to look at something they've never looked at, to see their world a little differently." The modernist ambiguity of his images constitutes the lure that potentially enables, rather than denies, the viewer's development of a critical consciousness about the industrial exploitation of the natural world and the larger ramifications of late capitalism. However, Burtynsky's reluctance to articulate a specific environmental politics also finds a pragmatic explanation in that he relies on the permission of industrial corporations to gain access to most of the sites he photographs. In a telling scene of *Manufactured Landscapes*, Burtynsky's translator struggles to convince a Chinese bureaucrat to allow him to shoot at a coal-mining facility. The authorities even ask Baichwal's crew to stop filming the negotiations, so they leave on the audio recorder and start taking photographs of the conversation. The bureaucrat contends, "It's very dirty, very dirty. I don't think it's a good day to make beautiful pictures." The translator responds by showing her a copy of a Burtynsky exhibition catalog and saying, "But through his camera lens, through his eyes, it will appear beautiful. For example, even this industrial waste, it's kind of like garbage. Still, it appears beautiful through his camera."

The reception of *Manufactured Landscapes* consistently contemplated whether the documentary critically engages the ambiguity of Burtynsky's images or merely replicates it. In her *New York Times* review, Manohla Dargis reads the film as "a Great Man documentary," but one with an occasional "rather tentative, perhaps even unconscious, critique" of Burtynsky and his vision.[53] Likewise, Gerda Cammaer understands the film as a generic hybrid of the artist portrait and the social documentary: "Piling up images both of construction and deconstruction, the documentary gradually becomes a multilayered puzzle of ethical questions, laid out for us as a constant pressing undercurrent to the uncomfortable beauty of Burtynsky's photos."[54] Cammaer argues moreover that the specific characteristics of the film medium allows the viewer "deeper insight into the problems at stake" than the stillness and silence of photography (123). Burtynsky has repeatedly acknowledged his satisfaction in finding a filmmaker who not only shared his resistance to documentary didacticism, but also fully understood and respected the medium of photography.[55]

Before teaming up with Baichwal, Burtynsky had been working with filmmaker Jeff Powis, who shot extensive DV footage of the photographer at work in Bangladesh and China between 2001 and 2004. From eighty hours of footage, Powis cut an hour-length documentary, but a dissatisfied Burtynsky shelved the project. The rough, hand-held immediacy of the DV footage contrasted sharply with the photographer's highly precise visual style. After meeting Baichwal, Burtynsky showed her Powis's rough cut. She agreed to take over the project but insisted new footage be shot. She understood the specific context Burtynsky sought in terms of the human narratives that his photographs obscure in their subliminal scale. "Because the resolution of these photos is extraordinary," she explains, "there are hundreds of narratives in these wide frames, and when you look in close and follow them, there are all of these inherent narratives."[56] Baichwal and her cinematographer Peter Mettler thus not only shot new footage of Burtynsky at work in China at a shipbuilding yard in Qili, a factory in Zhangzhou, and the Three Gorges Dam, but also travelled to places that he had already photographed, such as Shanghai, in search of footage that could flesh out the human details in his photographs. The film integrates this material with some of Powis's DV footage from China, Burtynsky's 2005 TED Prize talk (often merely heard in voiceover), shots taken at the Burtynsky retrospective at the Brooklyn Museum of Art, and his photographs themselves.

Throughout *Manufactured Landscapes*, Baichwal pursues an aesthetic mimicry that seeks cinematic equivalents for Burtynsky's photographic techniques through her use of cinematography, editing, and sound design. Nowhere is this more apparent than in the film's awe-inspiring eight-minute opening shot. A wipe cut from black introduces a tracking shot moving from right to left across an unnamed Chinese factory floor.[57] In steady linear motion, the camera passes by row after row of assembly lines with workers on each side of a conveyor belt.[58] Since the assembly lines are perpendicular to the direction of the camera's movement, we have little time to contemplate what individual workers are doing. Some of them glance inquisitively at the camera as it passes by (Figure 3.21). After several minutes, the regularity of the camera movement and the graphic repetition of the assembly line structure make us acutely aware of the duration of the shot and the space of the profilmic. Questions begin to arise: When will the shot end? Is this possibly a looped shot? How large is this factory? What is this massive factory in fact producing? After five minutes, we suddenly hear Burtynsky in voiceover reflecting, "Is there actually some way I can talk about nature and bring a certain appreciation for what it represents? We come from nature, and we have to understand what it is so as not to harm it and so ultimately harm ourselves." These lines jar at first, pushing us to reconsider what we are in fact looking at. Why is he talking about nature as we observe industrial mass production on a factory floor? Burtynsky continues his commentary by explaining his commitment to explore the industrial landscape as nature massively transformed by humanity. Baichwal's selection of these lines as the film's opening discourse defamiliarizes our perception of what we're seeing in this opening shot, but it also establishes Burtynsky's political commitment.[59] After eight minutes, a wipe cut to his

Figure 3.21 The eight-minute opening shot glides past a seemingly endless factory line in *Manufactured Landscapes* (Jennifer Baichwal, 2006).

Figure 3.22 The scene concludes with Edward Burtynsky's photographic diptych of the factory line in *Manufactured Landscapes* (Jennifer Baichwal, 2006).

photographic diptych of the same factory floor finally ends the momentous tracking shot (Figure 3.22). The factory floor is so vast that it needs two large-format prints to encompass the whole space. But since each shot is taken at a slightly different angle, the resulting bifurcated perspective disturbs our ability to orient ourselves in relation to the view before us. Mettler's cinematographic treatment of movement and duration as regularity and linearity achieves the filmic equivalence of Burtynsky's photographic articulation of scale. Yet he also adopts cinematic means to mirror the photographer's destabilizing of the viewer's perspective. The tight framing and frontal, perpendicular alignment of the continually moving traveling shot disrupts any possible sense of visual mastery of the scene on the part of the viewer. The shot provides no chance to scan the whole image within one's own time since the camera pulls us away from any detail at the very moment it is first noticed.

While Burtynsky's photographs illuminate the sheer scale of such Taylorized production, they cannot adequately depict the sheer repetitive nature of individual labor on the assembly line. *Manufactured Landscapes* acts to compensate for this oft-criticized aspect of his work by including several scenes that closely observe individual workers rapidly piecing together or testing components.[60] In one particular scene, a close-up of a young woman's hands demonstrates how she can assemble a complex electrical breaker in less than a minute (Figure 3.23). We watch her assiduously assemble one breaker after another in a long take lasting several minutes. Her voiceover reveals that she can produce over four hundred units a day without overtime. The durational aspect of film therefore permits a temporal articulation of scale that is just as significant as the spatial one presented by the photographs. Aesthetic mimicry expands into a form of intermedial complementarity: one medium appropriates and builds upon the aesthetic means of another. The film's editing consistently alternates in scale between the vast sublimity of Burtynsky's landscapes and the close-up vignettes of individual workers captured by Mettler's camera on the ground. Filmed footage fleshes out the tiny human detail discernable on the

Figure 3.23 A close-up of repetitive labor on the factory line illuminates the individual human scale occluded in Edward Burtynsky's photographs in *Manufactured Landscapes* (Jennifer Baichwal, 2006).

large-scale photograph. However, we are never quite given enough time at each end of the scale to settle into a comfortable perspective of either visual mastery from above or immersion on the ground before an edit pulls us to the opposite end of the scale (Video 3.5 ▶).

In the movement between still and moving images, Baichwal also employs editing and sound design to generate an intermedial ambiguity between them. Throughout the film, Dan Driscoll's ethereal score consistently incorporates various industrial sounds, which function to blur the distinction between the score and the ambient sounds of Mettler's documentary film footage. Sound bridges abound as the film shifts seamlessly between photographic and filmic images. Moreover, Baichwal intensifies this intermedial ambiguity by not only applying the Ken Burns effect to Burtynsky's photographs, but also editing them together with Mettler's film shots that present largely static subject matter, such as waste sites and city skylines, through various camera movements. In such sequences, we increasingly lose our ability to discern whether we are looking at film footage (Figure 3.24), or a photograph (Figure 3.25). By rendering both media through parallel forms of movement over stasis, *Manufactured Landscapes* enhances the modernist perceptual unmooring of the viewer that Burtynsky's images achieve by photographic means.

One of the most important moments of such blurring occurs close to the end of the film. Mettler's camera pans left across the skyline of Shanghai crammed with hundreds of skyscrapers on an overcast day. Like Burtynsky's photographs, the camera's position is elevated, and the foreground of the shot is at a substantial distance from the camera, thus eliminating the street level with its potential moving details from the image. This film shot could easily be mistaken for a photograph, despite the presence of background city sounds. In voiceover, Burtynsky comments, "We are changing the nature of this planet. We are changing the air, we are changing the water, we are changing the land. And that's not just China, that's the world at large." A cut introduces another image of the Shanghai skyline as the camera now pans laterally down toward the lower right. The sound bridge of ambient urban sounds obscures the transition from a film shot to a photograph. It is only when the head and shoulders of a gallery viewer appears on the right-hand side of the frame that it becomes apparent that we are not only looking at a Burtynsky photograph, but one on display in a gallery space (Figure 3.26). This transition is more than a visual trick on Baichwal's part. Just as Burtynsky's use of the first-person plural in his voiceover implicates us in his critical discourse, so too does the visual inscription of a gallery viewer, whose anonymity, from her obscured face, renders her as our on-screen proxy.

The documentary includes several scenes of gallery visitors looking at Burtynsky's large-format photographs and of the subjects of his photographs looking at small Polaroid test shots during his shoots. Their comparison facilitates a subtle critique of Burtynsky's relationship to the event of photography. In the gallery scenes shot on super-16mm color film, well-heeled visitors leisurely meander around the room,

Figures 3.24–3.25 Intermedial ambiguity between shots makes it difficult to discern the difference between Edward Burtynsky's photographs and Peter Mettler's cinematography in *Manufactured Landscapes* (Jennifer Baichwal, 2006).

pausing to lean into the pictures to discern their minute details or stepping back to contemplate the scale of the image (Figure 3.27). Burtynsky's voiceover commentary on the perceptual effect of his photographs confirms the emphasis he places on the relationship to his viewer. By contrast, the moments when Burtynsky's subjects are given an opportunity to contemplate their own images are shot on grainy monochrome video and appear marginal to his practice. In the first scene, children playing at a Chinese recycling site are given a Polaroid test shot of the photograph that Burtynsky has just taken of them. As they grab and pull at the picture to glimpse their own

Figure 3.26 A lateral pan reveals the location of the act of looking in an art gallery in *Manufactured Landscapes* (Jennifer Baichwal, 2006).

Figure 3.27 A gallery viewer scrutinizes an Edward Burtynsky print in *Manufactured Landscapes* (Jennifer Baichwal, 2006).

self-image, Burtynsky is seen with his back to the children as he scrutinizes another Polaroid test with a loupe. The final shot of the scene shows a single girl dismissively casting aside one of Burtynsky's more abstract shots. In the second scene, workers dismantling the city of Feng Jie for the Three Gorges Dam similarly crowd around a Polaroid test shot in which they are depicted. One worker plaintively holds up the

Figure 3.28 In *Manufactured Landscapes* (Jennifer Baichwal, 2006), Chinese workers complain about the difficulty in seeing details in Edward Burtynsky's photographs.

picture for Powis's camera after lamenting, "It is a very broad view. It's hard to see the details" (Figure 3.28). Although brief, these minor scenes nevertheless indicate not only the divergent engagements with Burtynsky's pictures by gallery viewers and the photographic subjects themselves, but also the priority that his photographic practice places on the viewer within the event of photography. *Manufactured Landscapes* replicates that priority by suffusing its presentation of Burtynsky's photography with multivalent ambiguity—between photograph and film, text and context, articulation and critique. Baichwal thus transforms aesthetic mimicry from a visual alignment with the photographer through filmic means into a form of aesthetic complementarity that seamlessly integrates filmic and photographic means to challenge viewers' normative perception.

Mimicry as Farce

Inevitably, the proliferation of aesthetic mimicry as a rhetorical strategy in photographer documentaries would end up in farce. While Van Dyke's *The Photographer* introduced aesthetic mimicry through the character of the young apprentice learning to see like the master photographer, Ben Lewis's short television documentary *Gursky World* (2002) takes it to a mischievous extreme as he cheekily plays the role of a naïve superfan who wants to impress the object of his obsession by showing that he can also create photographs just like the German master. Commissioned for the Channel Four series *The Art Show*, *Gursky World* became the model for Lewis's irreverent take on the television arts documentary, which he subsequently developed for the BBC as the award-winning series *Art Safari*.[61] Part of the idiosyncratic and anti-elitist strand of British television arts programming that was pioneered by producer and presenter Waldemar Januszczak in the late 1990s, Lewis infused the arts documentary with a performative naivety drawn from "klutz" documentarians like Nick Broomfield and Michael Moore.[62]

Lewis's presenter personality expresses an unrelentingly earnest desire to understand Andreas Gursky's aesthetic appeal as "the most influential photographer of our age." Invoking Gursky's totalizing vision of the ordinary in early twenty-first-century life, Lewis admits to being obsessed with Gursky: "I believe I'm living in a Gursky world. I can't help seeing Gursky where ordinary life should be."[63] He subsequently shows the view from the top of his apartment building, pointing out details and compositional elements that you could find in a Gursky photograph, particularly its paradoxical tension between bland flatness and monumental scale (Video 3.6 ⊙). This posture hovers between a parodic literalizing of modernist defamiliarization (Gursky's photography has successfully renewed our vision of the world) and an articulation of postmodern ambiguity (his work amplifies the blurring of reality and representation). The comic narrative alibi of the show is established when Lewis attends the opening reception of the Centre Pompidou's Gursky exhibition, for the filmmaker comes to the realization that, for all its totalizing imagination of our globalized age, none of Gursky's work on show was shot in Britain. Aping national shame, Lewis decides he must convince Gursky to come photograph Britain. A brief conversation with the photographer at the reception leads to an invitation to come visit his new studio in Düsseldorf. In preparation for the visit, Lewis meets an art collector, Anita Zablubowicz, who, after showing him the Gursky print in her collection, reveals that she had made her own "Gursky" of the South African resort Sun City before she had been able to acquire an original one. This inspires Lewis to create his own Gurskys in Britain as proof of its worthiness as a subject for his photography. Touring the city of Reading with the local council's public-relations officer and a large-format view camera, Lewis takes three photographs that imitate Gursky's subject matter and formal techniques: contemporary architecture, late capitalist work environments, rigorous symmetry, ambiguity of depth, and a preoccupation with color patterns. When Lewis shows them to Gursky at the end of his studio visit, the photographer entertains Lewis's gambit with politeness and good humor. Yet Gursky is not the real target of this farce.

If *Gursky World* used its aesthetic mimicry only to stage an elaborate joke on the artist, then it would not warrant critical consideration. But the documentary also shows great interest in explicating the work of the German photographer. In between scenes of Lewis, the art geek, awkwardly asking faux-naïf questions, he offers a more conventional art documentary discourse that formally analyzes Gursky's work and contextualizes it in relation to the history of photography and the contemporary art world. Lewis's mischief-making is ultimately directed at the political economy of the global art world, especially what he sees as the expressive vacuity of its key players—critics, curators, gallery owners, and collectors—whom he takes to task through comedy for failing to adequately explain why Gursky's photographs matter.

Lewis takes aesthetic mimicry to a comic extreme, but in the service of seriously testing Gursky's art world reputation. Similarly, the surfaces of *War Photographer*, *Witness*, and *Manufactured Landscapes* can be deceptive. These documentaries appear to deploy aesthetic mimicry to craft panegyric profiles of their photographer subjects. However, upon closer inspection, they ultimately reveal a potential contradiction within this device. In creating ways to see as the photographer does, aesthetic mimicry also creates various dynamics that can actually decenter the photographer, allowing the viewer to watch the multiple competing looks that constitute the event of photography. If Azoulay contends that to watch photography is to fundamentally see the medium otherwise, then photographer documentaries like the ones I have discussed paradoxically demonstrate the role that film can play in reorienting our attention away from the singularity of the photographer's vision of the world and toward the event of photography in all its complex multiplicity. In the next chapter, the critical interrogation of photographic authorship continues as I examine documentaries that mobilize specific photographic archives to challenge the conventional construction of the photographic artist within the history of the medium.

4

Discoveries and Restitutions of the Photographic Archive

In his 2017 film *On Photography, Dispossession and Times of Struggle*, Akram Zaatari includes a 1998 interview he conducted with Palestinian refugee Astra Abu Jamra about her mother's photo album, through which Jamra delicately leafs during the conversation (Figure 4.1). On the left-hand side of the screen, we see two iPhones on a bright white surface playing recordings of the interview from different angles: a high-angle shot over Jamra's shoulders that offers a clear view of the album's pages and an eye-level shot of Jamra from the presumed perspective of the interviewer across Jamra's dining-room table. On the right-hand side of the screen, gloved hands open archival file folders to reveal individual photographs or single pages from the album. Each of these objects bears a carefully inscribed archival cataloging number. This dual presentation of Jamra's family photographs aptly visualizes the displacement, fragmentation, and decontextualization produced by the archive. In the pristine space of the archive, the original object is severed from the social world of its original use (Jamra's home), the narrative complex of the album is shattered into individually cataloged images, and the archival folder preserves only the title or caption of the photograph, not the affectively rich meanings of oral narration engendered by family photo albums. Archivization preserves the physical photograph but not the social performances and affective relations that have produced and disseminated it.

In his foundational essay, "Reading an Archive," Allan Sekula posits the photographic archive as "a kind of 'clearing house' of meaning," in which the "possibility of meaning is 'liberated' from the actual contingencies of use."[1] However, this liberation must also be recognized as a loss: "an abstraction from the complexity and richness of use, a loss of context" (154). By failing to preserve the socially constructed looks that produce and circulate photographs, the archive establishes "a relation of *abstract visual equivalence* between pictures" (155, emphasis in original). This abstraction and decontextualization paradoxically push archival photographs further toward the contradictory poles that have historically shaped the understanding of photography as a medium: as objective record of the world and as subjective expression of an artist. Without the context that shapes the complex meaning of a photograph, it becomes more prone to be read simply as the empirical visual record of the event, person, or thing it appears to depict or as an aesthetic experience of sensual form shorn from its historical framework. Sekula further argues that the use of archival photographs as empirical illustrations of the past enhances the construction of history as visual spectacle, in which the viewer comes to identify with the camera offering a sensuous

A Medium Seen Otherwise. Roger Hallas, Oxford University Press. © Oxford University Press 2023.
DOI: 10.1093/oso/9780190057763.003.0005

From Jerusalem they went to Lebanon,
and then to Damascus.

Figure 4.1. Palestinian refugee Astra Abu Jamra discusses her mother's photo album in *On Photography, Dispossession and Times of Struggle* (Akram Zaatari, 2017).

experience of the past: "when photographs are uncritically presented as historical documents, they are transformed into aesthetic objects" (159). The seamless incorporation of archival photographs (and also moving image footage) into historical documentaries has often fallen into this particular trap, as I discussed in relation to Ken Burns's *The Civil War* in chapter 1. The archive is thus conventionally treated as a neutral repository of visual records that may provide historical documentaries with their obligatory visual illustrations of the past.

By contrast, this chapter examines documentary films that explicitly investigate and interrogate acts of collecting and archiving photographs outside the realm of the state (the next chapter will address films that engage state photographic archives). Some of these films apply archaeological tropes of excavation and revelation in relation to aesthetic discourse, namely the discovery of new photographic artists through the act of collecting vernacular photography or the recovery of parts of a photographer's oeuvre long considered lost. Others dwell on the nature of a photographic archive, probing how it actively transforms the meaning and value of the objects it holds. However, all these films emphasize the materiality of photography as they investigate the social biography and visual economy of both the photographic objects and the collections of which they are part. In her elaboration of the materialist turn in photographic studies, Elizabeth Edwards notes the usefulness of the anthropological concepts of social biography and visual economy for explaining how photographs do not merely signify as images, but also matter as objects.[2] The social biography of an object acknowledges that it cannot be understood through one single moment of its existence, for it is "marked through successive moments of consumption across space and time" (222). The concept of visual economy further accounts for the "double helix of simultaneous existence" of photographic objects, which are both singular and multiple (a photographic image can be reproduced in multiple forms, but each photographic object also holds its own unique social biography). Drawing on Deborah Poole's conceptualization of visual economy derived from her work in the Peruvian Andes, Edwards contends that the meaning of photographs is to be found "not in the content alone but in the production, consumption, material forms, ownership, institutionalization, exchange, possession, and social accumulation, in which equal weight is given to content and use value" (223). Documentaries about photographic archives and collecting are precisely concerned with these complex material dynamics of what people *do* with photographs through modes of exchange and transfer that shift their meaning and value. In this respect, they share common purpose with the work of many contemporary visual artists, such as Christian Boltanski, Fiona Tan, Santu Mofukeng, Akram Zaatari, and Walid Raad, whose gallery installations and photobooks interrogate photographic archives through their very materiality.[3] Moreover, Zaatari's films, which I discuss at the end of this chapter, circulate across the institutional borders of documentary and art worlds.

This chapter turns first to documentaries that participate in or critically interrogate the "discovery" of new photographic artists through the collection of work from outside of the institutional spaces of art photography and photojournalism. Whereas John Maloof and Charlie Siskel's *Finding Vivian Maier* (2013) played a significant role in Maloof's attempts both to establish Maier as a major twentieth-century photographer and to consolidate his authority as the professional and legal custodian of her photographic legacy, Jill Nicholls's *Vivian Maier: Who Took Nanny's Pictures?* (2013) takes a more critical look at the commercial and cultural transactions of photographic collection that posthumously propelled Maier from absolute obscurity to international fame. Commissioned by European public television, Paul Cohen and Martijn van Haalen's *Photo Souvenir* (2007) and Cosima Spender's *Dolce Vita Africana* (2008) each investigate a different studio photographer from postcolonial West Africa, namely Philippe Koudjina and Malick Sidibé, who have experienced radically different relations to the European art-photography market, as dealers and collectors (like André Magnin) have sought to transform such vernacular photography into limited-edition art photography since the late 1990s.[4] Whereas *Photo Souvenir* follows Koudjina's failed attempts to capture Magnin's market-legitimating approval, *Dolce Vita Africana* aims to counter the European recommodification of Sidibé's photographic archive by recontextualizing it back within the social world of postcolonial Bamako. Shifting tropes from discovery to recovery, Trisha Ziff's *The Mexican Suitcase* (2011) challenges the photo-historical framework the International Center of Photography (ICP) constructed for its exhibition and publication of recovered Spanish Civil War negatives by photojournalists Robert Capa, David "Chim" Seymour, and Gerda Taro.[5] While the ICP remained locked in an art-historical discourse of trying to parse the specific authorship of the images in the collection, Ziff's film resituates the Mexican Suitcase as a photographic object with a material history as important as the images it contains. Without Mexico's historic rescue of exiled Spanish

Republicans, the negatives would have been irrevocably lost, thus the film aligns their material recovery with the recent excavation of Spain's traumatic past, including the frequently overlooked role played by Mexico. The chapter concludes by interrogating the very process of archivization through three films by Akram Zaatari that reconsider his own founding involvement in the Arab Image Foundation, a project devoted to collecting, preserving, and creatively reframing vernacular photography in the Arab world. *On Photography, People and Modern Times* (2010), *Twenty-Eight Nights and a Poem* (2015), and *On Photography, Dispossession and Times of Struggle* (2017) put the space of the archive in tension with the original spaces of their production and circulation, namely the studio and the home, to not only consider what is lost in traditional methods of archiving, but also challenge the very conception of the photographic archive and what it should attempt to preserve.

Identifying Photographers and Collectors

In her meticulously researched study of street photographer Vivian Maier, Pamela Bannos examines the consequences and implications of what she calls Maier's "fractured archive."[6] After the elderly and impoverished Maier could no longer pay for her five storage lockers in Chicago's North Side, the storage company auctioned off their contents, which included her vast archive of photographs, negatives, undeveloped film rolls, and 8mm movies, as well as most of her other possessions. Local auctioneer Roger Gunderson bought them all for $260 and subsequently separated them into much smaller lots for sale at his auction house, turning a tidy profit of around $20,000 in the process. The vast majority of her photographic archive was bought by three men: vintage snapshot collectors Ron Slattery and Randy Prow, and John Maloof, a real-estate agent who was also a high-volume eBay seller.[7] In 2008, Maloof began selling digital prints and individual negatives to collectors on eBay, including Allan Sekula, who subsequently advised Maloof to stop selling the negatives because he recognized Maier as a potentially important discovery for twentieth-century photographic history, whose archive should thus not be further fragmented. As Slattery began to post Maier's photographs on his vernacular photography blog and Maloof created a photostream dedicated to Maier on the photosharing site Flickr, interest in her spread rapidly among photo buffs online. Bannos recognizes that the networked culture of the Internet not only contributed to the physical dispersal of Maier's archive (through Maloof's eBay sales), but it also played the decisive role in initially disseminating and popularizing her photography (through blogs and photosharing sites) (12). Although its archive is wholly analog, the phenomenon of "Vivian Maier" was ultimately a product of networked digital culture.

By 2011, Maier's photographs had begun to attract widening cultural interest. Maloof's exhibition of her work at the Chicago Cultural Center broke attendance records, he published the first of several books of her photographs, and his Kickstarter campaign to fund a documentary film about Maier raised over $100,000.

Premiering at the 2013 Toronto International Film Festival, *Finding Vivian Maier* was released theatrically in March 2014 and went on to be nominated for both Academy and BAFTA awards. The wide international release and broadcast of the documentary turned Maier into a globally recognized photographer. Maloof and Siskel structure their documentary around a dual narrative that moves backward and forward in time, delving into the biography of the mysterious Maier and charting Maloof's effort to preserve and promote her legacy. *Finding Vivian Maier* opens with a montage of talking heads who personally knew Maier describe her in a single word: "Paradoxical," "Bold," "Mysterious," "Eccentric," "Eccentric," "Private." Like much of the discourse that has constructed "Vivian Maier" in the public eye (of which Maloof had already played an outsized role), the film revels in the apparent paradox of a woman employed most of her working life as a nanny turning out to be such a prolific and talented photographer. As Rose Lichter-Mark has noted, it is patriarchy that constructs these circumstances as paradoxical, for it must place domestic labor in opposition to artistic ambition and creativity.[8] While the film indulges in a sustained pathologizing speculation about Maier's psychology and social behavior, ranging from her inveterate hoarding to her intensive secretiveness and alleged abusive treatment of her charges, it nevertheless constructs a set of parallels between Maier and Maloof—both are framed as amateurs and collectors.

Early in the film, Maloof shares his family history of amateur trading at flea markets in search of collectible discoveries: "I have a reflex and I can spot something down the road, and I know it is valuable." He also partially situates his interest in Maier's photographs as means to tutor his own amateur street photography. By positing Maier as an incredibly gifted, self-taught amateur (who never sold, exhibited, or published her photographs), the film creates a more compelling narrative of aesthetic discovery and enhances the value of Maloof's labor in facilitating it. Many of the interviewees in the film also spend considerable time talking about Maier's habits as a collector cum hoarder. Her cramped living quarters as a nanny overflowed with everything she kept, from bus tickets, receipts, and daily newspapers to audio tapes, 8mm films, and all her photographic negatives, as well as thousands of film rolls that remained unprocessed. The film's pre-credit sequence aligns Maloof with Maier's obsessive collecting in a fast-motion overhead shot that records him laying out all of his collection of her possessions on the floor of his small, finished attic (Figure 4.2). The film repeatedly returns to this attic floor, which parallels Maier's own limited living space (often in family attics), as Maloof lays out various categories of objects from his Maier collection in an iterative performance of both identification and ownership (Video 4.1 ▶).

Maloof's identification with Maier is critical to his claim of ethical commercial exploitation of her archive, about which he initially expresses some concern: "I can't help but feel a little uncomfortable or guilty exposing the work of a person who did not want to be exposed." One of Maier's few friends, Carole Pohn, reinforces this impression in her interview: "She would have never let this happen, had she known about it. That was her babies. She wouldn't have put her babies on display." Maloof

Figure 4.2. John Maloof unpacks Vivian Maier's possessions in his attic in *Finding Vivian Maier* (John Maloof and Charlie Siskel, 2013).

resolves his qualms through a letter he discovers in her possessions. During his trip to the French Alps to locate the "last of her cousins," from whom he claims to have bought the copyright of her oeuvre, Maloof meets the owner of a pharmacy whose grandfather had received a written request from Maier to print her photographs for potential sale as postcards. In voiceover, Maloof excitedly reports,

> Previously, we had thought that Vivian had no intentions of having anyone else print or show her work. This letter proves that assumption wrong. Vivian knew she was a good photographer, and she knew these photographs were good. She wanted to show them to people. She may not have had that happen while she was alive, but we're doing it now.

Maloof deploys this thin alibi to establish himself as the one to realize the artistic recognition that Maier had herself allegedly failed to achieve in her own lifetime. Although several other collectors, including Ron Slattery and Jeff Goldstein, had also contributed to the initial public interest in Maier, *Finding Vivian Maier* presents Maloof as the singular collector and lone champion of her work, who finds himself challenging art world institutions, like MoMA, that refuse to accept Maier into their canons.[9] Maloof acknowledges that museums want to deal with original prints made or commissioned by the photographer in their lifetime, not brand-new prints developed from original negatives. But he also counters that the art world has nevertheless embraced the previously undeveloped film rolls of the late Garry Winogrand and Berenice Abbott's posthumous reprints from Eugene Atget's negatives.

This comparison with Atget is revealing, given Rosalind Krauss's argument that Atget only came to be seen as an artist through the posthumous transformation of his photographic work from its original function as a topographical archive into an aesthetic oeuvre.[10] Krauss emphasizes the sheer size of Atget's archive as a profound challenge for its aesthetic status: "can we imagine an oeuvre consisting of 10,000 works?" (316). Although MoMA curator John Szarkowski tried to account for the uneven aesthetic quality of this vast body of work by applying art historical distinctions, such as "formal success/formal failure; apprenticeship/maturity; public commission/personal statement," Krauss argues that an archaeological examination (in the Foucauldian sense) of Atget's photography ultimately recovers its original archival, rather than aesthetic, function (317). Could we ask a similar question of Maier's even larger photographic archive? Was the imperative of Maier's photographic practice an archival rather than an aesthetic one? Did her photographs hold a similar status for her as the daily newspapers she so methodically collected? Her numerous rolls of film filled with shots of newspaper headlines suggest such a functional equivalence among the diverse objects she hoarded (Figure 4.3).

Although so much of *Finding Vivian Maier* is devoted to Maier's aesthetic legitimation, including favorable comparisons to Helen Levitt, Diane Arbus, and Robert Frank by Joel Meyerowitz and Mary Ellen Mark, the repeated visual trope of Maloof unpacking her "stuff" in his attic works not only to consolidate his identification with and ownership of Maier, but also to potentially reintegrate Maier's photographic practice into her everyday life. It reinforces the image of Maier the collector in which

Figure 4.3 Vivian Maier's photographs of newspapers in *Finding Vivian Maier* (John Maloof and Charlie Siskel, 2013).

photography functions primarily as a tool of archival collection rather than as a medium of aesthetic expression. While *Finding Vivian Maier* may present a close-up of a large plastic container filled with undeveloped film as both the tragedy of Maier's financial inability to realize her artistic potential and the promise of aesthetic revelation enabled by Maloof's labor, this shot also points to the possibility that her quotidian practice of shooting ultimately mattered more to Maier than producing photographic prints, the material platform of photography on which its aesthetic value is determined. "It was the *act* of photographing," suggests Abigail Solomon-Godeau, "rather than the production of a discrete image, that was the psychological imperative" for Maier.[11]

Produced for Alan Yentob's BBC arts series *Imagine*, *Vivian Maier: Who Took Nanny's Pictures?* devotes considerable screen time to the question of how Maier photographed but does so in the service of elaborating a case for Maier's aesthetic development as a photographer.[12] The documentary draws heavily from Bannos's research, and she becomes Yentob's principal expert witness as he travels to New York, Chicago, and the French Alps to narrate Maier's remarkable story. Similar to Bannos's book on Maier, the film builds both a critical investigation of the history of Maier's fractured archive and a meticulously researched argument about Maier's historical development as an artist, which serves as a foil against what Terry Castle has described as "the way Maier's male admirers have caricatured her as a kind of damsel in distress in need of posthumous rescue by chivalrous photo-daddies."[13] Bannos aims to restore aesthetic agency to this female photographer whose story has been wholly constructed by the male collectors who possess her archive. Although Maloof, the largest Maier collector, declined to participate in the documentary (because he was making his own film), Nichols was able to interview Slattery and Goldstein, as well as gallery owner Steven Kasher, who sold limited-edition prints made from Goldstein's collection.

Each of these arbiters of Maier's legacy holds their prints wrapped in plastic coverings before the camera as though they are showing them to Yentob while he interviews them. The sequences commence with a shot of the various containers that have held the photographs: an acid-free archival box in Kasher's gallery archive, Slattery's plastic Ziploc bags, and Goldstein's safe (Figures 4.4–4.6). While each container clearly foregrounds the theme of ownership, they intimate varying proprietary relations between collector and the object that the interviews elaborate. Kasher authoritatively holds up new print enlargements as he blithely shares the fundamental contradiction surrounding the trade in her work: "she made her work entirely for herself, a project entirely self-motivated, entirely self-fulfilling"; and "we believe that she never fully realized her work, so we are helping her to realize it." Slattery takes out his small original prints in hard plastic sleeves and spreads them randomly across a table in a classroom for Bannos and Yentob to view. He speaks of her photographs with the affect of the photo buff who cares more for their personal value to him than their increasing exchange value in the art market. At the end of the documentary, we return to this scene as he suggests to Bannos that he may start to give away some of his photographs, implying an act of amateur resistance against the rampant commercial

Figure 4.4–4.6 Three collectors/dealers of Vivian Maier photographs present their possessions in *Vivian Maier: Who Took Nanny's Photographs?* (Jill Nichols, 2013).

exploitation of Maier's archive. Resonating with the image of photographs as investments retrieved from a locked safe, Goldstein's interview focuses on the sensational narrative of purchasing his collection from Randy Prow, which included armed bodyguards and brick blocks of cash.

In contrast to this affective male performance of ownership, both literal and cultural, when Bannos appears holding Maier's photographs, she does so for the sake of understanding her photographic practice on the street by reconstructing her acts of photographing. The camera follows Bannos on an Upper East Side street as she uses a photocopy of a Maier print to locate the exact spot and angle where it was taken. Finding success, she holds the photocopy in one hand and in her other hand a Rolleiflex with the very same image in its viewfinder (Figure 4.7). Later in the film, Bannos charts Maier's movement through the Bowery as she tracks down the exact location of numerous photographs Maier took of indigent men on the infamous street. Whereas Maloof's identification with Maier revolved around the accumulative imperative of the collector, Bannos's retracing of Maier's steps through the materiality of her images and her equipment constructs an identification with the photographer at work, with the ephemerality of the photographic event, not the permanence of the photographic record produced by it (Video 4.2 ▶).

Even though both documentaries ultimately share an investment in using Maier's material archive to posthumously establish her as a major photographic artist of the twentieth century, their methods are tellingly gendered. Maloof constructs his narrative of Maier as a self-taught artist around masculinist notions of independence, autonomy, and interpersonal difficulty, which align with his own identification as a self-taught art historian and collector, yet he also frames her queer idiosyncrasy

Figure 4.7   Pamela Bannos tracks down the angle of Maier's photograph with her Rolleiflex camera in *Vivian Maier: Who Took Nanny's Photographs?* (Jill Nichols, 2013).

as neglect and abuse of her professional responsibilities as a nanny.[14] By contrast, Nichols marshals Bannos's feminist scholarship on Maier to claim her position within an aesthetic tradition in photographic history, while simultaneously making sense of her life and family history through a gendered optic, but without resorting to the psychopathology engaged by Maloof and other male champions of her work. Moreover, in *Finding Vivian Maier*, Maloof uses his possession of the majority of her material archive to ground his claims to define her legacy, whereas in *Who Took Nanny's Pictures?* Bannos demonstrates how the competitive rivalry between the male collectors of her fragmented archive has hindered the recognition of her aesthetic significance within the history of photography.

Studio Archives and the Global Art Market

The "amateur" and "accidental" frames attached to both Maier and her collectors were crucial to the narrative appeal of her discovery. Ever since photography became a serious commodity in the art market, most archival discoveries of new photographic artists, such as midcentury Arkansas studio photographer Mike Disfarmer, have been pursued by art professionals searching for archives of vernacular photography that can be recommodified into art photography.[15] West African studio photography became a key site for such recontextualization in the 1990s when international art dealers and curators made Malian photographers Seydou Keïta and Malick Sidibé into globally recognized artists. Susan Vogel's 1991 exhibition "African Explores" at the Center for African Art and the New Museum in New York first brought the art world's attention to West African vernacular photography with new prints made from negatives collected from studio photographers in the mid-1970s. Art collector Jean Pigozzi and his curatorial assistant, André Magnin, subsequently became the primary international agents for both Keïta and Sidibé, promoting and monetizing their archive of studio photography from the 1950s through the 1970s through high-profile exhibitions, books, and limited-edition new prints. Both photographers actively participated in their recontextualization, but not without a critical awareness of its economic and cultural dynamics. Sidibé was quite aware of how Magnin fostered a clear differentiation between Keïta as the preeminent studio portrait photographer and Sidibé as the principal reportage photographer for postcolonial Bamako, even though Sidibé was just as involved in studio portraiture as his older colleague.[16] As Candace M. Keller notes, Magnin's construction of Keïta and Sidibé as the quintessential artists of West African photography has made it far more challenging for other locally celebrated photographers to gain recognition in the global art world.[17] Keller further contends that to reframe these studio photographers as artists has depended on denying the complex authorial dynamics at play in such photographic practices, including the interaction between photographer and subject, as well as the labor of apprentices who took many of the photographs now credited in the art market to Keïta and Sidibé.

Whereas the original prints Keïta and Sidibé produced for their studio customers were suitably sized for mailing to family and friends as postcards, hanging in the home or placing in a family photo album, their transfer to the art market involved a profound formal and material transformation. Magnin's prints were matte, uncropped, significantly larger in size (for gallery hanging), and much higher in contrast compared to the rich tonal range of the original studio prints. The vast majority of the new prints lacked the names of their subjects, using the art-world moniker "Untitled" for most of Keïta's reprints and generic descriptions for Sidibé's pictures, which often recalled late nineteenth-century ethnographic photography in the region (e.g., *Peul Woman from Niger* and *Bathing at the Niger River*). This removal or reduction of context was not merely aesthetic and cultural, but also material: negatives were taken from the studio archives in Bamako and relocated to Europe for fine-art reproduction, often under ethically questionable circumstances.[18] Keller has argued that this appropriative reframing of the archives of West African photography is not only "neo-primitivist" on an aesthetic level ("its magnified, uncropped, graphic quality, developed for the scrutinizing pleasure of the foreign eye"), but also more profoundly primitivist in its material and economic exploitation of these local archives.[19]

Both *Dolce Vita Africana* and *Photo Souvenir* engage with this history of archival appropriation and recontextualization, but in significantly different ways. The latter explicitly foregrounds the transnational dynamics of this phenomenon in relation to Koudjina, while the former deliberately sidelines them to recontextualize Sidibé within his local Malian context. *Dolce Vita Africana* thus begins with an intertitle that introduces his international stature as a paradox: "Malick Sidibé is acknowledged as one of the great photographers of our times. He has been working from a tiny studio in Bamako, Mali, since 1962." Although the film ends with another intertitle, reporting that he won a Golden Lion for Lifetime Achievement in the Arts at the 2007 Venice Biennale, *Dolce Vita Africana* remains in Mali throughout its hour length.[20] At the beginning of the documentary, Sidibé offers a tour of his modest studio in Bamako and then pauses at his impressive collection of cameras (which cover an entire wall) in order to retrieve his first photo camera, a Kodak Brownie, which he proudly shows to the film camera. The title credits that follow are superimposed on a long shot of this camera collection (Figure 4.8). Although we later see Sidibé looking through boxes of his negative archive, *Dolce Vita Africana* clearly gives prominence here to the materiality of his tools, and thus to the act of photographing over its indexical product.

The documentary noticeably avoids any significant discussion of Sidibé's photographic aesthetics. Even in the one conversation that Sidibé has with friends about his reputation in Europe as "a great reportage photographer," he implicitly frames his own practice in terms of collaboration and its social relations: "I always tell them that I became a photographer thanks to the young people I followed and took photos of. They are the ones who gave me the subjects for my photos." Furthermore, Spender applies a set of optical effects to the presentation of Sidibé's photographs that downplay the aesthetic composition of his images: the 2½D effect detaches objects and bodies from midground and background, rapid camera movements and cuts between

Figure 4.8 The title credit of *Dolce Vita Africana* (Cosima Spender, 2008) present Malick Sidibé's collection of cameras.

photographic details emulate the rhythm of subjects dancing in the image (similar to Varda's *Salut les Cubains*), and special effects render objects in movement (such as an LP record on a disc-jockey's turntable). These techniques shift our attention from his compositional aesthetics to the dynamism of his subjects. Even photographs shown in full frame linger on screen only momentarily. By transferring the focus from aesthetic form to subject matter, the film detaches Sidibé from the art-world frame crafted by Magnin, reinstating his photographic practice within its local vernacular context in Mali.

   To visually emphasize the integral nature of Sidibé's studio within his community, Spender repeatedly shoots him sitting outside his studio from a camera positioned across the street, which captures his interaction with the street. In one of these long shots, four old friends arrive to reminisce with Sidibé about post-liberation Bamako. These four men then become significant characters of the documentary as they each draw on Sidibé's photographs to recall memories of the vibrant social life of the city that he documented in the 1960s and 1970s. They pass around Magnin's 1998 monograph on Sidibé as though it were a family photo album, pointing to particular pictures as souvenirs of cherished moments in their intimate histories. Nany, a former national footballer, later treats the book as a wedding album when he shows his wife and daughter-in-law Sidibé's photograph of his wedding. Fernand, a garage worker, also talks to a group of his younger colleagues about Bamako's former nightlife while he circulates the photobook along with a pile of his own faded and dog-eared Sidibé Studio prints (Figure 4.9). Although this scene brings together two very distinctive manifestations of Sidibé's photography—the

Figure 4.9 Fernand shows his younger colleagues Malick Sidibé's photographs of Bamako's golden years in *Dolce Vita Africana* (Cosima Spender, 2008).

fine-art publication and the modest studio print—Fernand makes no distinction between them in his oral narration, thereby returning all these images to their original vernacular context (Video 4.3 ▶).

Like many others in *Dolce Vita Africana*, this scene demonstrates Elizabeth Edwards's contention that vernacular photography is deeply entwined with oral narration because "photographs both focus and extend verbalizations, as they have dynamic and shifting stories woven around and through them, imprinting themselves in and being played back repeatedly through different tellings."[21] As Fernand waxes lyrical about his youth to a younger generation of men through a narrative performance with pictures, Sidibé's photographs function as "relational objects," connecting people through multisensory communication that includes the look of a dress worn in a photograph, the wistful tone of Fernand's voice recalling the nightclubs of yore, and the tactile gesture of generosity as he passes around his cherished snaps. *Dolce Vita Africana* is filled with such scenes of sociality organized around photographic objects, confirming Edwards's insistence on the need to study the multisensory qualities of photographs as "social objects."[22] The documentary emphatically restores Sidibé's photography as an archive of dynamic social objects, thus challenging its reduction by the art market to a collection of aesthetic objects available to distanced contemplation and the commodity fetish. Moreover, if Magnin's transformation of Sidibé's photography into art commodities had removed the names and particular identities of his subjects, Spender's decision to structure much of the film around his friends and subjects as documentary characters not only restores their names, but also reinforces the conception of photography as a complex of social performances that occur around the relational objects of the camera and the photograph. Although

Dolce Vita Africana frames the value of Sidibé's photography through its return to a local social context from a transnational aesthetic one, the terms of such restoration are highly gendered. Even though women constituted a substantial proportion of Sidibé's subjects, it is only men who are seen enacting social performances with photographs in the documentary, forging a male-centered, and largely apolitical, collective memory of post-independence Mali.

If *Dolce Vita Africana* offers a joyous, but almost exclusively masculinist, recollection of better days through photographs, *Photo Souvenir* dwells on the tragedy of the present for a disabled and impoverished studio photographer in Niamey, Niger: Philippe Koudjina. The documentary includes many similar scenes to *Dolce Vita Africana*, particularly those of elderly friends of the photographer reminiscing about their youth as they pass around his photographs of themselves. However, women are notably granted more opportunities to speak in *Photo Souvenir* than in Spender's film. Yet these scenes exude a melancholy tone, for they are intercut with shots of Koudjina hobbling along the streets of Niamey on crutches. Another comparable scene accentuates the tragedy of his fate compared to Sidibé: Koudjina unlocks a messy metal cabinet and pulls out random pieces of dusty, broken photographic equipment while he recounts how all his best cameras (including Hasselblads and Beaulieu movie cameras) were stolen when he was in hospital after the hit-and-run incident that crippled him. The thieves had only left the Polaroid cameras, which were now functionally useless, as Polaroid film was no longer available in Niger. As he piles up stacks of decrepit Polaroid cameras, his archive of broken machines mirrors the ruin of Koudjina's own body (Figure 4.10). Filmmakers Cohen and van Haalen

Figure 4.10 Philippe Koudjina's dilapidated collection of old Polaroid cameras echoes the degradation of his injured body in *Photo Souvenir* (Paul Cohen and Martijn van Haalen, 2007).

accentuate this corporeal analogy by including the photographer's admission in this scene that he now suffers from glaucoma. The deprivation of Koudjina's current life is blatantly contrasted with the conspicuous consumption of the global art world when the film abruptly shifts location to a ritzy gallery opening in Monaco that is showcasing Jean Pigozzi's collection of contemporary African art.[23] Although Sidibé is the guest of honor, the cinematographer consistently captures the photographer at moments when he is located at the margins, for example, as he sits alone in his majestic boubou in the empty gallery before the crowds arrive, or as he stands with the press photographers taking shots of curator André Magnin and Prince Albert, who is clearly the center of attention at the opening. While the film palpably contrasts Sidibé's recent international recognition to Koudjina's cultural oblivion (save his closest friends), its framing and editing choices in the European scenes also highlight the parameters of Sidibé's star power (Figure 4.11). Agency rests not with the discovered artist, but with his discoverers—the European curators, gallerists, and collectors who determine the criteria and procedures by which studio photographers from the Global South are transformed into visual artists.

Photo Souvenir subsequently alternates between Paris and Niamey, contrasting the discourses that frame Koudjina's practice in the former metropole and the postcolony (Figures 4.12–4.13). In Niger, his friends continue to treat his pictures as the personal souvenirs of vernacular photography, while in France photographer Philippe Salaun and journalist Jean Louis Saporito try to convince Magnin to support and represent Koudjina in the art market (Video 4.4 ⊙). His interest piqued, Magnin takes Koudjina's work to his fiscal sponsor, the French fashion designer agnès b. Although they both decide to pass on supporting Koudjina, their evaluative response to samples

Figure 4.11 Malick Sidibé sits in a Monte Carlo gallery awaiting the opening night reception in *Photo Souvenir* (Paul Cohen and Martijn van Haalen, 2007).

Figure 4.12 Ousmane Gindo looks at old portraits by his friend Philippe Koudjina in *Photo Souvenir* (Paul Cohen and Martijn van Haalen, 2007).

Figure 4.13 André Magnin inspects Philippe Koudjina's prints in *Photo Souvenir* (Paul Cohen and Martijn van Haalen, 2007).

of his work is strikingly similar to how we have heard them talk about Sidibé and Keïta. While the curator and the designer repeated circle around ahistorical humanist notions of "beauty," "dignity," and "tenderness," Koudjina's friends consistently situate his images, and the memories they incite, in relation to the historical moment of Niger's post-independence, just as Sidibé and friends recalled bygone Bamako through his photographs in *Dolce Vita Africana*. However, when Magnin does invoke historical time, it is to ask Salaun and Saporito if Koudjina has dated when the prints were taken, not in order to historicize the image, but to enhance its commercial value as an original fine-art print. *Photo Souvenir* concludes on a rather cynical note that acknowledges how the pecuniary values of the art world have seeped into Koudjina's social world in Niamey. One of his friends approaches him on the street and asks him to sign the back of his old portrait prints in the hope that they will increase in monetary value once Koudjina is recognized by the European art world. But the film's audience has already learned by this point that the value granted to his work will remain local and in the realm of the vernacular.

Both *Dolce Vita Africana* and *Photo Souvenir* challenge the exploitative dynamics of the global art world's interest in the archives of West African studio photographers by prioritizing local voices to situate and validate their photographic practices. Whereas *Dolce Vita Africana* exclusively interviews and films Malians who know Sidibé personally, *Photo Souvenir* does include outside French perspectives (particularly Magnin's) but deliberately frames and edits them in ways that enable critical perspectives on their discourse and action, especially in contrast to the Nigerien voices in the film. Sidibé's and Koudjina's photographic archives are particularly cherished in the films by the photographers' own generation for their capacity to engender nostalgia for the golden years of post-independence Bamako and Niamey, yet the films isolate such practices of memory from the political and economic realities of contemporary Mali and Niger. One could argue that *Photo Souvenir* posits Koudjina not only as victim of the art world's neocolonial economy, but also as a broader allegorical figure for the degradation and failures of African independence. His photographic archive is treated as part of the country's dwindling resource economy that is deemed insufficient in scale to deserve external investment from the Global North. Yet such a reading risks transforming still powerful, and potentially empowering, affect into the sentiment of tragic narrative.[24]

Exiled Archives and the Hierarchies of Photographic History

The narrative of recovering the lost archive of a major artist can be as culturally compelling as the discovery of a new artist in the vernacular archive. In 2010, the International Center of Photography (ICP) in New York opened the much-anticipated exhibition, *The Mexican Suitcase: The Rediscovered Spanish Civil War Negatives of Capa, Chim and Taro*, accompanied by the release of a two-volume catalog co-published with Steidl. The show marked the apotheosis of a decades-long search by the ICP and its founder, Cornell Capa, to recover his brother Robert's negatives from the Spanish Civil War. Cornell knew that Robert had tried to smuggle the politically sensitive negatives out of France in 1939 as he was fleeing from the

Nazi invasion, but multiple leads went nowhere, even after Cornell placed an ad in a popular French photo magazine in 1979. That same year, a suitcase containing a collection of Capa, Chim, and Taro prints from the war was discovered at the Swedish Ministry of Foreign Affairs. The valise, which had originally belonged to Juan Negrin, the prime minister of the Spanish Second Republic, had ended up in the Swedish legation in Vichy after the end of the civil war.[25] Cornell had dubbed this recovered collection "the Swedish Suitcase." Thus, when news came in 1995 that the negative collection might actually be in Mexico, it garnered the name "the Mexican Suitcase."

Shortly after Jerald Green, a Spanish-studies scholar in New York, had organized an exhibition of Spanish Civil War photography in Mexico City, he received a letter from Ben Tarver, an American-Mexican filmmaker, who informed him about a trove of civil war negatives he'd recently inherited from the daughter of General Francisco Aguilar González, the Mexican ambassador to Vichy France. Unlike the prior Swedish discovery, this collection was not contained in an actual suitcase, but rather three boxes: one repurposed box of Ilford photographic paper containing pockets of cut negatives and two custom-built boxes with a grid of compartments containing rolled film (with the box lids' interior serving as a hand-written key identifying the negatives' contents). The undeniable material beauty of the two hand-crafted boxes would feature prominently in the eventual press coverage, exhibition, and documentary film on the Mexican Suitcase.[26] After seeing Green's exhibition, Tarver was convinced that his negatives had been taken by Capa and Taro. Further correspondence to both Green and Cornell Capa followed with more substantiating evidence from Tarver, who wanted to find a suitable home for this undeniably valuable collection. Yet, over a decade of miscommunication and increasing mistrust ensued. Without having seen any of the actual negatives, the ICP retained a degree of skepticism about Tarver's claims,[27] while Tarver suspected that the ICP had hired a private detective to investigate him.[28]

The impasse was overcome due to a chance encounter in 2007 when Mexico City–based curator Trisha Ziff dropped by the ICP to see a friend, Chief Curator Brian Wallis, while she was briefly in New York.[29] Wallis casually asked Ziff if she could assist communicating with Tarver, which she did on returning to Mexico. After several months of discussions, Ziff convinced Tarver to transfer possession of the Mexican Suitcase to the ICP, which she argued had the greatest moral and legal claim to the negatives. In return, Tarver would have the film rights to use the 4,500 photographs in a documentary about the Mexican Suitcase as long as he completed it within two years. As time passed without Tarver making any progress on the documentary and the ICP eagerly waiting to be able to sell the rights to the BBC, Ziff persuaded Tarver to transfer the rights to her so that she could make the documentary.[30]

While the ICP was singularly focused on reuniting the negatives with the rest of Capa's archive to enhance understanding of this canonical photographer, Ziff insisted on acknowledging the material history of the Mexican Suitcase by delivering it to the ICP on December 19, 2007, in the hands of her son, Julio Meyer.[31] His father is the Mexican photographer and curator Pedro Meyer, born in 1935 to a German Jewish family in Spain, who, like tens of thousands of Spanish Republicans, were welcomed to Mexico as refugees from fascism by the Cárdenas government. Herein lies the crux of the difference between the ICP's exhibition (and catalog) and Ziff's documentary film on the Mexican Suitcase. Whereas the ICP sought to painstakingly identify the author of all the images in the collection (Capa, Chim, or Taro) and chart their groundbreaking use within the emergent practice of photojournalism (a project of consolidating photographic authorship), Ziff was fundamentally more interested in the material history of the Mexican Suitcase as a photographic object embedded in traumatic histories of migration, exile, and international responses to fascism (a project of historical contextualization).

Both projects prize the materiality of the Mexican Suitcase, but for entirely different reasons. The ICP positioned the negatives as one level materially closer to both the historical moment depicted and the aesthetic vision of their photographers, which the curators of the exhibition bind together in their claim that, in the Spanish Civil War, Capa, Taro, and Seymour forged a new conception of photojournalism as immediate witness to history.[32] Ziff treats the Mexican Suitcase as a material object whose survival indexes—and in fact was facilitated by—the physical salvation of Republican refugees by the Mexican state; it is a corpus that travelled along the very pathways of exile trod by those fleeing Spanish bodies. Its survival is no more or no less meaningful than the personal photographic archives collected by the refugees and their descendants.[33] The documentary thematically parallels this remarkable recovery of the Mexican Suitcase to the cultural and physical excavation of disappeared Republican soldiers that younger generations of Spaniards have demanded and partly achieved through the *Ley de Memoria Histórica* (Historical Memory Law) passed in 2007, which gives specific rights to the war's victims as well as their descendants. The film visually emphasizes this parallel several times when scenes of conservation with archivists and curators carefully unpacking the negative boxes precede or follow scenes of archaeological excavation with forensic anthropologists digging up and collecting the human remains of disappeared Republicans (Figures 4.14–4.15). The suitcase thus functions for Ziff as both index and metaphor to exile and historical reclamation.

Ziff hoped her film would challenge "the hierarchy of photographic history through a critique of the photojournalist as the purveyor of history." In short, to take Capa "off his pedestal." She criticizes the ICP exhibition and its catalog for its failure to account for why the negatives ended up in Mexico: "it was a revisionist version of the events, because it was precisely Mexico's relationship to the Republic in Spain that saved those negatives." Positing the Mexican Suitcase as "a metaphor of exile," Ziff explicitly connects the salvage of the negatives to the fate of Republican refugees: "For the ICP to omit this story both obscures the history of American foreign policy and diminishes Mexico's role in giving safe passage and asylum to Spanish Republicans." Ziff's contention that the ICP "consistently chose not to honor Mexico and its role in this narrative" was confirmed at an early stage by its leaking of the negatives' recovery to the *New York Times* in January 2008, contravening its agreement with Ziff to a

Figure 4.14 The archaeological excavation of a Republican soldier's remains at Rubielos de Mora in *The Mexican Suitcase* (Trisha Ziff, 2011).

Figure 4.15 An archivist opens one of the recovered boxes in *The Mexican Suitcase* (Trisha Ziff, 2011).

simultaneous reporting in the US and Mexican press. Even when the exhibition traveled to Mexico City in 2013, the ICP refused, despite Ziff's continued lobbying, to explicitly acknowledge and contextualize Mexico's key role in the negatives' survival.[34]

Drawing on a rhetorical strategy common within contemporary documentary film, the pre-title sequence of *The Mexican Suitcase* presents a handful of talking heads from the film to preview its organizing themes. Sitting below the iconic portrait of a smirking Capa and beside stacks of photographic monographs, Wallis emphatically prioritizes Capa's aesthetic vision with a gushing analogy: "It's like you discovered the Picasso notebooks from the most important period of his work." As the camera pans across a contact sheet showing an ongoing battle, Wallis waxes lyrical about the viewer's capacity to follow Capa in "a kind of virtual reality" that aligns with his physical trajectory, his visual perspective, and the decisions he made on the ground. He champions the tremendous value these negatives hold for the history of photography due to Capa's "novel, revolutionary way he was using visual techniques to communicate a story." Ziff undercuts such authorial focus, though, by sandwiching this paean between two other voices that qualify and contest Wallis's discourse of the master. In the scene preceding, the anonymous gloved hands of an archivist carefully open one of the boxes containing the negatives, as Spanish screenwriter Anna Bofarull highlights the mythologizing qualities of the narrative: "It's a romantic story of some photos. Suddenly a suitcase disappears and is found seventy years later. The story is fantastic, like fiction." Mauricio Maille, Mexican art curator at the Televisa Foundation, follows Wallis with an earnest call to recognize the affective value of this photographic object beyond the images it contains: "The Mexican Suitcase holds so many memories beyond the photos which Capa took. We, in Mexico, have the chance to understand it because it's part of our history. We can get what's behind the images, the memory that transcends what is beyond a negative." As Maille speaks, the camera tilts down a page of family photographs in a ring binder, introducing the vernacular photographic archives that the film will later mix with the photographs from the suitcase. Mexican writer Juan Villoro concludes the pre-title sequence by explicitly aligning the fate of the suitcase with that of the Republican refugees saved by Mexico: "the route it followed, the exiles' route, I think it tells us a lot about the twentieth century and its upheavals." Moreover, he envisions the recovery of the suitcase as "symbolic of the resurrection of a whole era," which sets up the subsequent explanation for the earlier enigmatic opening credit shots of an archaeological excavation. After Villoro's comment and the title credit, the film travels to Rubielos de Mora in Aragon to witness the excavation of a mass grave, as we listen to a young woman, Conchi Esteban Vivas, describe her anxious anticipation at recovering her Republican grandfather's remains at the site. Her commitment to uncovering long-repressed familial and national memory is amplified by subsequent interviews with young archaeologists, college students, and athletes, who express a collective imperative to recover the disappeared history of their families and their country.

In stark contrast to the ICP's imperative to use the Mexican Suitcase to burnish the photographic historical significance of Capa, and to a lesser extent, Taro and Seymour, Ziff's documentary employs several rhetorical strategies to decenter photographic authorship, including an oblique engagement with the mythos of Capa's most iconic image, a refusal to identify and differentiate images within and without the Suitcase, and a foregrounding of other photographic archives from the Spanish Civil War (particularly the family collections of Republican refugees).

Capa's most famous photograph, *Loyalist Militiaman at the Moment of Death, Cerro Muriano, September 5, 1936* (commonly known as *The Falling Soldier*), has been subject to intense scholarly and journalistic debate since 1975, when Robert Knightley published an account by South African journalist O'Down Gallagher, who claimed Capa admitted to him that the photograph of the soldier falling at the moment of his death was staged.[35] Capa's biographer, Richard Whelan, became his most ardent defender over the subsequent decades, drawing on the ICP's Capa archive in his efforts to prove the authenticity of the photograph.[36] As Vincent Lavoie notes, the debate has most recently shifted from the testimonial and the documentary to the forensic, as each side hired forensic experts to analyze the bodily trajectory of the falling soldier and the physical shape of the surrounding landscape.[37] Hugo Doménech and Raúl M. Riebenbauer's investigative documentary about the photograph, *La Sombra del Iceberg* (*The Shadow of the Iceberg*, 2007), literally stages a forensic examination of the image in a medical auditorium by pathologist Fernando Verdú (who is dressed in scrubs). Given its potential to imperil Capa's historical legacy, the decades-long debate about the *Falling Soldier* sustained the motivation of Cornell Capa and the ICP to find his brother's negatives. However, Ziff speculates that the uncertainty over what the negatives might reveal ultimately rendered the Mexican Suitcase into "a potential Pandora's box," which could explain why it took the ICP so long to recover it: "Was it going to fuel this debate further or was it going to solve it? Perhaps better not to know."

Ziff places the *Falling Soldier* twice very briefly in the middle of her documentary, but without explicit reference to the debate over the authenticity of the image. The photograph first appears as a postcard in the ICP store, referencing its reproducibility and commodification as one of the most iconic photographs of the twentieth century. It appears again a minute later, this time in full frame as the camera drifts almost imperceptibly across it. The voices that surround its presentation all work to interrogate Capa's mythologized status. ICP Curator Kristen Lubben discusses how Capa's reputation overshadows and appropriates not only the work of his female collaborator—a norm in Western art history—but also "Chim," his male collaborator. Pedro Meyer notes how the emergence of historical titans always produce the exclusion of others. Lluis Marti Bielsa, a Republican veteran, insists that most working-class fighters in the Civil War had little time or inclination to be photographed. Gabriel Weisz, the son of Capa's assistant, Chiki Weisz, blatantly rejects any coherent aesthetic idea in Capa's work. And finally, Juan Villoro argues that the Capa myth eclipses not only other witnesses, but also "the reality of the places where he'd been." To engage directly in the debate over the *Falling Soldier* would perpetuate the mythologization of Capa, thus Ziff presents the image merely as means to articulate various positions that decenter his authorship.

Throughout the film, Ziff also refuses to differentiate and identify the photographer of each image shown from the Mexican Suitcase, the opposite of the ICP's meticulous research that sought to attribute each and every image in the collection. Although the exhibition and its catalog provided extensive coverage of the diverse circulation of the photographs in the international press, the documentary's undifferentiated approach actually resonates more with the historical conditions that shaped the production of these images. As Simon Dell elucidates in the exhibition catalog, the photo editor—and not the photographer—was the primary creative force of the new illustrated press in the 1930s.[38] The task of photographers was to supply "unmarked materials," which encouraged them to choose "wide framing that could permit different kinds of cropping and montaging" by the editors in their construction of a compelling visual story through photographic images arranged on the page. A photo curator herself, Ziff performs a similar act of historical narrativization with diverse (and de-authored) photographs through the making of this documentary. In his book, *Memory Battles of the Spanish Civil War*, historian Sebastiaan Faber argues that the new photojournalism practiced by the trio was grounded in a constitutive tension between commitment and commodity, "a tension between the idea of photographs as documents of a historical reality made by politically committed photographers and their use as unmarked material generically and opportunistically included in photo features, albums and montages."[39] Faber also notes that, although Capa, Taro, and Seymour were attentive to "the aura of authorship," they often shared equipment as well as the images they produced, thus complicating the construction of their oeuvres (55).

While Ziff devotes significant screen time early in the film to the trio's political commitment, their photographic talent, and the commerce of their profession, her documentary situates these images within a larger photographic archive that includes not only other photojournalists but also the long-neglected vernacular collections of Spanish refugees.[40] For instance, in the sequence on the French concentration camp for Republican refugees in Argelès-sur-mer, Ziff seamlessly integrates Capa's documentation with images by an unknown photographer that she found in a Mexican archive, which reveal the atrocious conditions of the camp that remained outside of Capa's frame. Yet Ziff's integration of diverse photographic sources is not merely committed to democratizing the visual archive through the inclusion of marginalized and vernacular photographies, it also enables the documentary to differentiate distinctive modes of engagement with that wider archive. This latter project is most extensively elaborated in the film's conclusion by a range of voices.

Villoro sets up this differentiation with his contention that US culture fragments history by tearing things away from their original context, vacuuming them into "a sort of cosmopolitan galaxy where place doesn't matter, plot doesn't matter." The image track reinforces this assertion with a close-up of the completely decontextualized merchandise (plastic wallets, fridge magnets) produced by the ICP for the exhibition. Photographer Susan Meiselas then offers a counter-model that she has employed in her own work on the Nicaraguan Revolution—to bring a photograph back into the landscape in which it was taken, as a memory act.[41] She declares that "You can only do that in a community of concern, so you have to have a community that wants to embrace what was in order to bring what was into the what is." In several shots, laser-printed images from the Mexican Suitcase are held up in front of the Spanish landscapes in which they were taken. The people holding the photographs are not identified, although we may assume that they are descendants of Spanish

Republicans. These shots emblematize the larger work of the documentary as it situates the Mexican Suitcase within the emergent community of concern in Spain and Mexico devoted to recovering and remembering the Republican past. Catalan journalist Ernest Alós then explains how younger generations of Spaniards approach the visual archive of the civil war in a fundamentally different way than the ICP: "There is nobody for whom what happened then has not had a direct impact on their lives and on their families." For Alós, such history is inseparable from family biography.

Villoro, Meiselas, and Alós hereby consolidate the documentary's counter framework to the ICP's historical narrative about the heroic pioneers of twentieth-century war photography. In the film's concluding moments, Ziff inserts two scenes with descendants of Republican exiles that illustrate that counter-framework through strategies of displacement (Video 4.5 ▶). In the first, Victoria González-Román, the granddaughter of a Spanish exile, stands in front of a contact sheet from the Mexican Suitcase at the ICP exhibition and points to three consecutive photographs of her grandmother writing letters on a suitcase[42] (Figure 4.16). González-Román explains that her grandmother was a Basque refugee in Barcelona searching for her husband, a young Republican soldier, when the photographs were taken. The family was aware of the photographs but had never seen them and believed them lost. In this emotional testimony, González-Román displaces the exhibition's presentation of international history with her personal optic of family history. She treats these photographs in the public space of an international exhibition as though they are family photographs inviting the private discourse of familial oral narration. Yet this recourse to the private is not a retreat from the public, but rather a reclamation of the public memory of the nation from below. The following scene at Café Villerias in Mexico City inverts the

where she is writing on a suitcase.

Figure 4.16 Victoria González-Román points out photographs of her grandmother at the ICP exhibition in *The Mexican Suitcase* (Trisha Ziff, 2011).

direction of displacement, as Diego Villerias, the son of a Spanish exile, presents the little family museum of photographs and memorabilia on display in the café founded by his father. The private memory of a family's exile is here doubly made public— first, through its display in the café and, second, through Diego's emphatic presentation to Ziff's camera. If González-Román sees the public image of international photojournalism through the vernacular lens of the family photograph, then Villerias conversely places the private image of the family photograph in the public space of exhibition. Both contest the hierarchies of photographic history that subtend the ICP's framing of the Mexican Suitcase.

In the Café Villerias scene, as well as in several other shots of exiles and their descendants discussing their family photographs, Ziff notably chooses to retain the production clapperboard at beginning of the shot (Figure 4.17). This common self-reflexive device usually functions as a meta-cinematic trope to emphasize and acknowledge the construction of filmic reality, yet here it takes on an intermedial function. In its operative gesture, the clapperboard enacts both the instant and the flow of time that differentiate photography and film. Framing the convergence of the live witness and the preserved time of the photographic archive they narrate, the clapperboard here becomes a clarion emblem for "the community of concern" in both Spain and Mexico, which seeks, in Meiselas's words, "to bring what was into the what is" in the service of historical reclamation and collective memory.

The competing claims of cultural patrimony over the Mexican Suitcase remain at the heart of Ziff's documentary: Whose story does it tell? Who owns it? Who should be responsible for its material preservation? Although Ziff has always maintained that it was right, both morally and legally, to return the negatives to their photographers'

Figure 4.17. A clapperboard begins the interview with Diego Villerias, son of a Republican exile, in *The Mexican Suitcase* (Trisha Ziff, 2011).

estates, she does include several voices in the documentary, particularly Meyer's, that question the negatives' departure from Mexico and "return" to New York.[43] Meyer articulates a critique of cultural imperialism in which the cosmopolitan centers of power, such as Paris, London, and New York, conceive of the rest of the world as spaces in which "nothing important ever happens," consequently justifying the on-going material appropriation of culture by those centers. In his book, Faber counters with another possible framing of the negatives, as spoils of war, a claim enhanced by the unclarified circumstances in which they came into the long-term possession of General González. Moreover, Faber argues that the charge against the ICP for appro-priation and decontextualization could equally be leveled at the "nomadic and pro-miscuous" technology of photography itself: "What are these images by Capa, Chim and Taro if not pieces of Spanish reality that the photographers have appropriated, allowing them to be framed, frozen, decontextualized, manipulated, and circulated through the global media?" (44). Through its assiduous attention to photographic materiality and its affective significance across generations, Ziff's documentary seeks to repatriate the meaning and significance of the suitcase from its cosmopolitan posi-tion in the global art world (as touring exhibition and collectible catalog) to the places in which it continues to matter most—Mexico and Spain.

Rethinking Photographic Preservation

The question of photographic repatriation has become a central concern for Lebanese artist Akram Zaatari, but less in an international context of patrimony than in a do-mestic one that could challenge the very meaning of photographic preservation. In the nineteenth and early twentieth centuries, photographic archives of the Middle East were predominantly constructed by Western outsiders in the service of Orientalist scholarship and colonial administration. Access to national archives in the region has been tightly controlled by the postcolonial state, while few photographic archives exist within the non-governmental sector.[44] Moreover, private collections have suffered serious precarity and the risk of destruction, particularly in Lebanon and Palestine, under conditions of war, forced migration, and political instability.[45] Thus when Zaatari and photographers Fouad Elkoury and Samer Mohdad established the Arab Image Foundation (AIF) in 1997, they sought not only to preserve photography from the Arab world, but also to reconceptualize its histories through the artistic and scholarly projects generated by their specific practices of collection. A large research grant from the European Commission in Lebanon funded two years of collecting and researching photographic history across the Mashriq region (the Eastern Arab world), necessitating the development of a legal entity for ownership of the collec-tion and a central administration to manage its archiving and preservation. Over the following two decades, the collection grew substantially in size to over 600,000 pho-tographic objects. In its early years, the Foundation's collection was shaped primarily by the artistic and scholarly priorities of its founders, which, as Zaatari notes, were quite divergent: "I remember that Fouad in particular was invested in the idea of fore-grounding the photography of a 'modern' Arab world.... I was interested in family history, in discovering the details of photographic practices, and the links between photography and other aspects of Arab visual culture, notably popular film."[46] This initial idiosyncrasy as a "light, nimble and independent" organization suited the rap-idly changing cultural environment of postwar Beirut, which was experiencing an influx of external funding to support capacity building.[47] Although the absence of public institutions for visual culture in Lebanon often caused instability and discon-tinuity, it also provided a certain freedom from orthodoxy and tradition for new or-ganizations like the AIF.[48] The Foundation would subsequently play a significant role in both Beirut's burgeoning postwar art scene (particularly with artists such as Walid Raad, Joanna Hadjithomas, and Khalil Joreige) and in the wider debates about history, memory, and cultural production in the Middle East at the turn of the millennium.[49]

Zaatari has always insisted that the AIF was "not an archive of photographic arte-facts but one of collecting practices," in that it served "as an engine for producing groups of photographs, ensembles of images tied to one another through the desires and interests of artists or scholars" (43). This singularity allowed the Foundation to become, in Kaelen Wilson-Goldie's words, "a laboratory for rebellious ideas about the archive, the collection and the document."[50] For instance, in 2005 Zaatari con-vinced the Foundation's board of directors to recognize collecting as an art prac-tice, thus transforming the issue of a photograph's provenance, which would include not only the city and studio from which it came, but also the practice that brought it into the collection. Yet, with its growing collection and international reputation, the Foundation moved toward an increasingly conservative institutionalization, es-pecially in the realm of preservation. On the recommendations of an external con-sultant, the AIF changed the organization of its holdings in 2008. To maximize the use of archival storage space (following best practices in the field of conservation), objects were no longer to be stored according to their original collecting practices, but by similar size. For Zaatari, this had "the effect of scrambling the DNA of parts of the collection," thus weakening the collection's capacity to challenge prevailing concep-tions of the archive.[51] Moreover, the Foundation's online visual database as the public interface of its collection has consistently simplified the presentation of the holdings by omitting information about the researcher or artist who brought the material into the collection. Non-photographic materials related to the histories of collection have been separated from the photographs themselves and transferred to the library, or in some cases lost altogether.[52]

Zaatari's work in the 2010s returned to the photographic research and collecting practices he had undertaken in the late 1990s and early 2000s in order to interrogate the very dynamics of archivization in the AIF which had emerged in what Zaatari called the "shady area" between art and research practices on the one hand, and preservation and library science on the other (175). In a 2013 interview with Mark Westmoreland in *Aperture*, Zaatari elaborated on his idea of "Against Photography," which would eventually become a major exhibition shown in Barcelona, Düsseldorf,

Seoul, and Sharjah (2017–19).[53] In language that resonates with the reconceptualization of photography by both Ariella Azoulay and Elizabeth Edwards, Zaatari proposes this idea as "an invitation to look at the larger ecosystem in which a photograph is produced, diffused, consumed, and thus to look at photography as set of relationships converging in the object of a photo."[54] He plays off the multiple meanings of "against" as not only "in opposition to" but also "in comparison to" and "in contact with," by challenging the singular focus on the photograph as representational document and embracing photography's relationship to other media and cultural practices (177). Primarily interested in vernacular photography, Zaatari devoted considerable attention to the work of studio photographers Van Leo (in Cairo) and Hashem El-Madani (in Zaatari's hometown of Saida in Southern Lebanon), investigating the studio as an economy and a space of social performance in front of a camera, rather than as the originating site of artistic creation.

Zaatari also began to rethink the meaning of photographic preservation through two propositions. First, he contested the alignment of preservation with restoration, namely that photographic objects needed to be carefully restored to as close as possible to their original condition. People and time leave their marks on photographs, which a conservator sees as damage, whereas an archaeologist, artist, or anthropologist could see it otherwise, namely as the accrual of new layers of meaning: "By damaging something photographic in a picture, one might be preserving something else; a non-photographic element maybe in the realm of emotions."[55] Second, he proposed to the board of the AIF that the organization should offer to return collections to the families who had donated them, arguing that such domestic repatriation could preserve elements that conventional archival preservation disassembles: "If emotions can be preserved with pictures, then maybe returning a picture to the album from which it was taken, to the bedroom where it was found, to the configuration it once belonged, would constitute an act of preservation in its most radical form."[56] Zaatari explored such provocative ideas about preservation and his wider reconceptualization of photography in three documentaries he made in the 2010s: *On Photography, People and Modern Times* (2010), *On Photography, Dispossession and Times of Struggle* (2017), and *Twenty-Eight Nights and a Poem* (2018). While they share both similar thematic concerns and aesthetic strategies, each reconceptualizes the photographic archive along a different axis: spatio-temporality, materiality, and performance.

A split-screen documentary predominantly shown as a gallery installation, *On Photography, People and Modern Times* is structured around two sets of visual objects: photographic prints preserved in the AIF archive and video recordings of interviews Zaatari conducted with donors to the archive (primarily in their homes), who were either the photographers themselves or their relatives. The interviews address what people do with photography, ranging in topics from popular attitudes and assumptions about vernacular photography to labor practices within the studio to individual emotional attachments to particular photographs. Adopting a technique that recalls Harun Farocki and Hartmut Bitomsky's earlier visual inscriptions of archival research, Zaatari presents the interviews on a video monitor within the archive while a conservator's gloved hands remove photographs from their archival folders and places them next to the monitor.[57] The same photographs are carefully handled in both spaces (of the home and the archive), but within starkly differing social and affective frameworks (Video 4.6 ▶).

The split-screen architecture of the documentary generates a parallax perspective on the space depicted in both images on the screen: the reading room of the Arab Image Foundation (Figure 4.18). The camera in the left screen has been positioned on a vertical visual axis producing an overhead view of the white table on which the photographs and equipment are placed. The camera in the right screen is aligned on a horizontal visual axis providing a frontal view of the table and the objects behind it. This parallax structure remains constant with a few exceptions when both screens briefly present the vertical axis. The left screen provides the clearest view of the prints laid down on the table by the conservator while also offering a slightly angled view of the interview footage on the camcorder's small display screen. Alternately, the right screen clearly shows the interview footage on the monitor but offers only an oblique view of the prints on the table. This parallax perspective emphasizes a tension between the two-dimensional flatness of the left screen and the three-dimensional depth of the right screen in which we can also see midground and background, even though they remain out of focus. This particular technique is not just a visual trope for the loss of photography's social dimensions through archivization (Sekula's "abstract visual equivalence"), but also a call to recognize the interviews as just as much a part of photography in need of preservation as the photographs themselves.[58] Moreover, the row of digital videotapes placed in front of the monitor reinforces a sense of equivalent archival value between interview and photographic print.

Zaatari creates a further parallax structure on a temporal plane as he digitally embeds the moving images of the interview footage into successive digital freeze frames of the archive space (like an attenuated form of step printing). This generates an uncanny and ambiguous visual effect in which the image appears simultaneously still and moving. On the one hand, we might read this visual effect in terms of denying these archived photographs the kind of materialization in time and space that filming photographic objects produces, especially when compared to the interview footage

Figure 4.18 Studio photographer Van Leo discusses his work in *On Photography, People and Modern Times* (Akram Zaatari, 2010)

in which we see the physical movements of the donors as they touch the photographs they are discussing. On the other hand, some of these freeze frames engender a kind of special effect animating the photographic prints, which seem to magically materialize on the table without the aid of the conservator's hands. The constitutive ambiguity of this special effect around stillness and motion encourages us to contemplate what is preserved and what is lost in the process of archivization. The video's conclusion suggests how Zaatari might want to answer that question. On the video monitor we hear Zaatari attempt to persuade studio photographer Van Leo to donate three more prints to the Foundation, but the photographer seems deeply ambivalent about giving up more prints. He promises to look for them, turns off the light, and exits the frame. We then see the camcorder, tapes, and finally the monitor disappear from view, rendering the left-hand screen an abstract white blankness. The archive sanitizes as much as it preserves.

On Photography, Dispossession and Times of Struggle carries over several aesthetic continuities from *On Photography, People and Modern Times* as it once again brings together archived photographs and interviews with their donors, but its aesthetic engagement with photographic archive shifts from the spatio-temporal to materiality. Although it lacks the parallax structure of the split-screen division between vertical and horizontal perspectives, the film retains the aesthetic tension between the moving images of the video-taped interviews and the stilled filming of the photographs in the archive (Figure 4.19). In this film, the perspective remains resolutely vertical as the camera gazes down upon a blank white surface, which spatially flattens the film image and metaphorizes archivization in a more abstract manner than in the earlier

Figure 4.19 Dr. Sami Khoury writes names on the verso of photographs he is donating to the Arab Image Foundation in *On Photography, Dispossession and Times of Struggle* (Akram Zaatari, 2017)

film. The grayscale and color test pattern that appear on the left margin of the screen suggest the process of archival photographic reproduction. By invoking the distanced stasis of the photographic copy stand rather than the immersive (and seductive) mobility of the rostrum camera used in the Ken Burns effect, *On Photography, Dispossession and Times of Struggle* foregrounds the materiality of the archival photograph over its representational status.

The interviews focus on how photography has been embedded within experiences of dispossession, expulsion, and exile, primarily among Palestinians. Early in the film, Samieh Khayri describes how her family lost all their photographs during their expulsion from their Jerusalem home in 1948. Friends who stayed reported finding their family photos discarded onto the street. Khayri follows this story of material loss with one of unexpected recovery as she recounts how her aunt smuggled out the family's silverware hidden in rolled carpets. Her testimony thus positions the photographs among the most cherished possessions that expelled Palestinians lost during the Nakba. Astra Abu Jamra's subsequent interview amplifies the alignment between the fate of photographs and exiles: "But the albums were originally in Jerusalem. From Jerusalem they went to Lebanon, and then to Damascus. And from Damascus they came here. These are the stations we went through. We were displaced." The photo albums become totems for the trauma of exilic displacement and loss, which was exacerbated after Jamra's mother lent many photographs to someone who was making a book about Jerusalem but who never returned them. Zaatari's camera lingers over the gaps in the albums where photographs once resided, highlighting the material marks of absence (the mounting corners that no longer attach a photograph to the page or the handwritten caption for a missing image). The film also repeatedly focuses on the verso of photographic prints, revealing the scrawled names of the depicted subjects or the small chunks of paper that ripped from the album page when the photograph was removed in order to enter the archive. Both operate as further inscriptions of displacement. Zaatari also films Dr. Sami Khoury carefully writing the names of his friends in the photos on their verso before he donates them to the AIF, memory and meaning that remained embodied until that moment of the photograph's displacement into the archive, when inscription was required for their future preservation (Video 4.7 ▶). Even in the presentation of photographic images themselves, Zaatari employs visual strategies to highlight the materiality of the physical object, such as magnifying glasses, which enhance haptic visual access to the photochemical surface of the picture. The final set of photographs presented in the film are negatives from Syrian writer Abdel Salam El Ujayli's service in the Arab Liberation Army in Palestine in 1948. Although archival negatives are often treated, particularly by historians, as bearing a closer and more direct relationship to historical truth than photographic prints produced from them, negatives paradoxically require greater visual deciphering than positive images, placing more immediate perceptual emphasis on the material surface of the image, including its tonal range, sharpness, and chromatic qualities (Figure 4.20). The attention to materiality extends to the mediation of the

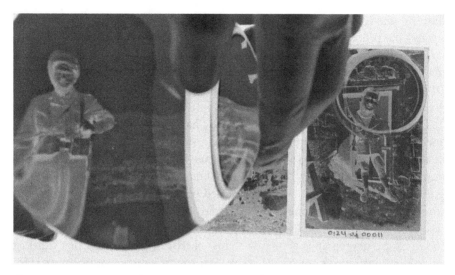

Figure 4.20 Negative images require greater visual deciphering than positives in *On Photography, Dispossession and Times of Struggle* (Akram Zaatari, 2017).

interviews that are screened on iPhones and iPads laid flat on the same blank white surface on which the conservator places the archived photographs. These thin rectangular media objects visually resemble the shape of the photographs themselves; the smart-screen devices are moreover often visually aligned with the photographs within the film frame. Furthermore, these devices also suddenly appear and disappear on screen through similar "magical" vitality as the photographs. To transmit the interviews through tablets and smartphones also implicitly acknowledges that such devices are now central to our haptic consumption of vernacular images as we hold them in one hand and use the other to navigate them by touching the screen. In its multifaceted attention to the materiality of not only the archived photographs but also the digital devices through which the interviews are mediated, *On Photography, Dispossession and Times of Struggle* expands the definition of photographic preservation to include the documented traces of photography's affective economy and the network of social and political relations it engenders. These are registered in the words and gestures of the interviews as well as the extra-pictorial marks and signs inscribed on the photographic objects.

Zaatari has had a longstanding interest in Hashem El Madani, a studio photographer from Saida, South Lebanon, since he first interviewed him in 1998; he has included Madani's photographs in numerous exhibitions and publications, beginning with one of the first AIF projects, *The Vehicle: Picturing Moments of Transition in a Modernizing Society* (1999).[59] Zaatari consistently positions Madani's images within the generic frameworks of vernacular photography, such as in the subgenres of portraiture explored in his 2002 collaboration with Walid Raad, *Mapping*

Sitting: On Portraiture and Photography.[60] Even when he dedicated a whole exhibition to Madani's studio photographs in 2004, Zaatari situated the work in relation to various "studio practices" rather than as aesthetic evidence of a newly discovered photographic artist. The exhibition catalog prefaced the images with an interview in which Zaatari asked Madani detailed questions about the economy and social practice of his Studio Shehrazade.[61] Zaatari later noted that he became ever more interested in Madani because he was "not a perfectionist 'high end' photographer," but a self-taught professional who would come to develop his own unmannered signature style in the service of product differentiation in the marketplace rather than aesthetic authorship.[62] Unlike André Magnin's highly profitable transformation of Seydou Keïta's and Malick Sidibé's vernacular photography into art, Zaatari resists the move to turn Madani into an artist, yet he also refuses to frame his curatorial work with the photographer as a form of artistic collaboration. Rather, he positions it as a mode of creative and self-reflexive displacement that produces a challenging dual authorship to the images: "they are products of a photographer's practice, tradition, and economy, and at the same time an artist's project that displaced them into another time, another tradition, another economy, while studying them and producing around them works that aim to change their initial perception completely. And that is what I like to call theater."[63] Performance is thus central to Zaatari's engagement with Madani in two significant interrelated ways. First, Zaatari wants to investigate the complex historical conditions that shaped photography as a social performance between photographer and subject in a specific time and place, namely Zaatari's own hometown of Saida in the latter half of the twentieth century. Second, rather than occlude the dynamics of displacement produced by the collection, preservation, and archiving of Madani's vernacular photography, Zaatari's projects use performance to engage these processes directly as fundamental aesthetic and conceptual concerns of the artwork itself: "I see my work with Madani as an ongoing performance. It's an intervention in this photographer's work and life: a reanimation of his economy and a displacement of his practice."[64]

Commissioned by the Musée Nicéphoré Niépce and premiered at the Berlinale, Zaatari's feature-length film *Twenty-Eight Nights and a Poem* presents itself as "An interpretation of Hashem El Madani's photographic archive," reflecting Zaatari's transformed conception of the photographic archive after working for almost a decade with Madani to move his hundreds of thousands of negatives to the AIF archive for digital scanning and preservation. In that time, Zaatari came to question not only the prevailing values of archival preservation, but also the very concept of what actually constitutes photography.[65] By recognizing the studio as a space of social performance and economic transaction (not merely the site of material image production), Zaatari argued to the AIF Board, unsuccessfully however, that the collection should also accept Madani's equipment as an important component of his archive. In his exhibitions, Zaatari began to incorporate large-scale photographs of Studio Shehrazade as well as various audio-visual equipment that Madani used and leased to customers. As new audio-visual technologies emerged in the mid- and late twentieth century, photographic studios in Lebanon began to offer their clients an array of machines for sound and image capture and diffusion—the photo studio became a multimedia site integrating the consumption of popular culture and the production of vernacular media. Zaatari's strategy of multimedia display exceeds the normative gesture in exhibitions to contextualize an artist through visual documentation of their creative space, equipment, and cultural context. He places these items as primary objects in the installations alongside Madani's photographs, granting them equal, rather than merely contextualizing, status and also highlighting photography's relation to other modern vernacular media.

As a digressively structured essay film, *Twenty-Eight Nights and a Poem* both replicates and extends Zaatari's integration within his installation work of the diverse components constituting Madani's archive. While the first forty minutes of the film examine Madani's photographic practices and interactions with clients in the studio (in a similar audio-visual style to the interviews and photographs in *On Photography, Dispossession and Times of Struggle*), the subsequent sixty minutes shift to the audio and moving-image technologies that became part of the studio's economy in the late twentieth century, specifically audio tape and super-8 film. Madani's clients used both media to consume popular culture as well as document their own lives, which Zaatari humorously highlights with a reel-to-reel tape that begins with a recording of a client testing the machine (that he claims had previously misfunctioned), before the tape abruptly cuts to a popular song. If much of Zaatari's earlier installation work had investigated the influence of popular culture on vernacular photography in the Arab world, *Twenty-Eight Nights and a Poem* considers how the photo studio became a multimedia economy to address new consumer media, which would eventually wholly displace the work of the studio photographer. The film combines scenes of Madani discussing his studio practices, intertitles offering metaphorically resonant definitions of different media and historical contextualization about media consumption in Saida, and staged scenes in Studio Shehrazade and the archive of the Arab Image Foundation, in which Zaatari and Madani perform gestures of archivization and preservation. It is the last of these aesthetic strategies that I will examine here since they provide the most generative articulation of Zaatari's reconceptualization of photography and its preservation.

The very title of the film alludes to contemplative reflection derived from performative gesture: the twenty-eight nights and a poem refer to Mohammed Abdel Wahab's 1935 *mawwal* "Fil Bahr (In the Sea)," in which the majority of the song is devoted to the singer's vocally elongated repetition of the phrase "Oh night" before it concludes with a single-line poem.[66] At the Berlinale, Zaatari emphasized the embodied, affective dimension to this vocal genre: "A *mawwal* is a prelude. It aims to prepare you to hear the song and normally there's one word you keep on repeating until you reach some kind of trance."[67] Such non-narrative recursion is reflected in the film's essayistic return to particular performative gestures by Zaatari and Madani that revolve around the question of preservation. In the opening minutes, Wahab's *mawwal* is played on an old reel-to-reel tape recorder while Zaatari's hands set up a digital audio recorder and microphone to record the playback. The audio switches between the soundtracks captured on the digital audio recorder itself and on the digital video camera filming the act of analog-to-digital transfer. This emphasis on the mechanical materiality of playback and recording is repeated time and again whenever the film presents archival material as we see and hear Zaatari's hands press buttons, spool film reels, and insert tapes and cartridges in machines. Such a move constitutes more than merely a Vertovian or Farockian political reflexivity around technological representation. The sounds of the machine and the haptic contact that operate it displace some of our attention from the content of the recording to the machine that presents it. While this points to the displacement that occurs in preservational reproduction, it also registers that the affective sensation and memory produced by media equipment and its use should be preserved as much as the content it communicated. Zaatari's performative gestures allude here to affective dimensions to photography (and modern vernacular media) that exceed the recording itself, making them all the more challenging to preserve.

Arguably the most provocative performative gestures around preservation occur near the end of the film. On a laptop Zaatari's hands type in a YouTube search for Abdel Halim's song "Tekhounouh (You Betray Him)" from the Egyptian film *The Empty Pillow* (Salah Abouseif, 1957); cut to a close up of Zaatari's hands holding a smart phone as it plays the song. He carefully places the phone in a wooden box (while the song still plays) and puts it on a shelf in the AIF archive; cut to Madani sitting at the desk in his studio as he takes the smart phone out of the desk drawer and continues watching the song. By this point, we have already seen several scenes of the retired Madani whiling away time in his studio that is stuffed full of old equipment and sample photographs from its heyday. But in this particular scene, the contrast between archival spaces is emphasized by the magical cut that transports the mobile phone from the AIF archive to Studio Shehrazade (Video 4.8 ▶) (Figure 4.21). It is a gesture of preservation as repatriation, albeit one mediated through the new digital archive of the internet (YouTube). At the end of the film, Zaatari locates a later Halim song on a laptop, "Ahlef bi samaha/I Swear by Its Sky" (1967), but this time he plays it through a Bluetooth speaker and records it on a Walkman cassette recorder, thus reversing the conventional transfer from analog to digital within archival preservation. Zaatari then places the still playing Walkman in a plastic container with a potted basil plant and puts it on another shelf in the AIF archive (Figure 4.22). This enigmatic and evocative gesture intimates the potential vitality of the archived object, its capacity to continue living and to change within the archive. Halim's lyrics confirm this notion: "If only I could have a second life!" An intertitle then describes the online virtual world Second Life, followed by the final shot of the film as Zaatari and Madani watch a laptop screen (hidden from our view), while colored lights dance around the

Figure 4.21 Hashem El Madani watches an Abdel Halim song on a mobile phone in his photo studio in *Twenty-Eight Nights and a Poem* (Akram Zaatari, 2017).

Figure 4.22 Akram Zaatari performs a gesture of radical preservation in *Twenty-Eight Nights and a Poem* (Akram Zaatari, 2017).

studio behind them (Figure 4.23). It is a droll and allusive performative gesture, reinforced by Melhem Barakat's song, "Aala babi waèf amarein (Two Moons Are Standing at My Door)." Their authorship is dual but parallel: Zaatari displaces Madani's archive into a second, parallel life as art after its vernacular use has become obsolete. Zaatari resists making Madani into an artist, for to do so would occlude the very significance that Zaatari finds in Madani's work as an artist himself, namely its illumination of

Figure 4.23 Hashem El Madani and Akram Zaatari presented as parallel authors at the end of *Twenty-Eight Nights and a Poem* (Akram Zaatari, 2017).

photography as a complex of social and affective relations mediated through perfor-mances around cameras and photographs. Indeed, for Zaatari's aesthetic engagement with Madani's archive to work as art, he needs it to retain its vernacularity.

However much any of these documentaries on photographic archives and col-lections embrace the vernacular, aesthetic value remains tenaciously in the picture, whether it be in the collector as artist in Zaatari's work or in the challenge to the he-gemony of aesthetic value in *The Mexican Suitcase*. The vernacular continues to be dialectically bound up with art, as its other. In his essay "Vernacular Photographies," published in 2000, Geoffrey Batchen provocatively argued for a radical overhaul of the history of photography by recentering it on the vernacular, which paradoxically characterizes the overwhelming majority of photographs ever taken but has also con-stituted photography's *parergon* in the study of the medium, "the part of its history that has been pushed to the margins (or beyond them to oblivion) precisely in order to delimit what is and is not proper to this history's enterprise."[68] In the twentieth century, the history of photography was written almost exclusively in terms of work defined by its aesthetic value, "excluding all other genres except as they complement a formalist art-historical narrative" (262). By shifting focus from the aesthetic qual-ities of the image to the morphology of the ordinary photographic object, Batchen asserted the importance of materiality and multisensory experience to the medium's history. However, at a symposium on vernacular photography almost two decades after his original essay, Batchen worried how easily the vernacular had become "a new collecting category" for the twenty-first-century art world, now so easily subsumed into such aesthetic categories and structures as the readymade, the found, and the grid.[69] He thus asks if the vernacular is still a useful category if it loses its capacity to contest the hegemony of the aesthetic, due to its continual absorption into the space of art. The study of vernacular photography shifted scholarly attention from defining what photography is to analyzing what people do with it, a methodological realignment of the field toward materiality that Batchen argues should be applied to all photography, including art photography.[70]

The documentaries in this chapter all attest to the multifaceted capacity of film to record and illuminate how the material practices of photographic collecting and archiving engender intersecting acts of displacement, identification, redefinition, revalorization, recommodification, preservation, and destruction. This is perhaps no better illustrated than in the close-ups of a small gesture repeated several times in Lorca Sheppard and Cabot Philbrick's *Other People's Pictures* (2004), a documentary about the trade in vernacular photography at New York's Chelsea Flea Market at the turn of the millennium (Video 4.9 ▶) (Figure 4.24). The camera homes in on the hands of a potential customer as they rapidly flick through a small stack of random snapshots they have picked up from the unordered mass of photographs laid out by the vendor.[71] The customer occasionally pauses briefly on a specific photograph, brings it closer to their eyes, and either puts it aside or throws it back into the mass, before continuing to flick through the rest of their stack. This seemingly simple haptic encounter with photographs in fact constitutes a complex array of economic, social, and affective processes. While holding other people's old photographs generates an

Figure 4.24 A customer flips through a stack of snapshots at Chelsea Flea Market in *Other People's Pictures* (Lorca Sheppard and Cabot Philbrick, 2004).

uncanny affective pleasure in the simultaneous experience of familiarity and ano-nymity, the movement of flicking through them enacts integrated processes of cate-gorization, distinction, and extraction around thematic interest, material condition, economic valuation, and affective stimulation. Given the significance of subjective taste in the flea-market economy of vernacular photography, these close-ups thus po-tentially capture the very moment of displacement in which a photograph changes in meaning, value, and possession as it is extracted from one collection to enter another of a completely different order.

5
Encounters with Photographic Portraits

If one of the central concerns of this book has been documentary film's capacity to capture what people actually do with photographs, then it seems fitting to conclude with a consideration of the photographic portrait, given its multiplicity of uses across the history of the medium. Indeed, as a fundamental pictorial genre of modernity, the portrait has served many public and private functions throughout its history: as biography, document, proxy, gift, commemoration, political tool, and work of art.[1] Although the invention of photography in the nineteenth century exponentially proliferated the production of the portrait and democratized its affirmative presentation of the modern self, the new medium also enabled whole new systems of modern surveillance, categorization, and subjectification. These "honorific" and "repressive" functions were not separate developments of photographic portraiture, argues Allan Sekula, but rather integrated within "a generalized, inclusive archive, a shadow archive that encompasses an entire social terrain while positioning individuals within that terrain."[2] Underpinned by the scientific discourses of physiognomy and phrenology, photographic portraiture offered "an essential hermeneutic service" to read the visual surface of bodies for signs of virtue and vice through mutual comparison of honorific and repressive portraiture (12). While the scientific authority of physiognomy and phrenology fell away in the twentieth century, the shadow archive persisted, as illustrated, for instance, by the infamous, doctored mugshot of O. J. Simpson on *Time* magazine's cover in June 1994 (the repressive contrast to the honorific 1994 "Men of the Year" cover featuring "The Peacemakers": Yitzhak Rabin, Nelson Mandela, F. W. de Klerk, and Yasser Arafat).[3]

The occasion of the photographic portrait involves an encounter among photographer, camera, and subject with varying degrees of agency, volition, and interaction at either end of the shadow archive. Whether an officially commissioned portrait or a family snapshot, the ceremonial presentation of the subject in the honorific tradition constitutes a negotiated collaboration between the subject's performative presence before the camera and the photographer's technical and aesthetic management of the occasion. By contrast, the repressive tradition compels the subject through either discipline or force to be subjected to the camera's registering gaze. Resistance to such subjectification may arise from the subject's vociferous return of the camera's gaze or gestural presentation of their face as mask. Indeed, the subject's facial performance of a social mask can also occur in more subtle ways within the honorific tradition depending upon the interpersonal dynamics of the collaboration between photographer and subject. Being the primary focus of most portraits, the face may conceal as much as it reveals. As Noa Steimatsky aptly summarizes in her book on the face in

A Medium Seen Otherwise. Roger Hallas, Oxford University Press. © Oxford University Press 2023.
DOI: 10.1093/oso/9780190057763.003.0006

cinema: "The face is naked: it *expresses*, it is open, it opens. But it is also a mask: the Latin, *persona*, could suggest that the face is where the *person* begins."[4]

The portrait establishes specific relationships among the participants in the event of photography. Willing or enforced, the subject's act of self-presentation before the camera and photographer generates a presence to be captured and preserved. "Each photograph," noted Barthes, "is a certificate of presence."[5] Hans Belting ties the portrait's conveyance of presence to the inscribed gaze of the portrait's subject: "Not only does the person portrayed gaze, but the portrait itself also gazes. The gaze in the portrait is, like the presence, a legacy of the icon, but here it has been redefined."[6] This alignment of gazes permits the materiality of the visual object to recede from our perception: "With the gaze the portrait loses its character as an object and appropriates the presence of a real face with which we—the viewers—can establish contact through our gaze" (121). Yet Belting emphasizes that such "iconic presence" does not constitute a magical or animistic return of the absent body through the visual object, but rather the presence of an absence. He writes,

Images traditionally live from the *body's absence*, which is either temporary (that is, spatial) or, in the case of death, final. This absence does not mean that images revoke absent bodies and make them return. Rather, they replace the body's absence with a different kind of presence. *Iconic presence* still maintains a body's absence and turns it into what must be called *visible absence*. Images live from the paradox that they perform *the presence of an absence* or vice versa (which also applies to the telepresence of people in today's media).[7]

In fact, all media involve producing such presence-absences. Iconic presence does not constitute a direct unmediated experience, even if it can feel like one for the viewer. Yet, it is more than just a mere "reality effect" created by specific media practices. Visual studies scholars such as Belting and W. J. T. Mitchell have expressed skepticism toward the historical premise that pre-modern magical thinking about images was wholly replaced by scientific reason in modernity.[8] They contend that some pre-modern magical thinking remains latent in our contemporary assumptions about the power and vitality of images. Mitchell even cites André Bazin's seminal essay, "The Ontology of the Photographic Image," as an example (54). With the reciprocal address between camera and subject aligning with that between image and viewer, photographic portraits are precisely the kind of modern images that lend themselves to the production of iconic presence.

Just as photographic portraits engender iconic presence, so may a face's direct address to the camera in film or video do likewise. Interviews and autobiographical testimonies before the camera in documentary film draw much of their affective power from the iconic presence of the filmed subject, which "compels attention and recognition," notes Steimatsky, "through the spatio-temporal weave of the image, its layering of presence-absence."[9] Given their divergent spatio-temporal weaves, photography and film manifest presence-absence in different ways. Through its embalming of time and space in the still image, photography registers and attenuates the intensities of the ephemeral present (for Roland Barthes, the "pure contingency" of photography), while preserving it as an absolute and already past (the "noeme" of "that has been") that simultaneously points to future mortality.[10] The presence-absence of the photograph occurs in its constitutive tension between "this is" and "that has been." In film, by contrast, the ephemeral present is experienced by viewers not as capture or embalming, but as escape and unspooling—during a continuous film shot the present appears to pass before their eyes and into their ears, simulating our embodied experience of duration. Yet viewers watch with an anticipatory awareness that such an unspooling present may be punctured at any moment by an edit or sound from another time and space. The cinematic present is thus charged with relativity. Moreover, viewers of documentary film also recognize the unspooling present on screen to be a documented event elsewhere that has now passed.[11] Presence-absence in documentary film thus occurs in the tension between the viewer's experience of an unspooling present on screen and their awareness of the spool (the recording of a prior event) from which it emerges. Thus the durational qualities of film, along with the relativity of the cinematic present, offer generative opportunities to reframe photography's iconic presence.

This chapter examines what transpires when filmmakers and artists structure documentary films around explicitly doing things with photographic portraits and their iconic presence, rather than merely embedding them as a form of visual evidence on the image track. It looks both up and down the shadow archive, considering how documentary film can redemptively engage the compelled portrait of the repressive tradition to bear witness to historical trauma and how its capacity to document the production and reception of the collaborative portrait within the honorific tradition can extend its impact.[12] The three documentaries analyzed in the chapter all facilitate an expansive understanding of the event of photography by staging and documenting encounters with photographic portraits that exploit the tension between their iconic presence and their materiality. Although the portraits in each of the documentaries derive from different historical contexts, they do share some formal qualities. Two of them involve prison mugshots, and the third features honorific portraits that play with the form of the identification photograph. The photographs are unadorned black-and-white facial portraits, almost all in direct frontal address with flat abstract backgrounds. Their formal simplicity is dual edged, pointing to the signification of a disciplinary function (to identify, to pathologize, to criminalize), but also to the potential to encounter the iconic presence of their subject.

Using photographs from historical contexts in which their production directly formed one of the very mechanisms of totalitarian violence has posed a particular challenge for documentary filmmakers: how can one incorporate such images in ways that can enable acts of bearing witness rather than merely reiterating the violence of their totalitarian gaze? Or, in Azoulay's words, how can we potentially watch such photographs? The films of Rithy Panh and Susana de Sousa Dias offer powerful examples of just such testimonial cinema wrought from complex engagements with prison identification photographs taken by the Khmer Rouge regime in Cambodia and the Portuguese fascist dictatorship of António de Oliveira Salazar, respectively. Panh's *S21: The Khmer Rouge Killing Machine* (2003) documents the atrocities of the notorious Tuol Sleng (S-21) Prison in Phnom Penh, where over 18,000 political prisoners of the regime were systematically tortured before being executed in the Killing Fields of Choeung Ek on the outskirts of the city.[13] Panh brings back to the prison two of its handful of survivors to engage their former guards and the material remains of the site. The prison identification photographs taken at S-21 become key stimuli for such witnessing encounters between perpetrators and victims at the site of atrocity. De Sousa Dias's *48* (2009) brings former political prisoners who survived torture by the Polícia Internacional e de Defesa do Estado (PIDE), Salazar's secret police, into an engagement with their multiple prison identification photographs taken at various times during their periods of imprisonment. The imagetrack consists solely of these portraits (save one brief sequence at the end of the film that includes a nocturnal landscape), thus we never see the survivors in the present, but only hear their voices on the soundtrack, which are excerpted from the interviews de Sousa Dias undertook with them. Both films facilitate a space of witness through the interplay of photographic materiality and iconic presence. Whereas *48* both amplifies and disrupts iconic presence for the viewer in its cinematic presentation of the portraits through sound and cinematography, *S21* observes how the dynamics of iconic presence play out as the documentary's social actors (both victim-survivors and perpetrators) interact with the materiality of the photographic objects.

The final section of the chapter turns to the collaborative photographic practice of French artist JR, which draws heavily on iconic presence in its disruptive reframing of urban visual space. Azoulay insists that collaboration is the "photographic event's ground zero," since "photography always involves an encounter between several protagonists in which the photographer cannot a priori claim a monopoly over knowledge, authorship, ownership and rights."[14] Collaborative photography projects emphatically embrace such distribution among their protagonists, yet they usually inscribe their collaboration in non-photographic traces, such as accompanying testimonial text in a photobook and on a wall display in a gallery exhibition, or through audio and video recordings embedded in a web documentary. Given that the most significant impact of a collaborative project may be in the ephemeral processes of collaboration themselves as much as it is in the photographs that they generate, documentary film can serve as a supplement to the project by documenting the event of photography while simultaneously extending it. Alastair Siddons's *Inside Out: The People's Art Project* (2013) is a prime example of this kind of art documentary. The film documents the eponymous global art project initiated by JR, in which he expanded the collaborative dynamics of his own well-established street-art practice of pasting enlarged black-and-white facial portraits of ordinary people in public spaces into an open-access process that enabled hundreds of thousands of people across the globe to collaborate in thousands of local manifestations of the project. Like of all JR's work at the time, *Inside Out* was grounded in the potential for the iconic presence of its magnified photographic portraits to temporarily dislocate urban landscape, and in doing so, incite a public space of engagement and discourse. Highlighting manifestations of the project in Tunisia, Haiti, and the United States, Siddons's film documents the collaborative, and at times antagonistic, dynamics at work in the production and reception of the project's local "actions." Photographic materiality also plays a significant role in such encounters with portraits, but in ways that differ substantively from the other two films.

Iconic Presence and the Ethical Address of Bearing Witness

Every incoming prisoner to the Tuol Sleng Prison (S-21) had their mugshot taken. "The meticulous production of the prisoner portraits was an important element of administrative control," notes Rachel Hughes. "The photographs were, for both prisoners and their masters, emblems of the regime's omnipotence and efficiency."[15] Applying an Arendtian framework of the "banality of evil," archivist Michelle Caswell argues that, along with other forms of "obsessive documentation," these mugshots played a key role in enabling mass murder by "alienating decision-makers from the violence of their decisions."[16] Caswell outlines three principal aspects of this alienation: reducing prisoners to pieces of bureaucratic documentation, allowing specific actions to be routinized and compartmentalized, and promoting a pervasive culture of thoughtlessness in the prison. As a closed and secretive totalitarian regime, the Khmer Rouge was motored by an incessant paranoia that sought to annihilate any suspected trace of a potential enemy within. Thus, photographs served as a bureaucratic technology to verify that decisions made higher up the command structure, such as arrest, imprisonment, and torture, had been carried out below. When a Khmer Rouge leader suspected someone of being a traitor, he would order them to be arrested so that torture could elicit a confession to prove the suspicion. The truth of the confession mattered little, as long as a document supporting the charge could be generated. As Caswell contends, "documentation surpassed truth, replacing lived reality with a dangerous and steadfast belief in the infallibility of records" (55). Moreover, in a regime that valued total obedience to hierarchy, obsessive documentation of carried-out orders became a means for subordinates to ingratiate themselves with their superiors. The commander of S-21, Kaing Guek Eav (known as Duch), prided himself on personally annotating the prison records to prove his efficiency and trustworthiness to the regime.[17] Photography was also used to document any deviation, mistake, or malfunction of the system of torture and extermination. For instance, when a prisoner was able to snatch a makeshift weapon and harm themselves, their guards, or both, the crime scene was systematically photographed with an obsessive forensic attention, so that the "killing machine" could learn from its supposed errors. Although the visual documentation of the prison system was assiduously produced, it remained very closely circulated within the Khmer Rouge hierarchy, as part of the prison's strictly enforced visuality, which included blindfolding prisoners to prevent them from communicating with others or comprehending the carceral structure in which they were imprisoned.

During the fall of the Khmer Rouge regime in 1979, the photographs were discovered by Vietnamese soldiers along with a wealth of written documentation in the abandoned prison. Most of the photographs had been anonymized by their separation from the prisoner files and the numbering system failed to re-identify them since the prison photographer had attached a daily batch number to the prisoner rather than a systematic identification number. The new Vietnamese-supported state, known as the People's Republic of Kampuchea, commissioned Vietnamese museum expert Mai Lam in 1980 to create an archive and museum at the site, where enlargements of some of the identification photographs were mounted on wall displays. The museum served an important geopolitical function for the new regime in justifying Vietnamese incursion into Cambodia as necessary to end the Khmer Rouge's genocide of its own people. The visual rhetoric of the display supported the charge of genocide by transforming the individuated identification photographs into a grid of faces signifying the collectivity of the regime's victims. "By emphasizing collective rather than isolated suffering," notes Thy Phu, "the exhibit projected a vision of shared trauma that connects prisoners with each other and links spectators with prisoners."[18]

Throughout the 1980s, historians began to use the S-21 archive as a crucial body of evidence for understanding the workings of the Khmer Rouge dictatorship. In 1993, two US photojournalists, Douglas Niven and Chris Riley, visited the museum and its archive, where they found thousands of negatives of identification photographs that had not been publicly seen before. Their self-declared discovery of these negatives initiated a transnationally funded restoration and preservation project, which also generated archival print sets of a hundred representative photographs from the archive that would significantly proliferate the transnational circulation of these images.[19] In 1996, Niven and Riley published *The Killing Fields*, a lavishly produced art book containing a selection of the identification photographs without captions. The following year, the Museum of Modern Art in New York mounted a small show of twenty-two portraits, simply titled *Photographs from S-21: 1975–1979*. The MoMA show faced substantial criticism for barely providing any context for the images and their history. Guy Trebay wrote in his *Village Voice* review, "Who are the people in the Tuol Sleng photos? Who are their families? What is the role of our own amnesiac culture in the atrocities that took place in a former public high school and beyond it in the killing fields?"[20] Ultimately, such transnational circulation of the photographs within the art world led to their historical decontextualization, as it increasingly framed them in universal humanist terms as icons of late twentieth-century genocide. In her analysis of contemporary artworks that have appropriated the S-21 photographs, Stéphanie Benzaquen similarly argues that they have been transformed into "emotional portraiture, icons of atrocity and injustice that make us feel and even project ourselves into such suffering."[21]

In all three of his documentaries about S-21 (*Bophana: A Cambodian Tragedy* [1996], *S21: The Khmer Rouge Killing Machine* [2003], and *Duch: Master of the Forges of Hell* [2012]), Panh has emphatically resituated the photographs back in their specific historical context. In the first of these, Panh focuses on female prisoner Hout Bophana, whose tragic love story with Ly Sitha (Comrade Deth), a former monk and revolutionary convert, was first uncovered by *Washington Post* journalist Elizabeth Becker in her 1986 book on the Khmer Rouge.[22] Not only does Panh frame Bophana in this film as an allegorical figure for Cambodia's fate under the Khmer Rouge, but, according to Vincente Sánchez-Biosca, she also becomes "an emotionally charged figure who runs through almost all his films in such a subtle manner that she has reached a kind of subliminal presence."[23] Sánchez-Biosca reads Bophana as "an instigating voice," "a figure of affliction," and "a metaphor for 'the missing picture'" that drives Panh's cinema of witness to the Cambodian genocide, which killed his entire family (175). Although neither *S21* nor *Duch* takes up her story, Bophana's mugshot appears in numerous scenes of both films on top of the stacks of photographs and documents that surround the perpetrators called to testify by Panh's camera. As one of the thousands of victims whose death had never been appropriately mourned within Buddhist tradition, Bophana's iconic presence haunts the space of testimony, quietly addressing the perpetrators to take responsibility for the torture, trauma, and death they caused. In his memoir, *The Elimination*, Panh recounts how Duch questioned why the filmmaker kept showing him so many photographs. Panh's answer affirms his faith in the capacity of the photographic portrait to bring its subject into iconic presence: "they are listening to you. Koy Thourn is here. Bophana's here. Taing Siv Leang too. I believe they're listening to you."[24]

Bophana opens with her photographic portraits retrieved from her prisoner file, which included photographs from both ends of the shadow archive: her mugshot and a faint photocopy of a studio portrait taken before the dictatorship (that was probably confiscated from her husband on his arrest). Shortly after, S-21 survivor and artist Vann Nath appears in a scene painting a large diptych based on these two portraits. The magnification and intermedial transfer of this representational act restore the honorific function of Bophana's studio portrait and reverse the repressive function of her mugshot. Nath's presence in *Bophana* initiates a witnessing dynamic that would prove foundational to Panh's subsequent film, *S21*. Originally, Panh had tried to avoid any contact between survivors and their former guards for ethical reasons. When Panh was interviewing Him Houy, the former deputy head of security at S-21, he explicitly told Nath to stay away from the site, but when filming was delayed a day, Nath ended up coming to the prison and encountering Houy accidentally. Although very nervous, Nath insisted on guiding Houy around the museum's display of his paintings depicting the torture that had been perpetrated in the prison. At each painting, Nath challenges Houy on camera to verify that the picture depicts the truth of what happened at S-21. Panh thus came to the realization that "testimony was not complete unless it was a testimony from both sides of the situation."[25] Critically, Panh's S-21 documentaries stage such witnessing encounters between victim and perpetrator in the co-presence of images, either Nath's searing canvases or the documentation photographs taken by the prison bureaucracy.

Whereas *Bophana* and *Duch* focus on a victim and a perpetrator, respectively, *S21: The Khmer Rouge Killing Machine* brings a group of former prison guards together with the surviving victim Nath at Tuol Sleng. The film took many years to make while Panh tracked down the prison personnel, and then interviewed and filmed them in their villages, in order to build trust before ultimately bringing them to S-21. After a summary of the history of the Khmer Rouge, the first real scene of the film establishes the former guards' motivation for participating in Panh's project: Houy sits in his rural home bemoaning his chronic headaches while his parents beg him to tell the truth, confess to the killings he perpetrated, and hold a ceremony to rid himself and his family of the bad karma haunting them. The film then cuts to Nath painting a brutal scene depicting the prisoners' arrival at S-21 as he describes the process, including the obligatory mugshot that was taken. Nath becomes the film's primary protagonist, its moral conscience, and Panh's proxy. He escorts fellow S-21 survivor Chum Mey into the museum to help him work through his traumatic memory and survivor's guilt. With patience but also gentle insistence, Nath questions Mey about his false confession and denunciations that were procured by torture. Nath continues this affective demeanor as the former guards return to the site where they engage in extensive conversations with Nath and reenactments of their prior duties in the prison. Panh brings the traumatic past into presence by drawing on the power of the original site and its material remnants to release the embodied traumatic memory of both victims and perpetrators. As Deirdre Boyle argues, the site and its artifacts propel them to "live beyond reenactment to 're-live' the past" in the present.[26] This mobilization of what William Guynn calls "psychodramatic mise-en-scène" has been the principal focus for much of the scholarship devoted to the film.[27] In interviews Panh has also emphasized the multiple layers of survivor co-presence within the production process (including himself, Nath as his on-screen proxy, and a film crew who have all lived through the genocide) to maintain the demand for perpetrators to bear witness to the truth of the past.[28] Although neither Panh nor scholars have discussed at any great length the significance of the photographs in the testimonial encounter that brings together perpetrator, victim, site, and document, they undoubtedly play an important role in the film's witnessing dynamics.[29]

For *S21: The Khmer Rouge Killing Machine*, Panh developed several specific strategies for reframing the photographs produced by S-21. First, Panh emphasizes the materiality of the photographs and their uses in the museum as archival objects. In a scene early in the film, Nath searches through a stack of mounted enlargements of the mugshots, which appear to be obsolete wall displays from a previous installation of the museum. Picking up each layer, he carefully brushes away the dust and disintegrating pieces of particle board, and then begins to split the boards into individual portraits. (Figure 5.1). At the bottom of the pile, obscured by the mugshots, is a photograph documenting the tortured body of a prisoner. The S-21 archive contains voluminous photographic documentation of the regime's torture procedures, but the

Figure 5.1 Vann Nath searches through a stack of mugshot enlargements from a former museum display in *S21: The Khmer Rouge Killing Machine* (Rithy Panh, 2003).

transnational circulation of the S-21 portrait photos has rarely included them. This brief scene thus allegorizes the multiple and contradictory processes at work with the mugshots as archival objects: decay, obscuration, recovery, and re-individualization. The second strategy appears shortly afterward as Nath sifts intently through a pile of prisoner files with their original identification photographs still attached, while Mey looks on. (Figure 5.2). Nath is looking for the file of his cousin, Say Sarak, who was arrested and imprisoned at the same time as him. If he finds it, he tells Mey, he will make a photocopy of the mugshot to give to his aunt, who always cries when she sees him. Nath here aspires to transform the repressive photographic document into two interrelated honorific functions: as gift and as memento mori (functions that leans heavily on the iconic presence of photographic portraits). Nath's failure to find his cousin's file is implied by the bitter irony of the cut to the next scene as Nath declares, "Here it is!" Yet he is not referring to his cousin's file, but to a prison log, in which Duch had annotated the phrase "Keep for use" alongside Nath's name.

In the following scene, arguably the most visually complex in the whole film, Nath explains why he was spared from execution. (Figure 5.3). A long shot reveals a spacious room in the S-21 museum with a very large mural by Nath of Khmer Rouge mass torture. On the left-hand side, a large photographic portrait of Duch is propped up in an armchair. On the right-hand side sits Nath painting a canvas that depicts Duch

Yes. She cries when she sees me.

Figure 5.2 Vann Nath searches for the file of his cousin in *S21: The Khmer Rouge Killing Machine* (Rithy Panh, 2003).

watching him paint a portrait of Pol Pot from a photograph. Nath is holding a photograph of Pol Pot as reference while he paints this self-reflexive picture. Although the secrecy around the structure of the Khmer Rouge during its early years in power prevented a public cult of personality developing around Pol Pot, within S-21 artist prisoners were continually forced to paint honorific portraits and sculpt busts of Brother No. 1. As he paints, Nath painfully discloses that other imprisoned artists were more talented than him, but unlike them, he was spared from execution because Duch had a fondness for his paintings of Pol Pot and would enjoy talking about art while watching him paint. The iconic presence of Duch's photographic portrait "sitting" on the chair facilitates Nath's act of remembering Duch's physical co-presence as he painted Pol Pot. Nath relives that experience in the present as we observe him painting Pol Pot's face in the picture that depicts that very act. This third formal strategy of Panh's thus involves the complex intermedial play of film, photography, and painting, welding together acts of memory, reenactment, and representation in the service of bearing witness through the perpetrator's portrait, rather than that of the victim.

Panh also stages several of Nath's interrogative conversations with the former guards in the museum's archive in which honorific portraits of Pol Pot, Duch, and other leaders of the regime adorn the glass doors of storage cabinets lining the walls of the archive. (Figure 5.4) Their iconic presence is contrasted with that of the mugshots

Figure 5.3 Vann Nath paints a depiction of his painting a portrait of Pol Pot in the presence of the prison commander, Duch, in *S21: The Khmer Rouge Killing Machine* (Rithy Panh, 2003).

and torture photographs on the table (the other end of the shadow archive), which Nath urges the former guards to contemplate alongside reports on the prisoners and their written confessions. This fourth strategy brings two sets of photographic gazes and their iconic presence to bear on the perpetrator. The look of the honorific portraits that surround the former guards invoke both the surveillant gaze of "Angkor" (the party structure) and its demand for complete obedience, while the look of the prisoners in their mugshots addresses the former guards with an ethical call to recognize their humanity. If Nath and Panh work to mobilize the bureaucratic tools of dehumanization (mugshots, logbooks, reports, and confessions) against themselves, to invert their alienating function, then the photographs play an outsized role for their iconic presence permits them to surpass the function of documentary evidence of atrocity. They engender a command to remember a particular person and a set of circumstances around them, but also to fundamentally recognize the other as human. Panh's mobilization of iconic presence in the service of recognizing humanity is far from the universalizing, dehistoricized dynamics of the mugshots' transnational circulation, for his project aimed not only to restore the victims' humanity, but also "to bring the torturers back to humanity" through witnessing encounters he stages with their victims both alive (Nath) and dead (the photographic portraits).[30]

For instance, when a prisoner had been interrogated,

Figure 5.4 Vann Nath questions the former prison guards in the museum's archive surrounded by photographs of Pol Pot and other Khmer Rouge leaders in *S21: The Khmer Rouge Killing Machine* (Rithy Panh, 2003).

Panh's camera captures the perpetrators' differing engagements not just with Nath's patient but insistent questioning, but also with the direct address of the mug-shots (Video 5.1 ⏵).[31] Some have difficulty looking at the portraits, while others look askance at them as they continue to resist taking responsibility for their perpetration of torture and murder. A notable exception is former prison interrogator Prak Kahn, who talks at length in two scenes about a female prisoner, Nay Nan, whom he interrogated and tortured. In each scene, Kahn holds the photocopied enlargement of her mugshot in both hands as he returns her look rather than looking at the other men in the room, who are listening to him. In holding the picture away from his body, the two-handed grip locks him into a scopic reciprocity with Nan (Figure 5.5). In the first scene he numbly describes his brutal beating of Nan to extract a false confession, while in the second he acknowledges his sexual attraction and feelings for her: "I had feelings for her and felt sorry for her." Although this disclosure is prefaced by his defensive patriarchal rationalization that all the guards were boys or young men deprived of exposure to the opposite sex, Kahn's testimony shows initial signs that, unlike his peers, he is beginning to consciously acknowledge his own human responsibility for his actions. He identifies and takes ownership of his own affect, as well as recognizes that his brutal treatment of Nan was exacerbated by his displacement of forbidden sexual desire. Of

My heart was aching,
I was full of lust.

Figure 5.5 Former prison interrogator Prak Kahn contemplates the iconic presence of Nay Nan's mugshot in *S21: The Khmer Rouge Killing Machine* (Rithy Panh, 2003).

all the former prison personnel in the film, he is the one who tellingly engages most with the direct address of the mugshots, indicating that Nan's iconic presence in the photograph has delivered an effective ethical address to bear witness.[32]

In an interview shortly before he died in 2011, Nath contested one of the most common interpretations of the S-21 mugshots, namely that the prisoners' anxious facial expressions articulate an indictment of the Khmer Rouge regime. He pointed out that the photographs were taken while the prisoners were in a traumatized, disoriented state, often after beatings and starvation: "These expressions that people empathize with are just pure shock from the flash."[33] Nath's claim also challenges readings that detect the recognition of imminent death in the prisoners' faces.[34] The production of mugshots in S-21 was as much part of the physical procedures of brutalization as it was an element of bureaucratic dehumanization. The redemption of these mugshots in Panh's documentary comes not from resolving their representational muteness—for giving them voice—but for enabling their iconic presence to engender an ethical address to the perpetrators to bear witness to their crimes.

Between Iconic and Auditory Presence

When Susana de Sousa Dias was researching her first documentary on the Salazar dictatorship in Portugal, *Criminal Case 141/53* (*Processo-Crime 141/53*, 2000), which told the story of two nurses fighting for improved conditions and the right to marry, she came across a massive ledger of PIDE's prison identification photographs in the state archive that completely fascinated her. This discovery would inspire her deeper interrogation of the fascist visual archive in her next film, *Still Life* (*Natureza Morta*, 2005), which subjects the photographs and various archival film footage to a rigorous set of visual manipulations in order to free them from "the shackles of the gaze that produced them."[35] While de Sousa Dias was researching the archival material for *Still Life*, the management of the state archive insisted on applying individual image rights to each of the prison identification photographs, forcing her to track down each former prisoner whose portrait she wanted to include in the film. Although de Sousa Dias argues that such a move to protect the right of image ironically denied the prisoners their status as historical subjects by obscuring the photographs' actual condition as "a political corpus" belonging to the *res publica*, she also recognizes that the state's requirements to secure image permissions generated new opportunities for her to critically interrogate the fascist archive.[36] Meeting former prisoners and extensively interviewing them built relationships of trust that became the foundation for a new film, *48*, which would focus on their experience of torture, drawing on both the prison portraits and her interviews with their subjects decades after their imprisonment.[37]

The meaning and function of prison identification photographs taken under a totalitarian regime differ from those taken in a democratic one. In writing about twentieth-century prison portraits in the United States, Bruce Jackson argues that whereas arrest photographs (regular mugshots) are filled with uncertainty in "a moment rich in possibility," identification photographs taken in prison after sentencing reveal faces that are "almost uniformly tranquil" as prisoners recognize the certainty of their removal from ordinary life for an extended period of time.[38] By contrast, the practices of arbitrary arrest and detention in the permanent state of exception under a dictatorship produce prison identification photographs full of affective ambiguity, ranging from shock and anxiety to resistance and resilience. Moreover, political prisoners are subject to being photographed at any given time during their incarceration as the practice becomes an integral part of the state's comprehensive psychic subjugation of the prisoner. Although the principal function of the PIDE photographs was to be archived—and thus removed from potential circulation—they were not to display any visible evidence of torture perpetrated on the prisoner, for, as de Sousa Dias notes, "(d)ictatorships will admit to anything but torture" (485). In bearing the tensions among these various functions, such photographs present faces latent with the trauma of torture.

In *Still Life*, de Sousa Dias had already begun to grapple with the challenge of detaching images in the fascist archive from the ideological gaze that produced them, thus opening them up through aesthetic means to reveal the violence that their visual surface concealed. After watching hundreds of hours of propaganda films produced by and for the Salazar regime, de Sousa Dias whittled down the material to about twenty hours to work with in the editing room. By her rigorous application of slow-motion techniques to such footage, what she calls "decelerated movement," the finished seventy-two-minute film incorporates only twelve minutes of original archival footage.[39] Through the combination of three formal devices—slow motion, reframing, and fading in/out—*Still Life* cleaves open multiple temporalities in the image, which break the naturalized linkage between the film image and its referent, disconnecting the narration of the past from "its punctual location in time" and opening up "the microdramaturgy within the events themselves" (29). De Sousa Dias treats such spatio-temporal decomposition of the image as "montage *within* the shot," which, she argues, can render visible the affective dynamics of the dictatorship by isolating gestures of violence, subjugation, charity, or adulation within the microdramaturgy of rituals performed for the camera by the church, the bourgeois family, and the military (the three ideological foundations of Salazar's *Estado Novo* [New State]).[40] *Still Life* alternates between this decomposition of the fascist film image and brief sequences of the PIDE prison mugshots (Video 5.2 ▶). Their emphatic stasis contrasts sharply with the decelerated, and thereby accentuated, movement of the archival film footage. Each prison portrait remains on screen for several seconds before a fade or cut to black transitions to the next portrait of a different prisoner or the same one from a different angle. PIDE photographed each prisoner from three standardized angles (frontal, profile, and half-profile), following the Bertillon system for photographic identification.[41] The affective range of facial expressions is diverse and at times highly ambiguous. In *Still Life*, these anonymous faces both testify to the systematic repression of the state and present a collective counter-gaze that dialectically looks back with incrimination at the archival film footage with which it is interspersed.

If the PIDE prison portraits functioned in a supporting role in *Still Life* to pry open obscured meanings and affects within the fascist film archive, de Sousa Dias centered them in *48*. She faced two principal challenges in constructing a whole film around the prison portraits: first, how to sustain viewers' engagement with a photographic portrait for more than several seconds; and second, whether to show the former prisoners' contemporary image from the interviews she had conducted with them. The aesthetic solutions she developed would ultimately enhance the iconic presence of the portraits. After experimenting with shooting the photographs on 35mm film, de Sousa Dias discovered that within a very short time the film viewer ceases actively looking at the still image itself once they have absorbed its visual information. Realizing that she needed a form of motion, "something to keep the eye and mind involved," she asked her cinematographer, Octávio Espírito Santo, to move within and across the photos, yet these movements appeared far too abrupt, "like violence against the images."[42] By shifting from film to digital video, de Sousa Dias was able to gain more precise control in animating the still image. The motion of the pans across and zooms into and out of the photographs is so decelerated that it becomes barely perceptible. Over the course of a shot that may last several minutes, the scale of the face hardly changes. This visual technique generates a kind of uncanny animation, in which the viewer senses a vitality to the still image without being able to immediately locate it, or, as de Sousa Dias puts it, "images can be opened up to the disruptive and epistemological effects created by this undecidability between movement and stasis."[43] The technique deviates sharply from the cinematization of the photograph produced by the normative Ken Burns effect, in which camera movement and sound effects applied to a photograph aim to imitate film's dynamic spatio-temporality.

In watching *48*, we remain aware of our visual contemplation of photographic images. The infinitesimal movement of the frame does not enhance the impression of depth, especially since all the identification photographs were taken with flat black or white backgrounds. Indeed, de Sousa Dias repeatedly uses slow fades to and from black to introduce and withdraw photographic portraits with black backgrounds. Like the barely perceptible camera movement, such fading devices subtly imbue the photographic image with the temporal duration and dynamic luminosity of film, which augment its iconic presence (Figure 5.6). The luminescent figuration of a face that emerges from or submerges into darkness works moreover to allegorize the very paradox of absence-presence within iconic presence, especially after a slow fade to black in which the afterimage of the disappeared face momentarily lingers in our visual perception.

However, the extremely subtle motion of the camera does gradually make us aware of the edges of the original photograph, rendered all the more apparent because the

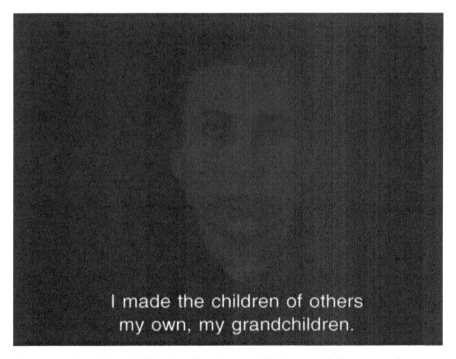

Figure 5.6 Slow fades subtly imbue the photographic image with the temporal duration and dynamic luminosity of film in *48* (Susana de Sousa Dias, 2009).

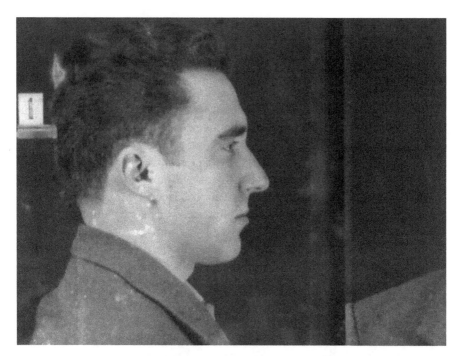

Figure 5.7 Slow camera movement across the portraits gradually reveals the edges of the frame and the adjacent image in *48* (Susana de Sousa Dias, 2009).

three separate portrait angles (frontal, profile, and semi-profile) were always printed together in a row on a single photographic sheet (Figure 5.7). In conjunction with the magnification of scale applied to these small photographic objects, camera movement also delicately highlights the material surface of the photograph because creases, folds, and chemical discoloration become noticeable as they slowly shift across the screen. A partial fingerprint on the surface of Conceição Mátos's portrait even catches our attention as a haptic trace of the photograph's material history within the bureaucracy of the state. (Figure 5.8). De Sousa Dias's uncanny animation of the photographs thus moves simultaneously in two seemingly opposite directions: to enrich the iconic presence of the photographic image and to foreground the materiality of the photographic object. Turning to the sound-image relations in the film illuminates the significance of this delicate tension.

De Sousa Dias grappled with the ethical dilemma of whether to include the present faces of the former prisoners whom she had interviewed, but ultimately decided to withhold them for several reasons. To incorporate filmed interviews, she contended, would depict the former prisoners firmly rooted in "the concrete time of the present" with their spoken descriptions "automatically being relegated to the past in which they occurred and which their words try to reconstitute" (498). Similarly, by alternating

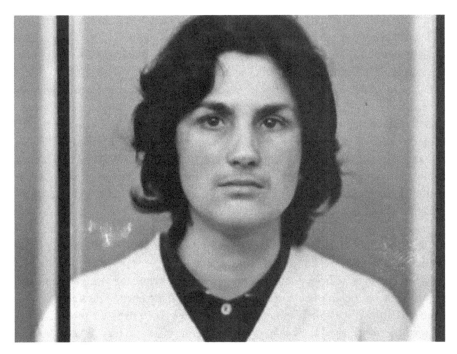

Figure 5.8 A fingerprint on Conceição Mátos's portrait marks the material history of its usage in the prison in *48* (Susana de Sousa Dias, 2009).

the present faces of the former prisoners with their prison identification photographs, these archival images would suffer a reduction to the mere illustration of the past. These parallel diminutions would counter the entire project of the film, which sought "to bring viewers face to face with the political prisoner" through "the co-presence of multiple and heterogeneous temporalities."[44] As viewers listen to the soundtrack their relationship to the image shifts among several potential positions. The former prisoners alternate between what de Sousa Dias calls "perception and memory," which is to say, between talking about the photographic object that is before them in the present moment of their interview with de Sousa Dias and responding to the photographic image as an incitement to bear witness, an aide-memoire, which envisions the prisoner's traumatic experience of torture well beyond the photograph's visible threshold. For example, Mátos begins her segment of the film by situating the moment when the identification photo was taken (Video 5.3 ⓹). She notes that it was seventeen days after arrest that her picture was finally taken at PIDE headquarters. She comments on aspects of her physical appearance in the picture, such as her hairstyle and the hairy lip that she had developed during her incarceration. But then she begins to elaborate the circumstances of the brutal interrogation that followed by Inspector Tinoco, who proclaimed, "Well, from here it's either the morgue or the mental hospital." Mátos vividly describes how her interrogators forced her to urinate, defecate, menstruate, and vomit in her cell, after which she was forced to strip, and her clothing was used to clean up her bodily excretions. She then specifically notes that it was the very clothes she is wearing in the mugshot that they used.

Such a mental image as the one Mátos verbally describes constitutes the true space of testimony, in which the witness brings their traumatic experience into a presence that is shared with the listener. As Dori Laub contends, "the listener to trauma comes to be a participant and a co-owner of the traumatic event: through his very listening, he comes to partially experience trauma in himself."[45] Yet the persistent iconic presence of the prisoner's face looking directly back at the viewer prevents such delicate dynamics of bearing witness from degrading into mere vicarious identification with the traumatized subject. The viewer of *48* remains in a face-to-face visual encounter with an other, whose facial expression presents a mask of affective displacement, pointing to a truth that remains elsewhere beyond the frame. In his testimony, Antonio Dias Lourenço mentions that the PIDE officers loved to see pain on prisoners' faces, so he maintained a perpetual mask before the camera: "From me, they did not get the pleasure of seeing a tortured face." By pursing his lips, he developed a habitual expression of contempt for the state's repressive gaze (manifested in his tormentors' eyes and their camera). For the film's viewer to read the resistance in this returned look is also to potentially recognize their own implication in the perpetrator's gaze at the prisoner. There are even moments in *48* when former prisoners cannot even recognize themselves in their prison identification photographs. For instance, Antonio Gerváso admits at the beginning of his segment, "That's funny, this one I do not know. I don't remember ever having my hair like that. I would not be able to recognize me. Oh no" (Figure 5.9). In that instant, the former prisoner momentarily sees himself through the perpetrator's gaze, but as an unrecognizable other.

In combination with her application of camera movements to the photographic portraits, de Sousa Dias understands the film's soundtrack as enabling a "montage in temporal depth."[46] The surface of the photographic image is penetrated by the supplement of recorded speech, which entails language, sound, and duration. It thus opens up the photographs to the act of watching. If watching photography reinscribes the dimensions of duration and movement into the interpretation of the still photograph, then *48* thereby permits its viewers to contemplate the "montage of heterogeneous viewpoints" that participate in the temporally and spatially manifold event of photography.[47] Moreover, the material traces of use inscribed on the photographs point to their bureaucratic circulation within PIDE files passing before many eyes of the security state, but also to their contemporary circulation as photographic objects within the context of de Sousa Dias's film: her investigative gaze in the archive, the former prisoner's testifying gaze in interview and the film viewer's listening gaze (as the recipient of the mediated act of witness). If the iconic presence of the prisoners' faces binds these multiple gazes and temporalities together within the experience of watching these photographs through the film, their foregrounded materiality ensures

This one I don't remember.

Figure 5.9 Antonio Gerváso does not recall anything about this mugshot of him in *48* (Susana de Sousa Dias, 2009).

that we recognize their historicity as visual objects, while the voiceover soundtrack facilitates our spectatorial mobility across different positions and temporalities in relation to the faces on screen.

However, the significance of sound in *48* exceeds the testimonial discourse offered by the former prisoner. De Sousa Dias has noted the film's explicit interest in paralinguistic communication—voice as gesture—as critical to the prisoners' capacity to bear witness to the trauma of torture. In the editing room, she paid careful and precise attention to "repetitions, hesitations and pauses, as well as all the sounds occurring parallel to the discourse (sighs, groans, different cadences of breathing, intonation, modulation)."[48] Since testimony emerges, as Laub explains, from the "black hole" of silence and the impossibility of speaking trauma, enunciative difficulties and challenges are as integral to the true articulation of traumatic experience as successfully realized narrativization.[49] Fulfilling the listener's role in testimony, de Sousa Dias respects such silence by permitting the audience of *48* ample time to listen to the presence of the former prisoner before they first speak in their segment. In addition to the sounds of their breathing body, we hear their haptic engagement with their surrounding space (the rustle of their clothes, their handling of the photographs they're discussing and the sounds of their body occupying a seat) as well as various environmental sounds (such as the street noise outside their home). Rather than close-miking the prisoners during interview, de Sousa Dias placed a microphone in front of them, enabling the construction of an auditory space of encounter with the listening viewer. "Just by resorting to sound," claims de Sousa Dias, "the viewer can have a more physical and sensorial perception of the witness."[50] Such auditory presence (that is separated from image) generates a "being with" that can traverse spatial and temporal difference on the one hand, while engendering a paradoxical absence-presence on the other—a contradiction amplified by the soundtrack's interaction with the uncanny animation of the prison mugshots.

48 concludes by addressing the question of how to watch prison identification photographs that are no longer extant. In her research, de Sousa Dias discovered that all the prison photographs taken in Portuguese colonies had been destroyed after the end of the Salazar regime. Torture perpetrated by the security services was far more brutal in the colonies than the metropole, which thus cast an ethical dilemma for her: how to adequately represent the infinitely greater "black hole" of colonial atrocity? De Sousa Dias includes interviews with two former prisoners in Mozambique, Amós Mahanjane, and Matias Mboa, whose testimonies are dominated by the pervasion of death in the colonial prison, where sickness ran rampant, and murder by torture was a regular occurrence. Unable to show their lost prison portraits, de Sousa Dias presents a black screen on which specks of light glimmer momentarily before disappearing again into the darkness. At various points, the edge of a white frame, a vertical scratch, and a couple of hairs appear on the black screen, suggesting the material surface of a projected film (inverted to a negative image). This subtly haptic image resists figuration until a roving light illuminates a wire fence and a twisted tree trunk at night in the foreground of the image while the background remains pitch black (Figure 5.10). Taking Portuguese military surveillance film that scanned the perimeters of an army camp for the presence of African guerilla fighters, de Sousa Dias transforms its signification of terrorist threat from the unseen insurgent in the night to a visual allegory of the threshold of visibility for the colonial violence being testified to on the soundtrack.

The threshold of visibility constitutes one of the film's central preoccupations. What can be done with such an archive of compelled portraits to make present what the photographs occlude, namely the systematic torture of their subjects? Moreover, how can film allow us to see beyond the rigid institutional signification of the mugshot, to encounter the iconic presence of the prisoner? De Sousa Dias addresses these challenges by placing the viewer in a cinematic present constructed from multiple temporalities across sound and image. Its unspooling duration provides sufficient time to visually contemplate the photographic portrait beyond its original signification, allowing its iconic presence to be felt by the viewer (abetted by the film's uncanny animation of the still images). At the same time, the viewer senses the auditory copresence of the former prisoners as they pry traumatic memory from their engagement with those same images.

Screams... Dilacerating.

Figure 5.10 Stills from Portuguese military surveillance footage stands in for the aporia of the discarded identification photographs in the Portuguese colonies in *48* (Susana de Sousa Dias, 2009).

Playing with Iconic Presence in Public Space

The collaborative art practices of the French artist JR draw significantly on both the iconic presence of photographic portraiture and the materiality of the photographic object. JR's consistent production of documentary films about his projects evolves from his longstanding preoccupation with documentation; he began his street art in the early 2000s by photographically documenting himself and his fellow graffiti artists at work and then pasting the photocopied pictures on the streets of Paris, which he dubbed *Expos 2 Rue* (*Sidewalk Galleries*). His turn to portraiture in his next project, *28 Millimeters: Portrait of a Generation* (2004), would establish the foundations of his collaborative practice for the following decade. Using a 28mm wide-angle lens, he shot close-up portraits of young people from Les Bosquets, one of the many impoverished and socially marginalized *banlieues* that French politicians and media in the mid-2000s had pathologized as gang-ridden, immigrant ghettos filled with "*la racaille*" (rabble).[51] The wide-angle lens required JR to get really close to his photographic subjects, to come face-to-face with them, which thus necessitated the cultivation of trust and collaboration between photographer and subject. JR asked his subjects to ham it up, to pull funny faces, and to caricature themselves before the camera. Finding agency in appropriation and self-distortion (which is amplified by the wide-angle lens), they project back a parodic mimicry of the clichés that construct their representation in news media and political discourse. The portraits evoke the visual frame of an identification photograph in their stark frontality, "isolated in a shallow, contained space."[52] They lie somewhere between wild parodies of the mugshot and the kind of playful self-presentation adopted in casual photobooth portraits. Although photobooths were originally developed to produce cheap identification photographs that were demanded by the institutions of the twentieth-century state, they were quickly appropriated and subverted as a popular recreational "tool for experimental self-fashioning."[53] It is hardly surprising that JR converted six vans into portable photobooths for the *Inside Out* project, which were able to generate large single posters of their subjects (rather than a strip of miniature portraits). Magnification is indeed one of JR's central aesthetic strategies. Beginning with *Portrait of a Generation*, he has blown up his collaborators' portraits into large, and sometimes massive, black-and-white posters, which he then pastes in public spaces within their communities and beyond (for *Portrait of a Generation* he posted them not only in the banlieues but also bourgeois districts of central Paris). JR adapted and expanded these techniques in his subsequent projects, such as *Women are Heroes* (2008–9), which focused on empowering women in conflict zones around the world, and *Wrinkles of the City* (2010–13), which foregrounded the lives of the elderly in diverse urban landscapes in Havana, Shanghai, Los Angeles, Istanbul, and Berlin.

JR's method is grounded in the local materiality of face-to-face encounters. Deliberately avoiding the support of sponsors, government agencies, or NGOs, he seeks collaborators and participants for his projects through on-the-ground meetings and encounters.[54] His aesthetic practice intervenes in the dense visual field of urban space through a visual distinction between his images and the outsized faces seen on advertising billboards and political posters. Graphically, the monochrome images stand out in whatever setting they are pasted. Moreover, in their bare simplicity as closely cropped photographic portraits, they lack the framing words, symbols, or graphics that bind faces to particular ideological messages in advertisements, election posters, and public portraits of authoritarian leaders. Without language to anchor signification, JR's facial portraits encourage viewers to respond to their iconic presence. As Petra Eckhard contends, they also invert the invasive aesthetics of social documentary by allowing the marginalized subject to raid public space, to claim presence there: "Rather than staging (or aestheticizing) the urban poor within their 'typical' environments of poverty or war, JR's portraits are reduced to facial close-ups, which are only added a physical backdrop when pasted onto the city's architecture."[55] Through his production of massively scaled photographic images and application of them directly onto the irregular surfaces of architectural structures (including walls, roofs, stairs, and towers), JR transforms landscapes into portraits.[56] Like other street artists who wish to reclaim urban space from private corporate interests, JR treats the entire material structure of the city as "a projection surface" on which a genuinely public, but highly ephemeral, visual space can be formed.[57]

JR's outsized but simple anonymous portraits offer the iconic presence of the face as ethical address in Emmanuel Levinas's sense: unique and infinite, the face as pure alterity rather than binary otherness.[58] JR's street art thus shares in the "ethical turn" that art historian Claire Bishop argues is a key quality of contemporary participatory art practices.[59] Situating participatory art within the historical context of neoliberalism, identity politics, and global human-rights discourse, Bishop remains skeptical of such a turn in which "an ethics of interpersonal interaction comes to prevail over a politics of social justice" (25). Moreover, Jennifer Orpana asks if the group actions of JR's *Inside Out* project have "the potential to capture how thoroughly entwined neoliberalism and its contestations are."[60] She reads *Inside Out* in relation to post-Keynesian political strategies that situate the responsibility of wellbeing onto the private individual and creative city agendas that have appropriated the celebration of diversity as a response to neoliberal austerity measures. Other critics, such as Bertie Ferdman, have argued, by contrast, that the power of *Inside Out* lies precisely in its critical engagement with the urban visual regime under neoliberalism: "*Inside Out*'s urban dramaturgy plays with the structure, rhythm, and flow of the city, via mediated performance practices, to enact new stories of what our cities are and for whom."[61] This art project thus both tactically reclaims privatized urban space as a temporary mise-en-scène for true public encounters and relocates the public performance of self within collective, community-building action.

The emphatic iconic presence of faces, unattached to any immediate framing message, functions as an empowering affirmation of self-presence for the portraits' subjects and as a lure for onlookers who must ask: who are they and why are they here? JR understands this dual impact to be central to his street art. His collaborators claim sovereignty of their own image in the space of their community, while the transformed landscape inspires visitors, such as journalists, to investigate the nature of this visual interruption of public space.[62] After installing "Women Are Heroes" in Morro da Providencia, the oldest *favela* in Rio de Janeiro, in August 2008, JR quickly vanished, forcing journalists to engage with the participants from the favela community.[63] Rooted in his origins in street art, JR has constructed an artist persona that is, at once, an instantly recognizable character and a disappearing figure. His fedora and sunglasses serve as a mask, which both characterizes and disguises him.[64] JR's justifications for his mask always point to the risks involved in the illegal aspects of his practice, which thus require his continued visual disguise. However, another reason remains unstated: keeping his own face masked keeps attention on the iconic presence of the faces in his photographic portraits. JR continually walks the tightrope of the Warholian conundrum: how to exploit the very means that construct the modern discourse of the artist in the service of actually disrupting its normative function in late capitalism? The *Inside Out* project is his most sustained attempt to square that circle.

With *Inside Out*, JR stepped away from the processes of taking the photographs and installing them in public space. Instead, he invited anyone in the world to take up his aesthetic practice for their own specific goals and provided them with the technological means of reproduction to realize their own "group actions," which would "convey a message or a cause that you are passionate about."[65] Any group of five or more people could upload portraits to the *Inside Out* website and within several weeks receive large printed posters of their photographs.[66] The project guidelines maintain the aesthetic continuity with JR's previous projects: single, closely cropped expressive faces with flat, abstract backgrounds.[67] In the decade since its launch in March 2011, *Inside Out* has produced posters of more than 400,000 participants for over 1,800 projects in 138 countries, making it the world's largest-ever global participatory art project.[68] Like all of JR's major projects, *Inside Out* is structured by a number of dialectic tensions: between the local and the global, between the embodiment of human encounter and the mediation of representation, between the ephemerality of the event and the posterity of documentation, and between the unifying aesthetic method of the artist and the infinitely diverse application of it by the project's participants.

Documentation of JR's installations is a crucial and integral component of the projects themselves. First, it creates a visual document of artworks that may be extremely ephemeral and last only a very short period due to weather-related erosion or to deliberate removal by property owners, the state, or opponents of the project. Second, it presents visual perspectives that may have been inaccessible to those physically present at the sites of installation, such as extreme long shots that capture the project's transformation of the cityscape from a distance. Third, it illuminates the global dimensions of each project by bringing into view the resonances among the various local group actions. Fourth, it permits the encounters engendered by the project to be witnessed by far more people than those who were physically present at the site during the life of the action. Like other contemporary street art, diverse forms of documentation constitute significant aspects of the mediation of JR's projects.[69] Documentation permits the project to be global and virtual as well as local and material. JR produces it on five different platforms: the fine-art prints that provide the principal funding for his practice; photobook publication by major art presses; his comprehensive website; his social media accounts, particularly Instagram; and the documentary films that his production company Social Animals have made for every project since *Women Are Heroes*.

Inside Out has generated diverse forms of documentation that served different functions as the project developed, including in a photobook published in 2017, a video-wall installation in the Brooklyn Museum's 2019 JR retrospective exhibition, and a website revamped several times over the past decade (the 2021 update includes comprehensive documentation of every group action) (Figures 5.11–5.12).[70] Following the first local group action, *Artocratie en Tunisie* (*Artocracy in Tunisia*), which took place immediately after the 2011 revolution, Social Animals produced a thirteen-minute short film about it to help promote the *Inside Out* project online. Within three months, a photobook documenting the Tunisian group action was co-published in Paris and Tunis, which included the black-and-white portraits, photographic documentation of the installations, and short personal essays by the organizers.[71] As the number of

Figure 5.11 A video-wall installation of the Inside Out project in the Brooklyn Museum's 2019 JR retrospective exhibition (photo: Roger Hallas).

Figure 5.12 2021 redesign of the Inside Out website.

local projects grew across the globe, the project website hosted a selection of short video documentation produced by the organizers of group actions.[72] Premiered at the Tribeca Film Festival and later broadcast on HBO, Alastair Siddons's seventy-minute documentary film *Inside Out: The People's Art Project* (2013) provides significantly more aesthetic and political contextualization for the project than the short videos. Moreover, it consistently articulates the vision of JR's project through his relationship with his collaborators. For instance, the pre-title sequence presents JR's TED Prize speech in which he first publicly announced the *Inside Out* project in Long Beach, California, but it is introduced and narrated in voiceover by members of Teleghetto Haiti, a guerilla media collective, which collaborated on the *Inside Out* project in Port au Prince (Figure 5.13). Embodying the reversal of the mediated gaze that is central to Teleghetto's tactics on the ground in post-quake Haiti (which involve "cameras" constructed from discarded plastic oil cans), it is the postcolonial periphery that gets to introduce and frame the European-American center.[73] Similarly, when JR returns to his studio in Paris, we hear his telephone conversation with Ladj Ly, one of JR's earliest collaborators in Les Bousquets and the subject of his first well-known image (in which Ly points a camcorder at JR's camera as though it were a gun). Ly is the one to skeptically ask, "Do you really believe it will work?"

Although the documentary includes brief footage and photographs of *Inside Out* projects in many different sites across the globe, it devotes most screen time to just three sites: Tunisia (2011), Port au Prince (2012), and Standing Rock, North Dakota (2011).[74] Tunisia garners the greatest attention for several reasons. It was the very first manifestation of *Inside Out*, undertaken only weeks after the revolution, thus providing an already dramatic setting. Although JR's own Tunisian family background may have motivated his interest in being personally involved in this project, the documentary never mentions this context. The revolution and its aftermath are initially framed in the documentary through two sets of portraits. First, we witness the grainy cell-phone footage of a massive poster of President Zine El Abidine Ben Ali being ripped from the wall of a fort in La Goulette, a wealthy suburb of Tunis (Figure 5.14).

Figure 5.13 The guerilla media collective Teleghetto Haiti introduces the footage of JR's 2011 TED Prize speech in *Inside Out* (Alistair Siddons, 2013).

Figure 5.14 Cellphone footage of the iconoclastic destruction of a massive poster of President Zine El Abidine Ben Ali during the Tunisian Revolution in *Inside Out* (Alistair Siddons, 2013).

This iconoclastic action was understood as a key symbolic event in the early days of the revolution. Then, amid the ruins of an abandoned and looted police station in La Goulette, Aziz Tnani and Serine Nazer, two Tunisian photographers, peruse the thousands of discarded police files and identification photographs scattered across the floor, as they reflect upon the permanent state of surveillance endured by Tunisian society for decades (Figure 5.15). In the Tunisian regime, both forms of portraiture served as tools of state surveillance at different ends of the shadow archive; the iconic presence of Ben Ali's image dominated public space while the identification photographs in the police records criminalized a whole society outside of public view. It is within this fraught visual terrain of revolutionary iconoclasm that the Tunisian *Inside Out* project would take place. Over a montage of Tnani, Nazer, and other photographers shooting close-up portraits of ordinary Tunisians on the street, Tnani and Sophia Baraket explain their aim of replacing the dictator's singular image with faces of the Tunisian people in all their diverse multitude, a counter visuality that would be replicated in different ways and by different people in subsequent Arab revolutions across the region.[75] Later in the sequence, we hear JR joke with the Tunisian photographers about the dictatorship preselecting the best walls for the project and the revolution clearing space for its posters.

While JR's photographs of the finished installations published in *Artocratie en Tunisie* record how the group action transformed the visual landscape of postrevolutionary Tunis, it is Siddons's documentary film that is best able to capture the project's installation as an *event*, a complicated encounter between people on the street and anonymous portraits in highly charged public space. At first, the camera

Look at all the photos

Figure 5.15 Tunisian photographers Aziz Tnani and Serine Nazer peruse thousands of abandoned police files in *Inside Out* (Alistair Siddons, 2013).

captures the euphoric sense of individual and collective empowerment among those pasting the posters. As one of the participants notes, "Who'd have thought that one day we could touch these walls." Such excitement extends beyond the recently won ability to experience in public space the iconic presence of ordinary Tunisians rather than that of the dictator. This moment is as much about touch as sight. Close-ups and oblique camera angles draw attention to the material surface of the pasted walls as hands carefully smooth out the creases of the paper (Figure 5.16). The tactility of paper and glue binds the people to the wall—and each other—in this collective act of spatial appropriation and co-creation. In fact, JR has repeatedly invoked "the power of paper and glue" as central to his aesthetic practice—he mentioned it in his TED Prize talk that opens *Inside Out*, and it provides the title of his 2021 documentary film about his work.[76]

Gradually the focus of the Tunis sequence shifts from the participants to the passersby who have spontaneously encountered the installations (Video 5.4 ▶). The initial responses are positive: "It's great that Tunisians can find themselves in these images." But dissent also begins to grow in the gathering crowds (Figure 5.17). At the highly politicized site in La Goulette, where Ben Ali's towering image had been torn from the wall, several older Tunisians challenge the photographers who have organized the project, asking whether the faces on the wall are martyrs or political candidates. Refusing or failing to recognize the portraits' iconic presence, they insist on identifying what specific meaning these faces signify. Suspicion is expressed that outsiders are imposing a new visual regime, an understandable concern given the long history of state surveillance in Tunisia.[77] When the photographers claim that the faces represent the Tunisian people, a man counters that the Tunisian map or flag

Figure 5.16 *Inside Out* (Alistair Siddons, 2013) draws attention to haptic encounter with photographic images as participants smooth out paper and glue on the wall.

Figure 5.17 Dissent grows toward the pasting as the first day progresses in *Inside Out* (Alistair Siddons, 2013).

would serve as better images of the nation. In the tense iconoclastic mood of post-revolutionary Tunisia, even the mere faces of ordinary citizens are caught in the long shadow of the dictatorship's visual regime. Intercutting across the three main installation sites of the first day emphasizes the mounting hostility toward the project from local residents who claim ownership of public space appropriated by the project and accuse the organizers and participants of not being Tunisian. As menacing crowds assemble around the installations shouting accusations at the participants, the tactile engagement with the portraits abruptly shifts to an aggressive tearing away of the posters. After the crowds have left, the camera dwells on the remaining fragments of the posters left on the walls. Iconoclastic violence has failed to completely destroy the iconic presence of the portraits and ironically even subtly enhances it, giving the faces the appearance of tenaciously peeking through the remaining fragments of the poster (Figure 5.18). On their drive home at dusk, photographers Tnani and Nazer recount how the crowd started to throw stones at them, turning its violent response from the images to the participants themselves.

Despondent at the violent rejection of their postrevolutionary countervisuality, the photographers confer over how to proceed the following day. While Tzani suggests finding quieter places away from densely populated neighborhoods in order to avoid the threat of violence reactions, JR argues for doubling down on their original target, the iconic Porte de France on the edge of the Medina, which he insists they could paste in an hour and a half during the middle of the night. JR wins out, and the rapid overnight installation is presented in fast-motion cinematography. As the morning begins, local men congregate around the monument, contemplating the multitude of faces before them. Photographer Sophia Baraket defends the project against the suspicions and questions raised by the onlookers in a debate that is rigorous but good-humored (Figure 5.19) The men begin to tear off pieces of the posters, but without the aggressive affect of the previous day; they do it silently, patiently, and methodically. These moments of literal iconoclasm provide stark reminders of Azoulay's assertion that no party within the civil contract of photography has complete control over the claims to be made by the image. The scene concludes with a bystander who comments (in French): "Some Tunisians felt free to paste pictures up. And others feel free to destroy what was pasted. That's democracy. We are now free to enjoy this."[78] Even

Figure 5.18 Fragments of the torn posters retain some sense of iconic presence in *Inside Out* (Alistair Siddons, 2013).

You can't just tear them down
without a thought

Figure 5.19 Photographer Sophia Baraket defends the project to a group of men who want to remove it at the Porte de France in *Inside Out* (Alistair Siddons, 2013).

though the iconoclastic response of many Tunisians clearly upsets the local organizers of the project, the documentary ultimately frames the event as a brand new, if short-lived, public space of political freedom in post-revolutionary Tunisia. The final images of Tunisia are not the torn remains of the project, but the material ruins of the dictatorship enlivened by the iconic presence of ordinary Tunisians: a young boy's smiling face is pasted over a Ben Midi poster on the ransacked headquarters of the former ruling party; massive piercing eyes envelop several burnt-out vehicles; a middle-aged man's inquisitive glance presides over the abandoned police files and identification photographs seen earlier in the film.

If the scenes devoted to Tunisia permit the film to document the often tense relations between the photographers and the local community, the scenes in Port au Prince focus primarily on the relationship between the project organizers and the participants, who are mostly members of Teleghetto. The collective's co-founder, Jean-Pierre Romel, explains the rationale of its combative stance: "We started it as a response to the invasion of foreign camera crews. We use images like a weapon." Teleghetto then interrogates Mackenley Benoit, a local photographer who organized the *Inside Out* group action in Port au Prince, about the question of visual sovereignty: "You came here, and we gave you our faces. But what will Haiti get out of it?" The documentary concludes with a rather playful argument between Romel and JR about the significance of *Inside Out* as Romel is installing a massive pair of eyes on the side of a building and JR serves as his assistant (Figure 5.20). Romel taunts JR with the idea of losing his authorship: "So JR, if you give away all your secrets, then you'll have nothing left to offer." JR counters that this is precisely the idea of *Inside Out*: "No longer a secret, but a movement." As they're climbing down through the rubble, Romel teases JR about his supposed irrelevance: "Now we feel so involved,

Figure 5.20 While pasting a massive pair of eyes in Port au Prince, JR and participant Romel playfully discuss the meaning of the project in *Inside Out* (Alistair Siddons, 2013).

we've forgotten JR. Sorry, my friend." Imitating the visual style of JR's own photographic documentation, the final shot before the end credits lingers on the completed installation of the giant pair of eyes staring out across the cityscape, while Romel affirms in voiceover the visual sovereignty they have achieved: "We prefer the project. JR is just a person. But *Inside Out* is the thing.... We're inside and you're out." Just as in the beginning of the film, the hierarchies between center and periphery have been inverted through Teleghetto's playful reframing of the project's title. The documentary thus best articulates the very ethos of the project, not in JR's words, but in the words of those who have made it their own. This concluding scene reiterates how *Inside Out*, like JR's practice in general, involves a materially ephemeral play with iconic presence in public space. Documentary film is crucially able to record, preserve, and disseminate how affective responses to such iconic presence are transformed into social and political discourse by collaborators and those who encounter the visual intervention into public space.

The three films in this chapter document engagements with photographic portraits, recording what filmmakers and artists *do with* them rather than merely *represent through* them. A dynamic relationship between the portraits' iconic presence and their materiality as photographic objects is critical to each of the encounters captured within the documentaries. Iconic presence is grounded in a conceptualization of the image as a presentation rather than a representation.[79] It is not a matter of what the image signifies—the signified behind the signifier—but what form of presence it engenders in the moment of its reception as an encounter between image and viewer. Portraits are particularly imbued with the potentiality of iconic presence due to the alignment between the visual address of the image and that of its subject—photographic portraits even more so given their embalmment of the present moment. Both *S21* and *48* appropriate photographic portraits whose original functions were bound to specifically defined forms of signification: identification, categorization, criminalization. In staging encounters between prison mugshots and perpetrators (in *S21*) and victims (in *48*), Panh and de Sousa Dias create the conditions in which the iconic presence of the portraits can stimulate acts of bearing witness to atrocity. In *S21* the former guards begin to enact genuine testimony when they engage with the portraits of the victims not merely as the visual evidence of their dehumanization and extermination but as their iconic presence persisting beyond death. In *48* the encounter with the iconic presence of their own former selves enables the victims of the PIDE to bear witness to that which the photographs themselves explicitly occlude, namely their torture.

Whereas *S21* draws on the observational affordance of documentary film to render an experience of being present to the space and time of the encounter with photographic portraits in the Tuol Sleng prison, *48* exploits film's capacity to construct its own effect of cinematic presence from the editing together of sounds and images recorded in diverse times and spaces. Viewers of *48* do not watch the victims' encounter with their own prison mugshots as a profilmic event but rather are situated within a cinematic present constructed from the multiple temporalities of the film's sounds and images. Thus, the experimental form of *48* positions its viewers directly in an encounter with the portraits' iconic presence. De Sousa Dias mitigates against this opportunity lapsing into a vicarious, dehistoricized, and ethically compromised identification with the victim-survivor by maintaining visual attention to the materiality of the mugshots as photographic objects bearing the physical traces of their historical use and circulation. Similarly, Panh places considerable emphasis on the mugshots as photographic objects with material histories. Although Panh's film works to redeem the portraits from the repressive tradition so that their iconic presence may stimulate perpetrator testimony, this transformation avoids the dehistoricizing universal humanism so often applied to these particular photographs in their transnational circulation as icons of atrocity. The film's redemption of these mugshots occurs within their very historicization, not beyond it.

If *S21* and *48* deploy the materiality of the photographic object to register its accrued history, its endurance across time, *Inside Out* attends to the very opposite: the material ephemerality of the photographic portraits in JR's global art project. Participants and bystanders are seen to engage with the portraits' iconic presence in public space in profoundly haptic ways—participants lovingly applying paper and glue to walls with their hands and some bystanders aggressively tearing off damp shards of these recently pasted photographs. Material ephemerality is key to JR's aesthetic practice as the contingent encounters generated by the creation and public installation of the portraits constitute the core of the work rather than the photographs themselves, which will perish within a relatively short period of time. With documentation a crucial aspect of his practice since he began, JR relies on documentary film to preserve and disseminate at least fragments of such encounters. Like de Sousa Dias and Panh, what JR does with photographic portraits in *Inside Out* is to facilitate encounters with them that mobilize their iconic presence, not to merely dwell in the affective responses it generates, but to facilitate the transformation of such affect into a public discourse on social justice, collective memory, and other political issues raised by the historical circumstances of the local action.

Conclusion

As the chapters of this book have shown, documentary film's engagement with photography extends well beyond the incorporation of photographs as indexical evidence and visual illustration. However, even in that respect, media makers, such as Forensic Architecture, have developed new frameworks for presenting photographic evidence in documentary that rely on the extravisual dimensions of digital materiality (such as metadata) as much as the indexicality of the image itself. Although most popular and academic attention to photography continues to prioritize the individual photograph and the photographer, documentary films demonstrate a capacity to illuminate the complex relations that constitute photography, even when the filmmaker's approach is conventionally authorial and hermeneutic. The deployment of cinematic elements in documentary film—namely mise-en-scène, cinematography, editing, and sound—recognizes photography not only as an aesthetic practice, but also as a social, cultural, and political one. These formal elements foreground the relational qualities of the medium in several ways: mise-en-scène highlights the camera and the photograph as social objects that mediate relations between the participants of photography; cinematography both supplements the temporal experience of a photograph with a layer of mediated duration and permits us to observe the relations engendered by photography in their duration; editing relates the diverse times and spaces of the event of photography, connecting photographer, photographed, camera, photograph, and viewer; and sound resituates photography, particularly of the vernacular variety, within social relations mediated through oral communication.

My argument about documentary film's affordance for seeing (and hearing) photography otherwise draws on theoretical frameworks grounded in anthropological and political conceptions of photography's relationality. The work of Elizabeth Edwards, Christopher Pinney, and Geoffrey Batchen constructs an anthropology of the photographic object as a mediating agent within social relations, whereas Ariella Azoulay's conceptualization of the event of photography posits the medium as negotiating political relations among its participants rather than constructing political meaning within the photographic image itself. As *Picturing Derry* amply demonstrates, the lines between social and political relations often overlap in provocative and revealing ways. Ultimately, what both frameworks share is a fundamental turn away from the question of defining the photographic image to asking what people do with photography and what forms of relation it enables—a shift from ontology to performativity. Documentary film is particularly well suited to elaborating these latter endeavors because its observational capacity to record profilmic time, space, and sound in a dimensional richness permits it to capture multisensory encounters with

A Medium Seen Otherwise. Roger Hallas, Oxford University Press. © Oxford University Press 2023.
DOI: 10.1093/oso/9780190057763.003.0007

cameras and photographs, which produce the relations of photography. Moreover, in its alternation between presentation and representation, the documentary itself becomes a platform on which people can do things with photography. The double gaze between photographic and cinematic modes of seeing the world when watching photographs (and cameras) on film facilitates the creative treatment of *intermediality* in multiple ways, including, as I have elaborated in the previous chapters, intermedial ambiguity, aesthetic mimicry, and iconic presence.

A medium seen otherwise works in both directions, for it is not only photography that comes to be seen in a different light, but also documentary film. Intermedial studies of cinema have primarily attended to fictional narrative and experimental film, yet documentary is arguably just as intermedial, if not more so, than these other modes of film. The "creative treatment" invoked by Grierson's seminal definition of documentary very much includes its propensity toward intermedial incorporation. Documentary film's inscription of photography provides a case in point. It does not merely reproduce the photograph's indexical claim on actuality; rather it positions the photograph within an intermedial frame that is able to center multisensorial experience, particularly touch and hearing, and emphasize the dynamics of presentation and presence over representation.

The reconceptualization of photography in terms of these three dynamics—the event of photography over the singular photographic image, performance over ontology, and presentation over representation—has moreover become key to theories of photography in the age of social media, what Nathan Jurgenson has dubbed "social photography."[1] Digital photography's embedding within the electronic networks of social media has proliferated the continuities and discontinuities between analog and digital photography. With cameras playing such a significant function within the smartphone, photography becomes ever-more integrated into everyday life and its diverse activities; it has turned into a ubiquitous medium.[2] Smartphones are single devices that incorporate "the whole process" of photography for the first time, from capture to edit to dissemination to consumption.[3] The immediacy and instantaneity of production, distribution, and consumption of the networked image transforms photography into almost a live medium, in which images are circulated on networks as simultaneous expressions of presence, albeit always in different visual flows given the algorithmic control of image feeds in most social media applications. Photography thus moves from being a mode of commemoration and preservation to a mode of visual communication. The selfie arguably constitutes the quintessential social photograph since it "points to the performance of a communicative action rather than to an object, and it is a trace of that performance." As Paul Frosh further explains, "It says not only 'see this, here, now,' but also 'see me showing you me.' "[4] In that sense, "it is not necessarily about performing identities," argues Martin Hand, "but rather meeting the *basic needs of social recognition*."[5]

Given documentary film's proven capacity to illuminate what people do with photography, how has it engaged with these most recent transformations generated by social photography? Despite the use of a few new visual tropes to convey the user's

Figure 6.1 Ben (Skyler Gisondo) immerses himself in the visual flow of social media in *The Social Dilemma* (Jeff Orlowski, 2020).

immersion into an image flow rather than the durational contemplation of individual images (Figure 6.1), documentaries that address social photography have been surprisingly conventional on a visual level. They tend to prioritize talking-head interviews over examination of image flows or observation of social-media behavior. For instance, Jonathan Ignatius Green's documentary *Social Animals* (2018) about Instagram focuses on interviews with three subjects, two who have become Instagram influencers and one who experienced high-school bullying through the application. Jeff Orlowski's Netflix feature documentary *The Social Dilemma* (2020) and Erica Jenkin's BBC program *The Instagram Effect* (2022) are both dominated by the perspectives of former high-level employees of the major social-media companies, who warn of the broad-ranging social and political dangers of the algorithms and machine-learning that ground the digital architecture of social-media platforms.[6] Their discourse of the exposé is reinforced by visualizations of a fundamentally nonvisual process, the algorithmic sorting of posts in social-media feeds. Whereas *The Instagram Effect* uses animation to illustrate AI researcher Josh Simon's explanation of the algorithmic process (Figure 6.2), *The Social Dilemma* employs the sci-fi trope of a fictional user, Ben (Skyler Gisondo), as avatar, whose choices are controlled by three algorithmic logics (growth, engagement, and monetization) all personified by actor Vincent Kartheiser (most famous for his *Mad Men* role).

A notable exception to this generic conventionality is Ukrainian director Sergei Loznitsa's *Austerlitz* (2016), a slow observational documentary about Holocaust tourism at the Dachau and Sachsenhausen concentration camps. In static, black-and-white long takes, shot in the glaring summer sun, Loznitsa's camera impassively observes the behavior of tourists circulating through the camps. For most of the film, the object of their gazes is kept offscreen, focusing our attention on their multisensory engagement with the camp. We watch hordes of tourists file through the different spaces of the camp clutching audio and visual protheses (audio guides, cameras, and smartphones). Although the audio guide aims to teach them historical knowledge of

Figure 6.2 Animation illustrates the process of algorithmic sorting of a user's Instagram feed in *The Instagram Effect* (Erika Jenkin, 2022).

Figure 6.3 Tourists taking "Shoah selfies" at the Sachsenhausen concentration camp gate in *Austerlitz* (Sergei Loznitsa, 2016).

the camp, it also standardizes the tourists' experience into a fixed itinerary of points to be digested rather than as an unimaginable and unrepresentable event to be contemplated in all its impossibility. Moreover, the film's attenuated deployment of the observational mode gives us time to follow the gestures of the "Shoah selfie" in great detail (Figure 6.3). (Video ▶).[7] Watching this behavior closely reveals a paradox at the heart of so-called dark tourism: if social photography functions to communicate presence on the part of the photographer—a necessary requirement for the act of bearing witness to historical trauma—then the act of photographing also produces a filter through which to domesticate, tame, or even evade the confrontation with genocide. In his sustained deployment of one of cinema's foundational capacities—to observe the world in continuous time—Loznitsa demonstrates how documentary film can still provide meaningful tools for seeing the rapid, ongoing transformations of photography otherwise.

Notes

Introduction

1. See Annemarie Hürlimann and Alois Martin Müller, eds., *Film Stills: Emotions Made in Hollywood* (Ostfildern: Hatje Cantz, 1993); Steven Jacobs, "The History and Aesthetics of the Classical Film Still," *History of Photography* 34, no. 4 (2010): 373–86; Jan Baetens, *The Film Photonovel: A Cultural History of Forgotten Adaptations* (Austin: University of Texas Press, 2019); Gusztáv Hámos, Katja Pratschke, and Thomas Tode, eds., *Viva Fotofilm: Bewegt/Unbewegt* (Marburg: Schüren Verlag, 2009).
2. For a discussion of photography's use in the webdocumentary, see my essay, Roger Hallas, "Photojournalism, NGOs, and the New Media Ecology," in *Sensible Politics: The Visual Culture of Nongovernmental Activism*, ed. Meg McLagan and Yates McKee (New York: Zone Books, 2012), 94–114.
3. See Alain Bergala, "Magnum Meets the Cinema," in *Magnum Cinema: Photographs from 50 Years of Movie-making* (London: Phaidon, 1995), 7–19; and George Kouvaros, *Famous Faces Yet Not Themselves: The Misfits and Icons of Postwar America* (Minneapolis: University of Minnesota Press, 2010) which examines the agency's acclaimed multi-photographer assignment on the set of John Huston's *The Misfits*.
4. Documentaries about Magnum include *The Magnum Story* (Patricia Wheatley and Rosemary Bowen-Jones, 1989), *Magnum Photos: The Changing of a Myth* (Reiner Holzeimer, 1999), and *Cinema Through the Eye of Magnum* (Sophie Bassaler, 2017). In 1992, the agency commissioned *The Magnum Eye*, a series of seven short films by its photographers. Magnum collaborated with *Cahiers du cinéma* and Phaidon on *Magnum Cinema: Photographs from 50 Years of Movie-making* (1995) and with the National Cinema Museum in Turin on *Magnum Photographers on Film Sets* (2011). In 2007, Diane Dufour and Serge Toubiana curated the exhibition about Magnum photographers, *The Image to Come: How Cinema Inspires Photographers*, at the Cinémathèque Française. Magnum launched the webdocumentary platform *Magnum in Motion* in 2006.
5. David Green, "Marking Time: Photography, Film, and Temporalities of the Image," in *Stillness and Time: Photography and the Moving Image*, ed. David Green and Joanna Lowry (Brighton: Photoworks, 2006), 9–21.
6. Jürgen E. Müller, "Intermediality and Media Historiography in the Digital Era," *Acta Universitatis Sapientiae, Film and Media Studies* 2 (2010): 15–38, here 15. The International Society for Intermedial Studies was founded in 1996 and is based in Sweden. Romanian film scholar Ágnes Pethő's book *Cinema and Intermediality: The Passion for the In-Between* (Newcastle: Cambridge Scholars Press, 2011) was a key transitional text for developing the concept within film studies, while Ana M. López's article, "Calling for Intermediality," *Cinema Journal* 54, vol. 1 (2014): 135–41, urged wider engagement with intermediality by film scholars. Edinburgh University Press launched its series *Edinburgh Studies in Film and Intermediality* in 2015.
7. Müller, "Intermediality and Media Historiography," 18.

8. Lars Elleström, "The Modalities of Media: A Model for Understanding Intermedial Relations," in *Media Borders, Multimodality, and Intermediality*, ed. Lars Elleström (London: Palgrave Macmillan, 2010), 11–48, here 12.

9. Marion Schmid, *Intermedial Dialogues: The French New Wave and the Other Arts* (Edinburgh: Edinburgh University Press, 2019), 166.

10. See Jonathan Crary, *Techniques of the Observer: On Vision and Modernity in the 19th Century* (Cambridge, MA: MIT Press, 1992); Friedrich Kittler, *Film, Gramophone, Typewriter*, trans. Geoffrey Winthrop-Young and Michael Wutz (Stanford: Stanford University Press, 1999); Leo Charney and Vanessa Schwartz, eds., *Cinema and the Invention of Modern Life* (Berkeley: University of California Press, 1996); and Alison Griffiths, *Shivers Down Your Spine: Cinema, Museums, and the Immersive View* (New York: Columbia University Press, 2008).

11. See Laurent Guido and Olivier Lugon, eds., *Between Still and Moving Images* (New Barnet: John Libbey, 2012); David Campany, *Photography and Cinema* (London: Reaktion Books, 2008); Karen Beckman and Jean Ma, eds., *Still Moving: Between Cinema and Photography* (Durham, NC: Duke University Press, 2008); Brianne Cohen and Alexander Streitberger, eds., *The Photofilmic: Entangled Images in Contemporary Art and Visual Culture* (Leuven: Leuven University Press, 2016); Neil Campbell and Alfredo Cramerotti, eds., *Photocinema: The Creative Edges of Photography and Film* (Bristol: Intellect, 2013); Eivind Rossaak, ed., *Between Stillness and Motion: Film, Photography, Algorithms* (Amsterdam: University of Amsterdam Press, 2011); Damian Sutton, *Photography, Cinema, Memory: The Crystal Image of Time* (Minneapolis: University of Minnesota Press, 2009); David Green and Joanna Lowry, eds., *Stillness and Time* (Brighton: Photoworks, 2006); and Philippe Dubois, *Photographie & Cinéma: De la différence à la l'indistinction* (Sesto San Giovanni: Édition Mimésis, 2021).

12. David Campany, "Introduction: When to Be Fast? When to Be Slow?," in *The Cinematic*, ed. David Campany (London: Whitechapel, 2007), 10–17, here 16.

13. See Brian Winston, *Claiming the Real II: Documentary: Grierson and Beyond* (London: Palgrave Macmillan, 2008), 14.

14. For a summary of these debates within documentary photography, see Ian Walker, "The Problematic Possibilities of Documentary," in *A Companion to Photography*, ed. Stephen Bull (Oxford: Wiley Blackwell, 2020), 371–91.

15. Philippe Dubois, "Photography *Mise-en-Film*: Autobiographical (Hi)stories and Psychic Apparatuses," trans. Lynne Kirby, in *Fugitive Images: From Photography to Video*, ed. Patrice Petro. Bloomington: Indiana University Press, 1995), 152–73, here 152–3 (emphasis in original).

16. Garrett Stewart, *Between Film and Screen: Modernism's Photo Synthesis* (Chicago: University of Chicago Press, 1999), 10.

17. Raymond Bellour, "The Pensive Spectator," in *The Cinematic*, ed. David Company (London: Whitechapel, 2007), 119–23, here 120.

18. The only book in English devoted to the subject is Libby Saxton's *No Power Without an Image: Icons Between Photography and Film* (Edinburgh: Edinburgh University Press, 2020).

19. Haneke creates a similar ambiguity between sound and image in the credit sequence of *Caché (Hidden)* (2005) when we hear the unlocatable voices of Juliette Binoche and Daniel Auteuil over a static long take of a Parisian residential street, but the film ultimately

explains the relationship between their voice and the image when it reveals the long take to be a surveillance tape that they are watching on their television screen.

20. Later in the film, we witness Georges use a hidden camera to surreptitiously photograph fellow passengers on the Paris Metro. The black-and-white photographs subsequently presented directly to the viewer are also documentary photographs taken by Delahaye, which he published in the book *L'Autre* (London: Phaidon, 1999).

21. Bill Nichols, *Representing Reality: Issues in Documentary Representation* (Bloomington: Indiana University Press, 1991), 19.

22. Jaimie Baron, *The Archive Effect: Found Footage and the Audiovisual Experience of History* (New York: Routledge, 2014), 7.

23. Marion Schmid makes a similar point in her study of photography in French New Wave feature films and documentaries. See *Intermedial Dialogues*, 166.

24. Tory Jeffay, "Flat Out Formalism: *Strong Island* as Trans of Color Critique," *New Review of Film and Television Studies* 19, no. 2 (2021): 217–38, here 234.

25. See Edward Dimendberg, "Transfiguring the Urban Gray: László Moholy-Nagy's Film Scenario 'Dynamic of The Metropolis,'" in *Camera Obscura, Camera Lucida: Essays in Honor of Annette Michelson*, ed. Richard Allen and Malcolm Turvey (Amsterdam: University of Amsterdam Press, 2003), 109–26.

26. Campany, "Introduction," 13.

27. The sequence ends with several studio photographs of romantic couples, which Campany reads as the implication that "the itinerant photographer was replacing the formal studio." Campany, *Photography and Cinema*, 54.

28. Roland Barthes, *Camera Lucida: Reflections on Photography*, trans. Richard Howard (New York: Hill and Wang, 1981), 115.

29. I understand vernacular photography according to Clément Chéroux's definition as that which is "utilitarian, domestic, or popular": "It is generally understood as ordinary or mundane, tied to everyday life. Indeed, many vernacular images, such as those taken by amateurs, fit this definition. Many others, however, are rather out of the ordinary: postmortem photographs, medical images, or car accident pictures, to name a few. Consequently, the vernacular cannot be narrowly aligned with the ordinary. Vernacular photography constitutes a much larger body, one that includes family snapshots alongside photographs produced by scientists, the police, the military, insurance agents, studio operators, and photo booths. It encompasses press release photographs, fashion and wedding photographs, ID pictures, photographic objects, and many other applications of the photographic medium." "Introducing Werner Kühler," in *Imagining Everyday Life: Engagements with Vernacular Photography*, ed. Tina M. Campt, Marianne Hirsch, Gil Hochberg, and Brian Wallis (New York and Göttingen: The Walther Collection and Steidl, 2020), 22–32, here 24–5.

30. A comprehensive history of the photography documentary has yet to be written. Although this book aims to identify and analyze key aspects of the genre, it cannot offer complete coverage of the full diversity of the genre.

31. Roger Hallas, "Introduction," in *Documenting the Visual Arts*, ed. Roger Hallas (London: Routledge, 2020), 1–20, here 2.

32. See Elizabeth Edwards, "Objects of Affect: Photography Beyond the Image," *Annual Review of Anthropology* 41 (2012): 221–34; Christopher Pinney, *Camera Indica: The Social Life of Indian Photographs* (London: Reaktion, 1997); Elspeth H. Brown and Thy

Phu, *Feeling Photography* (Durham: Duke University Press, 2014); and Geoffrey Batchen, "Vernacular Photographies," *History of Photography* 24, no. 3 (2000): 262–71.

33. Batchen, *Photography's Objects* (Albuquerque: University of New Mexico Art Museum, 1997), 3.
34. Elizabeth Edwards and Janice Hart, "Introduction: Photographs as Objects," in *Photographs, Objects, Histories: On the Materiality of Images*, ed. Elizabeth Edwards and Janice Hart (New York: Routledge, 2004), 3.
35. Elizabeth Edwards, "The Thingness of Photographs," in *A Companion to Photography*, ed. Stephen Bull (Hoboken, NJ: John Wiley, 2020), 97–112, here 100. She borrows the term from Erving Goffman.
36. Margaret Olin, *Touching Photographs* (Chicago: University of Chicago Press, 2012), 17 (emphasis in original).
37. See Martha Langford, *Suspended Conversations: The Afterlife of Memory in Photographic Albums* (Montreal: McGill-Queen's University Press, 2001).
38. Edwards, "The Thingness of Photographs," 103.
39. Ariella Azoulay, *The Civil Imagination: A Political Ontology of Photography* (New York: Verso, 2012), 14.
40. Ariella Azoulay, "What Is a Photograph? What Is Photography?," *Philosophy of Photography* 1, no. 1 (2010): 9–13, here 11.
41. Ariella Azoulay, *The Civil Contract of Photography* (New York: Zone Books, 2008), 130.
42. Azoulay, *The Civil Imagination*, 18.
43. Azoulay further insists that the event of photography occurs even in the mere hypothetical presence of the camera or the hypothetical existence of the photograph since it is constituted as a set of relations rather than the necessary production of a finished photograph. See *The Civil Imagination*, 18–25.
44. Kristen Lubben, "An Interview with Susan Meiselas," in *Susan Meiselas: In History*, ed. Kristen Lubben (New York and Göttingen: International Center of Photography/Steidl, 2008), 12–20, 115–21, 239–47, here 116.
45. Martha Rosler, "Wars and Metaphors," in *Decoys and Disruptions: Selected Writings, 1975–2001* (Cambridge, MA: MIT Press, 2004), 245–58.
46. Drake Stutesman, "Connectivity: An Interview with Susan Meiselas," *Framework: The Journal of Cinema and Media* 51, no. 1 (2010): 61–78, here 65.
47. Elizabeth Edwards, "Thinking Photography beyond the Visual?," in *Photography: Theoretical Snapshots*, ed. J. J. Long, Andrea Noble, and Edward Welch (London: Routledge, 2009), 31–48, here 42.
48. Aside from my discussion of the fabled 1932 photograph, "Lunch atop a Skyscraper," in Chapter 1, I do not address documentaries about specific iconic photographs. Libby Saxton's *No Power Without an Image* has covered this subject extensively.
49. Sekula, "The Body and the Archive," *October 39* (1986): 3–64.
50. Hans Belting, "Image, Medium, Body," *Critical Inquiry* 31, no. 2 (2005): 302–19, here 312.

Chapter 1

1. Fatimah Tobing Rony discusses the fundamental ambivalence of that smile: "The enigma of Nanook's smile allows the audience to project its own cultural presuppositions: from the point of the view of an outsider he is childlike, from the Inuit point of view he may be

seen as laughing at the camera." *The Third Eye: Race, Cinema and Ethnographic Spectacle* (Durham, NC: Duke University Press, 1996), 111.

2. Steven Jacobs, *Framing Pictures: Film and the Visual Arts* (Edinburgh: Edinburgh University Press, 2011), 3. Jacobs provides an extensive critical assessment of these films and their significance to postwar cultural politics.

3. For example, see Luciano Emmer's *Racconto da un affresco* (1938) about Giotto's murals in Padua, Henri Stork's *The World of Paul Delvaux* (1946), and Alain Resnais's *Van Gogh* (1948).

4. Jacobs, *Framing Pictures*, 6.

5. André Bazin, *What Is Cinema?*, Vol. 1 (Berkeley: University of California Press, 1967, 1971), 166.

6. These oppositions are extensively analyzed in the most significant scholarship on the film: Richard Raskin, *Nuit et Brouillard by Alain Resnais: On the Making, Reception and Functions of a Major Documentary Film* (Aarhus: Aarhus University Press, 1987); Sylvie Lindeperg, "*Night and Fog*": *A Film in History*, trans. Tom Mas. (Minneapolis: University of Minnesota Press, 2014); Emma Wilson, "Material Remains: *Night and Fog*," *October*, no. 112 (2005): 89–110; Andrew Hebard, "Disruptive Histories: Toward a Radical Politics of Remembrance in Alain Resnais's *Night and Fog*," no. 71 (1997): 87–113; Sandy Flitterman-Lewis, "Documenting the Ineffable: Terror and Memory in Alain Resnais's *Night and Fog*." In *Documenting the Documentary: Close Readings of Documentary Film and Video*, ed. Barry Keith Grant and Jeannette Sloniowksi (Detroit: Wayne State University, 1998), 204–22; and Griselda Pollock and Max Silverman, *Concentrationary Cinema: Aesthetics as Political Resistance in Alain Resnais's Night and Fog* (New York: Berghahn Books, 2010). For a discussion of the film's role in the emergence of the essay film, see Timothy Corrigan, *The Essay Film: From Montaigne, After Marker* (Oxford: Oxford University Press, 2011); Paul Arthur, "Essay Questions" *Film Comment* 39, no. 1 (2003): 58–62; Philip Lopate, "In Search of the Centaur," in *Beyond the Document: Essays on Nonfiction Film*, ed. Charles Warren (Middleton, CT: Wesleyan University Press, 1996), 243–70; and Rascaroli, *The Personal Camera: Subjective Camera and the Essay Film* (New York: Wallflower Press, 2009).

7. Flitterman-Lewis, "Documenting the Ineffable," 214. Other scholars have read the camera with its roving movement as an investigator or an embodiment of transience and oblivion. See Wilson, "Material Remains," 96, fn. 31.

8. The translations of the French voiceover are from the Criterion Collection DVD of the film released in 2003.

9. Lindeperg, "Night and Fog," 97.

10. However, a number of the of the black-and-white shots were filmed by Resnais's crew, while several others were taken from Wanda Jakubowska 's fictional narrative film *The Last Stop* (1948).

11. Lindeperg emphasizes the need to recognize that our contemporary perception of such diverse archival sources as historically distinct from the period when Resnais was making *Night and Fog*: "Despite the brief time lapse between them, these two generations of images can no longer be considered interchangeable. Aside from showing two distinct events, they also present two radically opposed views of the camps: that of the criminals (and sometimes their victims) and that of the witnesses who arrived after the fact. Today these two points of view strike us as irreconcilable into a single moment of seeing" ("Night and Fog," 101).

12. Lindeperg, "Night and Fog," 60.

13. Vincent Pinel quoted in Lindeperg, "Night and Fog," 97.

14. For a discussion of the film's aesthetic and rhetorical deployment of traumatic form, see Joshua Hirsch, *Afterimage: Film, Trauma and the Holocaust* (Philadelphia: Temple University Press, 2003), 28–62.

15. Resnais modifies this rhetorical structure in a following sequence of film footage of the deportation trains from the Dutch internment camp at Westerbork. This extremely rare documentation of the deportation process from internment camps to extermination camps is presented without commentary. The richness of its visual detail must wordlessly bear the weight of representing all deportations to the extermination camps.

16. Michael Berkowitz, *The Crime of My Very Existence: Nazism and the Myth of Jewish Criminality.* (Berkeley: University of California Press, 2007), 103–5.

17. The shooting script published by Richard Raskin indicates the image to be a photograph from the Auschwitz Museum (Raskin, 105), yet the visual qualities of the shot appear closer to the black-and-white film footage that Resnais shot at Auschwitz. All subsequent identification of shots in the film I derive from Raskin's book.

18. One aspect of generational loss in technological reproduction of a photographic image is subtle flattening of the image.

19. Wilson, "Material Remains," 107.

20. For the definite account of these photographs, see Georges Didi Huberman, *Images in Spite of All: Four Photographs from Auschwitz*, trans. Shane B. Lillis (Chicago: University of Chicago Press, 2008).

21. Wilson, "Material Remains," 102.

22. Rascaroli, *The Personal Camera*, 35.

23. Corrigan, *The Essay Film*, 63.

24. The initial proclamation of the group asserted, "Next to the novel and other extensive works, there is the poem, the short story, or the essay, which often plays the role of a hothouse; it has the function of revitalizing a field with the contribution of fresh blood. The short film has the same role. Its death will also be the death of film, since an art that ceases to change is dead art." Quoted in Nora Alter, *Chris Marker* (Urbana: University of Illinois Press, 2006), 14.

25. Corrigan, *The Essay Film*, 68. Published in 1958, Theodor Adorno's "Der Essay als Form" (The Essay as Form) defines the essay in relation to these dual characteristics and several of the seminal attempts to define the essay film draw from Adorno's argument. See Corrigan, *The Essay Film*, 23; and Nora Alter, "Translating the Essay into Film and Installation," 47–9.

26. Varda would make several documentaries explicitly about photography later in her career: *Ulysse* (1982), a short film that contemplates a striking photograph she took in 1954 of a naked man and a dead goat on a beach; *One Image for One Minute* (*Une Minute Pour Un Image*, 1983), a series of television shorts each commenting on a single photograph; and *Ydessa, The Bears and Etc* (2004), which examines Canadian artist and collector Ydessa Hendeles' family-photograph installation *Partners (The Teddy Bear Project)*. Marker engaged extensively with photography in his CD-ROM project *Immemory* (1997) and his exhibition and book *Staring Back* (2007).

27. See Steven Ungar, "Quality Wars: The Groupe des Trente and the Renewal of the Short Subject in France, 1953–1963," *South Central Review* 33, no. 2 (2016): 30–43.

28. See Campany, *Photography and Cinema*, 74–82.

29. The slide projector would contribute even more significantly to intermedial dynamics in the late 1960s and early 1970s when it was taken up by artists working performance art, installation art, and expanded cinema. See Darsie Alexander, ed., *Slide Show: Projected Images in Contemporary Art* (University Park: Penn State University Press, 2005).
30. For a history of the genre, see Hámos et al., *Viva Fotofilm*.
31. Yuriko Furuhata, *Cinema of Actuality: Japanese Avant-Garde Filmmaking in the Season of Image Politics* (Durham, NC: Duke University Press, 2013), 25.
32. Although 16mm cameras introduced a level of mobility and accessibility that would facilitate direct cinema and *cinéma vérité* in this period, 35mm photographic cameras were still far more flexible tools for documenting the world. As Varda notes about making *Salut les Cubains*, she chose to take photo cameras to avoid "lugging around 16mm equipment." Sarah Moroz, "Socialism and cha-cha-cha," *The Guardian*, December 10, 2015, https://www.theguardian.com/artanddesign/2015/dec/10/agnes-varda-photographs-cuba-salut-les-cubains.
33. In an interview published in 2015, Varda noted, "In the general energy, I saw 'socialism and cha-cha-cha.' This element of dance is in the Cuban temperament. It's easy to say, but it's true. I was in the Soviet Union and other communist countries and it was different. It wasn't happy at all." Karolina Ziebinska-Lewandowska, "Socialisme et cha-cha-cha," in *Varda/Cuba*, ed. Clément Chéroux and Karolina Ziebinska-Lewandowska (Paris: Editions du Centre Pompidou, 2015), 7–12, here 9 (my translation).
34. Jane Gaines, "Political Mimesis," in *Collecting Visible Evidence*, ed. Jane M. Gaines and Michael Renov (Minneapolis: University of Minnesota Press, 1999), 84–102, here 91.
35. Valérie Vignaux, "*Salut les Cubains* d'Agnès Varda ou cinécriture et cinema politique," in *Varda/Cuba*, ed. Clément Chéroux and Karolina Ziebinska-Lewandowska (Paris: Editions du Centre Pompidou, 2015), 147–51, here 149.
36. Delphine Bénézet, *The Cinema of Agnès Varda* (New York: Wallflower Press, 2014), 2.
37. The film's title is a wry reference to *Salut les copains*, a French magazine about pop stars launched in the early 1960s. See Crista Blümlinger, "Postcards in Agnès Varda's Cinema," in *Between Still and Moving Images*, ed. Laurent Guido and Olivier Lugon, (New Barnet: John Libbey, 2012), 275–89, here 284.
38. Catherine Lupton reads this as a thematic divide between culture and nature. See *Chris Marker*, 104.
39. Jan Christopher Horak, *Making Images Move: Photographers and Avant Garde Cinema* (Washington, DC: Smithsonian Institution, 1997), 45.
40. Susan Sontag, *On Photography* (New York: Farrar, Straus, and Giroux, 1977), 153–80.
41. Tom Daly, "The Still Photo in Cinema," *Pot Pourri* (Summer 1977): 2–4, 4.
42. Jones writes, "The films contain an organic wholeness, a certain aesthetic integrity that avoids the imposition of forced connections to some larger issue, some greater relevance. But the avoidance of explicit relevance does not mean that these films were esoteric or trivial. Their popularity was enormous, and still is. These films did not *refer* to a wider world, but *spoke* to the wider world through their integrity of structure and material, or style and content. Perhaps their aim and effect were to find the universal in the particular." David Jones, "The Canadian Film Board Unit B," in *New Challenges for Documentary*, ed. Alan Rosenthal and John Corner, 2nd ed. (Manchester: Manchester University Press, 2005), 79–93, here 87–8.

43. William Bluem, *Documentary in American Television* (New York: Hastings House, 1965), 141.

44. Philip J. Lane coined the phrase "still-in-motion" to describe camera movement over still photographs in his dissertation, "NBC-TV's Project 20: An Analysis of the Art of the Still-in-Motion Film in Television."

45. Donald Hyatt quoted in Bluem, *Documentary in American Television*, 159.

46. Tom Roston, *Ken Burns: The Kindle Singles Interview* (Amazon Services, 2014), 390.

47. *The Civil War* would be referenced and parodied multiple times during the early 1990s, including on episodes of *Twin Peaks*, *Saturday Night Live*, and *thirtysomething* during the 1990–1 television season.

48. See Mikel Vause, "Capturing the American Experience: A Conversation with Ken Burns." *The Contemporary West* 23, no. 1 (2006), and Randy Kennedy, "The Still-Life Mentor to a Filmmaking Generation," *New York Times*, October 19, 2006.

49. Roston, *Ken Burns*, 395.

50. Gary R. Edgerton, *Ken Burns's America: Packaging the Past for Television* (New York: Palgrave Macmillan, 2001), 36.

51. Lucia Ricciardelli, *American Documentary Filmmaking in the Digital Age: Depictions of War in Burns, Moore, and Morris* (New York: Routledge, 2014), 90.

52. John C. Tibbetts, "The Incredible Stillness of Being," *American Studies* 37, no. 1 (1996): 117–33, here 129.

53. Anthony W. Lee and Elizabeth Young, *On Alexander Gardner's Photographic Sketch Book of the Civil War* (Berkeley: University of California Press, 2008), 29.

54. Tibbetts also draws a parallel between Burns and Gardner by reading the former in relation to Miles Orvell's argument that American documentary representation in the nineteenth century, such as Gardner's book, prioritized rhetorically convincing effect over factual accuracy. Tibbetts, "The Incredible Stillness of Being," 130.

55. David Thelen, "The Movie Maker as Historian: Conversations with Ken Burns," *Journal of American History* 81, no. 3 (1994): 1031–50, here 1037.

56. Jeanie Attie, "Illusions of History," *Radical History Review* 52 (1992): 95–104, here 97–100. For the range of perspectives among historians in the critical debate on the series, see Robert Brent Toplin, *Ken Burns's The Civil War* (New York: Oxford University Press, 1996).

57. Tibbetts, "The Incredible Stillness of Being," 126.

58. Roston, *Ken Burns*, 375.

59. Judith Lancioni, "The Rhetoric of the Frame: Revisioning Archival Photographs in *The Civil War*." *Western Journal of Communication* 60, no. 4 (1996): 397–414, here 401.

60. When presenting ambrotype and tintype portraits, the series does allow the accompanying metal frame to appear, but these are always partial views and we never see the whole object.

61. Although Brady's company produced stereoscopic images, this photograph was taken by French photographer Marc Antoine Gaudin in 1860.

62. The voiceover erroneously attributes the spoken commentary to Oliver Wendell Holmes. The oft-quoted text derives however from an anonymous *New York Times* review published on October 20, 1862.

63. The black mattes also invoke public rituals of mourning that drape images of the dead in black.

64. Alan Trachtenberg, *Reading American Photographs: Images as History, Matthew Brady to Walker Evans* (New York: Hill and Wang, 1990), 85. See also Cara A. Finnegan, *Making Photography Matter: A Viewer's History from the Civil War to the Great Depression* (Urbana: University of Illinois Press, 2015), 19–27.

65. Attie also criticizes the series for largely excluding important elements of the visual culture of the war, such as wood engravings, cartoons, and lithographs. See Attie, "Illusions of History," 101.

66. Allan Sekula, "Reading an Archive: Photography Between Labour and Capital," in *Photography/Politics: Two*, ed. Patricia Holland, Jo Spence, and Simon Watney (London: Commedia, 1986), 153–61, here 155 (emphasis in original).

67. Patricia Thomson, "Sundance 2002: New Directions: 'The Kid Stays in the Picture,'" *American Cinematographer* 83, no. 4 (2002): 102–6, here 103.

68. For example, Jun Diaz, "Moving Pictures: Creating Multiplane Animation from Photographs," *DV 11*, no. 5 (2003): 26–32; and Greg Gilpatrick, "Manipulated Reality: *The Kid Stays in the Picture*," *Independent Film and Video Monthly* 25, no. 5 (2002): 45–6.

69. John Caldwell, *Televisuality: Style, Crisis and Authority in American Television* (New Brunswick: Rutgers University Press, 1995).

70. Other documentaries about single iconic photographs include *Chevolution* (Trisha Ziff and Luis Lopez, 2008) about the life of Korda's *Guerrillero Heroico* photograph of Che Guevara; *Search for the Afghan Girl* (Lawrence Cumbo Jr, 2003) about Steve Curry's 1984 *National Geographic* cover shot of a young Afghan girl; and *Kim's Story: The Road from Vietnam* (Shelley Saywell, 1997) and *Das Mädchen und das Foto* (*The Girl and the Photo*, Marc Wiese, 2010) about Nick Ut's famous photograph of Kim Phúc fleeing a napalm attack during the Vietnam war.

71. For a vigorous critique of the film's ideological framework, see Darragh O'Donoghue, "Home Video: *Men at Lunch*." *Cineaste* 39, no. 3 (2014): 67–9.

72. Denis Murphy suggests that the film's substantive Irish funding likely motivated the inclusion of this dubious story line. "*Men at Lunch/Lónsa Spéir* (Seán Ó Cualáin, 2012)." *Estudios Irlandeses* 8 (2013). http://www.estudiosirlandeses.org/reviews/men-at-lunch-lonsaspeir-sean-o-cualain-2012/.

73. The differentiation between positive parallax (enhanced depth with the frame) and negative parallax (the perception of elements in the space between the screen and viewer) have become central to the critical and theoretical assessment of stereoscopic 3D cinema. See Barbara Klinger, "Beyond Cheap Thrills: 3D Cinema Today, the Parallax Debates, and the 'Pop Out,'" in *3D Cinema and Beyond*, ed. Dan Adler, Janine Marchessault, and Sanja Obradovic (Toronto: Public Books, 2013), 186–99.

Chapter 2

1. Batchen, "Vernacular Photographies," 262. Although the term "photographic object" was used earlier in Peter Bunnell's acclaimed 1970 MOMA exhibition, *Photography as Sculpture*, to define three-dimensional photographic artworks that challenged prevailing assumptions about the medium, my use of the term aligns with Batchen's concern with the objecthood of vernacular photographs. For a comprehensive account of Burrell's show, see Mary Statzer, *The Photographic Object, 1970* (Berkeley: University of California Press, 2016).

2. See Lev Manovich, *The Language of New Media* (Cambridge, MA: MIT Press, 2001), 27–30.

3. Eyal Weizman, "On Forensic Architecture: A Conversation with Eyal Weizman," *October*, no. 156 (2016): 116–40, here 125.

4. Elizabeth Edwards, "Objects of Affect: Photography Beyond the Image," *Annual Review of Anthropology* 41 (2012): 221–34, here 224.

5. See Mieke Bal, "Visual Essentialism and the Object of Visual Culture," *Journal of Visual Culture 2*, no. 1 (2003): 5–32, and W. J. T. Mitchell, "There Are No Visual Media," *Journal of Visual Culture* 4, no. 2 (2005): 257–66.

6. Batchen, "Vernacular Photographies," 263.

7. Edwards, "Objects of Affect," 228.

8. Elizabeth Edwards and Janice Heart, "Introduction," in *Photographs, Objects, Histories: On the Materiality of Images* (New York: Routledge, 2004), 4.

9. Edwards, "Objects of Affect," 224.

10. Manovich, *The Language of New Media*, 45–8.

11. Nicholas Negroponte, *Being Digital* (New York: Knopf, 1995), 14.

12. For example, Joanna Drucker, "Digital Ontologies: The Ideality of Form in/and Code Storage: Or: Can Graphesis Challenge Mathesis?," *Leonardo* 34, no. 2 (2001): 141–5; N. Katherine Hayles, "Translating Media: Why We Should Rethink Textuality," *Yale Journal of Criticism* 16, no. 2 (2003): 263–90; and Matthew G. Kirschenbaum, *Mechanisms: New Media and the Forensic Imagination* (Cambridge, MA: MIT Press, 2008).

13. Kirschenbaum, *Mechanisms*, 10–15.

14. Kirschenbaum cautions against wholly aligning forensic materiality with hardware and formal materiality with software, citing the blurred boundaries that constitute firmware (programmable hardware). Ibid. 13.

15. Langford, *Suspended Conversations*, 22–39.

16. See Mikolaj Jazdon, "Starring Photos: On Polish Iconographic Films Made from Photos," *Kwartalnik Filmowy* (2013): 140–58, here 141–4. Jazdon argues that these two films initiated what would become "a living tradition" in Polish cinema of documentaries based on wartime photographs.

17. Jazdon's translation, 143.

18. Jazdon, 143. See also Frances Guerin, *Through Amateur Eyes: Film and Photography in Nazi Germany* (Minneapolis: University of Minnesota Press, 2012), 75–6; Petra Bopp, "Images of Violence in *Wehrmacht* Soldiers' Private Photo Albums," in *Violence and Visibility in Modern History*, ed. Jürgen Martschukat and Silvan Niedermeier (New York: Palgrave, 2013), 181–97, here 181–5.

19. See Guerin, *Through Amateur Eyes*, 85–93.

20. I have been able to identify him as Gerhard Marquardt from an official report by the Berliner Landesbeauftragten für die Unterlagen des Staatssicherheitsdienstes der ehemaligen DDR (Berlin State Commission on the Stasi Documents). See Jörg Rudolph, Frank Drauschke, and Alexander Sachse, *Hingerichtet in Moskau: Opfer des Stalinismus aus Berlin 1950–1953* (Berlin: Der Landesbeauftragter für die Stasi-Unterlagen, 2007), 107. Although many of those convicted and executed by the Soviet military tribunals of the early 1950s were victims of a Stalinist purge of East German political dissidents and were subsequently rehabilitated posthumously, Marquardt was not. Gedrovich's decision to systematically obscure any visual reference to his full name functions both to respect the privacy of his family and to render his story more generally representative of Wehrmacht soldiers' experience.

21. Sylvie Lindeberg argues that Jaubert's film ultimately meditates on "the complex status of photography, the strength and the fragility, the absence at the heart of the visible, and the political motivation of the gaze." Sylvie Lindeberg, "The Strange Twentieth-Century Album." *L'Atalante: International Film Studies Journal* 12 (2011): 20–7, here 25.

22. For more detailed analysis of the full range of aesthetic devices that Jablonski used to challenge to the occlusion of violence in Genewein's images, see Guerin, *Through Amateur Eyes*, 151–7.

23. Alec Wilkinson, "Picturing Auschwitz," *New Yorker*, March 17, 2008, 48–55.

24. Critical debate has centered largely around Farocki's female-voiced commentary that speculates on the motivations behind the looks of both the SS photographer and the Jewish woman in the photograph: "The photographer has his camera installed and as the woman passes by, he clicks the shutter—in the same way he would cast a glance at her in the street, because she is beautiful. The woman understands how to pose her face so as to catch the eye of the photographer, and how to look with a slight sideways glance." Whereas Nora Alter questions what she sees as the commentary's sentimental over-narrativization, Kaja Silverman defends it by arguing that the dynamics of the male gaze pervade even within the structure of the concentration camp. See Alter, "The Political Im/Perceptible in the Essay Film: Farocki's *Images of the World and the Inscription of War,*" *New German Critique* 68 (1996): 165–92, and Kaja Silverman, *The Threshold of the Visible World* (New York: Routledge, 1996), 153.

25. In a close reading of Farocki's wide-ranging rhetorical use of hands in his work, Volker Pankenberg concludes, "the hand stands for the concrete and individual in contrast to the interchangeable and abstract rhythm of machines." Volker Pankenberg, *Farocki/Godard: Film as Theory* (Amsterdam: University of Amsterdam Press, 2015), 223.

26. These devices can be seen in Bitomsky's historical documentaries about Nazi-era Germany, *Deutschlandbilder (Images of Germany,* 1983) and *Reichsautobahn* (1986), as well as his essay films about cinema, *Das Kino und der Tod (Cinema and Death,* 1988) and *Das Kino und der Wind und die Photographie (Cinema and the Wind and Photography,* 1991). In the latter films, Bitomsky further defamiliarized the moving image by discussing film scenes through use of printed frame captures.

27. See Patricia Holland, Jo Spence, and Simon Watney, eds., *Photography/Politics Two* (London: Commedia, 1986); Victor Burgin, ed., *Thinking Photography* (London: Macmillan, 1982); and the journal *Camerawork* (1976–85).

28. Trisha Ziff, "Photographs at War," in *The Media and Northern Ireland,* ed. Bill Rolston (London: Macmillan, 1991), 189.

29. All six of the photographers Adam interviewed were male.

30. Faction Films, "Producing a Picture," in *Photography/Politics Two,* eds. Holland, Spence, and Watney, 133.

31. *Memory Pictures* explores the photographic work of British-Indian photographer Sunil Gupta, and *Looking for Langston* offers "A Meditation on Langston Hughes and the Harlem Renaissance" through a range of texts and images, including the photographs of James Van Der Zee, George Platt Lynes, and Robert Mapplethorpe.

32. Patricia Zimmermann, *States of Emergency: Documentaries, Wars, Democracies* (Minneapolis: University of Minnesota Press, 2000), 65.

33. Catherine Grant outlines this shift in the movement's deployment of photographs: "The aesthetic emphasis in the campaigns shifted, then, from the relatively straightforward

indexical function of the photographs ('Here pinned to my body is a picture of *my* daughter who has been 'disappeared': where is she?') toward an ever greater *iconic* significance ('Here are *masses* of photographs of all the disappeared children of our nation, criminally taken in the prime of their lives: where are they?')." Catherine Grant, "Still Moving Images: Photographs and the Disappeared in Films about the 'Dirty War' in Argentina," in *Phototextualities: Intersections of Photography and Narrative*, ed. Alex Hughes and Andrea Noble (Albuquerque: University of New Mexico Press, 2003), 63–86, here 68.

34. Diana Taylor writes, "Wearing the images like a second skin highlighted the affiliative relationship that the military tried to annihilate. The Madres created an epidermal, layered image, superimposing the faces of their loved ones on themselves. These bodies, the images make clear, were connected—genetically, affiliatively and now, of course, politically." *The Archive and the Repertoire: Performing Cultural Memory in the Americas* (Durham, NC: Duke University Press, 2003), 178.

35. Taylor, *The Archive and the Repertoire*, 176–7.

36. Barthes, *Camera Lucida*, 76–7.

37. Kris Fallon, "Archives Analog and Digital: Errol Morris and Documentary Film in the Digital Age," *Screen* 54, no. 1 (2013): 20–43, here 35.

38. Bill Nichols, "Feelings of Revulsion and the Limits of Academic Discourse," *Jump Cut* 52 (2010).

39. Linda Williams, "Cluster Fuck: The Forcible Frame in Errol Morris's *Standard Operating Procedure*," *Camera Obscura 25*, no. 1 (2010): 28–67, here 58–9.

40. See respectively, Williams, "Cluster Fuck," 32; Caetlin Benson-Allott, "*Standard Operating Procedure*: Mediating Torture," *Film Quarterly 64*, no. 4 (2009): 39–44, here 41–3; and Fallon, "Archives Analog and Digital," 36–40.

41. Williams, "Cluster Fuck," 32.

42. As Matilde Nardelli contends, digital photographs on screen have a duration: an image file can be open, closed, queued, or latent (for example, when the screensaver kicks in). Matilde Nardelli, "End(u)ring Photography," *Photographies* 5, no. 2 (2012): 159–77, here 161.

43. Frances Guerin outlines the continuities between the Abu Ghraib and Wehrmacht photographs as amateur images: "For example, both sets of images were never meant to be released to the world. They were private images of daily events made for a community of soldiers and their friends and families at home.... the Abu Ghraib photographs were reportedly used in the exact same manner as those taken by German soldiers in World War II: as keepsakes, passed around by soldiers to other soldiers within the unit as a document of their activities." Frances Guerin, "The Ambiguity of Amateur Photography in Modern Warfare," *New Literary History* 48, no. 1 (2017): 53–74, here 66–7.

44. Fallon, "Archives Analog and Digital," 37.

45. Errol Morris's Interrotron apparatus permits the filmmaker and subject to exchange direct eye contact through a synchronized two-camera setup, involving two-way mirrors and video monitors.

46. Benson-Allott, "*Standard Operating Procedure*," 41.

47. Martin Lister, "Introduction," in *The Photographic Image in Digital Culture*, ed. Martin Lister (New York: Routledge, 2013), 8.

48. See Nicholas Muellner, "The New Interval," in *The Versatile Image: Photography, Digital Technologies and the Internet*, ed. Alexandra Moschovi, Carol McKay and Arabella

Plouviez (Leuven: Leuven University Press, 2013), 75–85, and David Bate, "The Digital Condition of Photography," in *The Photographic Image in Digital Culture* (2nd ed.), ed. Martin Lister (New York: Routledge, 2013), 77–94, here 81–3.

49. A full articulation of the project's rationale can be found on its website: http://www.foren sic-architecture.org/project/.

50. Eyal Weizman, "Introduction: Forensis," in *Forensis: The Architecture of Public Truth*, ed. Forensic Architecture (Berlin: Sternberg Press, 2014), 9–32, here 9.

51. Weizman, "Introduction," 11.

52. Weizman, "Introduction," 12.

53. Weizman, "Theory Talk #69," 2015. http://www.theory-talks.org/2015/03/theory-talk-69.html.

54. Yves Alain Bois, "On Forensic Architecture: An Interview with Eyal Weizman," *October* 156 (2016): 116–40, here 136.

55. Eyal Weizman, "Interview with Eyal Weizman," *International Review of the Red Cross* 98, no. 1 (2016): 21–35, here 24.

56. Eyal Weizman, "Before and After Images: Eyal Weizman's The Image Complex," 2016, available at https://thephotographersgalleryblog.org.uk/2016/05/22/the-image-complex/.

57. Amnesty International released on its YouTube channel in July 2015 several advocacy videos derived from its collaboration with Forensic Architecture. Two videos elaborated the Black Friday investigation: *Black Friday* (15 minutes) and *How Do They Do It?: Forensic Architecture* (8 minutes). Two more videos, *Gaza Platform Findings* (10 minutes) and *CSI Gaza: Forensic Architects* (4 minutes), explained a second manifestation of the collaboration between the two organizations: the Gaza Platform, an online interactive map of all the Israeli attacks on Gaza during the 2014 war.

58. The voiceover emphasizes both unique value of the collaboration and the political scale of the narrative it documents: "It provides in unprecedented levels of detail what happened that day in depth and breadth that's unmatched by anything produced before and it reveals evidence of war crimes, and possibly crimes against humanity. It is the story of a manhunt, a controversial military order and the price that was paid by Palestinian civilians for the life of a single soldier."

59. "Black Friday," Report by Amnesty International and Forensic Architecture, available at https://blackfriday.amnesty.org/report.php.

60. After initially ratifying the Rome Statute, Israel withdrew from the ICC in 2002.

61. Weizman, "On Forensic Architecture," 126.

62. In its elaborate manipulation of time and space through editing, Dziga Vertov's seminal documentary *Man with the Movie Camera* (1929) exemplifies the influence of Einsteinian relativity on Soviet filmmakers. Lev Manovich take ups this resonance in Vertov's film for understanding the elasticity of the new media object in his seminal book, *The Language of New Media* (Cambridge, MA: MIT Press, 2001).

63. The documentary is here drawing on the cultural practices of Palestinian society to display portrait photographs of Palestinians killed in the conflict in a wide variety of private and public spaces. Anne Paq and Ala Qandil's web documentary *Obliterated Families* (2017) about the civilian casualties of the 2014 war both documents such practices and appropriates them in its own visual rhetoric.

64. Weizman contends that the surface of the earth is not "an isolated distinct, stand-alone object, nor did it ever 'replace' the subject; rather, it is a thick fabric of complex relations,

associations, and chains of actions between people, environments, and artifices." Eyal Weizman, *Forensic Architecture: Notes from Fields and Forums* (Berlin: Hatje Kantz, 2012), 6.

Chapter 3

1. Henri Cartier-Bresson, *The Mind's Eye: Writings on Photography and Photographers* (New York: Aperture, 1999), 27. Whereas Cartier-Bresson selected the French title of the book, which translates roughly as "images on the sly," from a list of forty-five possible titles, the American title of the book came from the eighteenth-century epigraph to the essay, which Cartier-Bresson's French publisher had originally suggested for inclusion. Richard Simon, the book's American publisher, insisted on using "the decisive moment" for its English title. For a detailed history of the book's publication, see Clément Chéroux, "The Bible for Photographers," pamphlet published with reprint of Henri Cartier-Bresson's *The Decisive Moment* (Göttingen: Steidl, 2014).
2. Most of the glass paintings produced by Picasso in this documentary, as well as the ones made in Henri-Georges Clouzot's more celebrated *The Mystery of Picasso* (1956), did not survive, which means they now exist, ironically, only as filmed images.
3. "À pas de loup" (tiptoeing) was at the top of Cartier-Bresson's typed list of possible names for his photobook. See Chéroux, "The Bible for Photographers," 15.
4. This conversational format has been adopted by many subsequent documentaries about photographers, including Peter Adam's BBC series *Master Photographers* (1983) and Paul Carlin's documentary *The Spectre of Hope* (2002), which hosts a conversation between public intellectual John Berger and photographer Sebastião Salgado.
5. Mimicry has been a key concept for both queer theory and postcolonial theory, specifically Judith Butler's argument that gender and sexual identity are imitations without an original and Homi Bhabha's contention that colonial mimicry creates the potential conditions for ambivalence and subversion in which mimicry can devolve into a form of mockery that undermines colonial authority. See Judith Butler, "Imitation and Gender Insubordination," in *Inside/Out: Lesbian Theories, Gay Theories*, ed. Diana Fuss, 13–31 (New York: Routledge, 1991); and Homi Bhabha, "Of Mimicry and Man: The Ambivalence of Colonial Discourse." *October* 28 (1984): 125–33.
6. Azoulay, *The Civil Contract of Photography*.
7. For instance, *Photography Fights!* (1944) uses dramatization to explain the invaluable work of photographic interpreters in the US Navy gleaning important strategic information from reconnaissance images.
8. James L. Enyeart, *Willard Van Dyke: Changing the World Through Photography and Film* (Albuquerque: University of New Mexico Press, 2008), 245. The films on Graham and Wright were never made, while the project about Georgia O'Keeffe morphed into *Land of Enchantment: Southwest USA* (Henwar Rodakiewicz, 1948), a nineteen-minute film that explores the landscape and culture of the Southwest, with Navaho cultural practices enjoying as much screen time as O'Keeffe and her paintings.
9. For a comprehensive account of this ideological project, see Greg Barnhisel, *Cold War Modernists: Art, Literature, and American Cultural Diplomacy* (New York: Columbia University Press, 2015).

10. "Group F.64 Manifesto," reprinted in *Seeing Straight: The f.64 Revolution in Photography*, ed. Therese Thau Heyman (Oakland, CA: Oakland Museum, 1992), 53.

11. Van Dyke had shifted from photography to film in the mid-1930s, convinced that it had greater potential for effecting social and political change.

12. Leslie Squyres Calmes, *The Letters Between Edward Weston and Willard Van Dyke* (Tucson: Center for Creative Photography), 52.

13. See, respectively, Robert Katz, "Documentary in Transition: Part 1: The United States." *Hollywood Quarterly* 3, no. 4 (1948): 425–33, here 433; and Lester Asheim, "The Affective Film," *Journal of the University Film Producers Association* 8, no. 1 (1955): 4–9, here 6–7.

14. At the very time of shooting the film, Weston had just hired a new assistant, Dody Harrison, who would later help Weston in his final years as he sorted his archive and produced his final portfolio.

15. Unlike the previous shot of Weston under the view camera's cloth, the landscape is not upside down (as it would be in a view camera), a manipulation on Van Dyke's part to avoid confusing or defamiliarizing the viewer.

16. See also Stephen Dwoskin's *Shadows from Light* (1983), a self-declared "cinematic journey through the atmospheres of Bill Brandt's photography," which recreates Brandt's distinctive lighting in its mise-en-scène.

17. These are all specifically staged for the camera since Weegee had moved to Los Angeles in 1946 to pursue filmmaking.

18. Barthes, *Camera Lucida*, 3.

19. The massive popularity of Weegee's photobook is the likely inspiration for the title *The Naked Eye*, which otherwise would seem an odd choice for a documentary so focused on photography's technological mediation of vision.

20. Alan Trachtenberg, "Weegee's City Secrets," *E-rea* 7, no. 2 (2010).

21. Azoulay, *The Civil Contract of Photography*, 14. She uses film here only as an analogy to describe a mode of engaging photography.

22. Azoulay deems Roland Barthes and Susan Sontag as the primary, and most influential, proponents of this position, which preserves "a stable meaning for what is visible in the photography and reduce the role of spectator to the act of judgment, eliminating his or her responsibility for what is seen in the photograph" (*The Civil Contract of Photography*, 130).

23. Barthes, *Camera Lucida*, 77.

24. "The photograph will always include something else that is not reducible to the photographer's viewpoint. It is a viewpoint, or perhaps it be termed a viewing position, that is not attributable to anyone but the camera" (Azoulay, *The Civil Contract of Photography*, 383–4).

25. Azoulay's subsequent book, *The Civil Imagination: A Political Ontology of Photography*, shifts from a discussion of the "civil contract" of photography to its "civil imagination," suggesting an acknowledgment that photography's political ontology is performative and potential, rather than a pre-existing set of conditions.

26. Azoulay, "What Is a Photograph?," 12–13.

27. Cornell Capa defined the "concerned photographer" as one who produced "images in which genuine human feeling predominates over commercial cynicism or disinterested formalism," Cornell Capa, *The Concerned Photographer: The Photographs of Werner Bischof, Robert Capa, David Seymour ("Chim"), André Kertész, Leonard Freed, Dan Weiner* (New York: Grossman, 1968), n.p. *War Photographer* features a section documenting the

installation of Nachtwey's exhibition *Testimony* at the International Center of Photography, which was founded by Cornell Capa.

28. This fracturing of perspective has been treated by some reviewers as evidence of a "disjointed" film that "lacks a solid structure." See Tammy Kinsey, "*War Photographer* (2001)," *The Moving Image* 3, no. 2 (2003): 108–11.

29. See Mark Reichardt, Holly Edwards, and Erina Dugganne, eds. *Beautiful Suffering: Photography and the Traffic in Pain* (Williamstown, MA: Williams College Museum of Art, 2007).

30. Sarah Boxer, "The Chillingly Fine Line Between Ecstasy and Grief," *New York Times*, June 9, 2000, E27.

31. Susie Linfield, *The Cruel Radiance: Photography and Political Violence* (Chicago: University of Chicago Press, 2010), 211.

32. Henry Allen, "Seasons in Hell: Reflections Through Unwary Eyes," *New Yorker*, June 12, 2000, 106.

33. Matthew C. Ehrlich and Joe Saltzman trace the roots of this particular characterization to the public image of Robert Capa in *Heroes and Scoundrels: The Image of the Journalist in Popular Culture* (Urbana: University of Illinois Press, 2015), 104.

34. Robert Koehler, "War Photographer," *Variety*, June 17, 2002, 27.

35. John Anderson, "A Photographer or an Exploiter," *Newsday*, June 19, 2002, B10. Hans-Michael Koetzle similarly commented on the microcam's revelation: "An ingenious little trick, had it not ultimately turned against its clever inventor. Because as a result we gain some rather blunt insight into a craft, the contradictions of which Frei exposes, unintentionally, it is to be assumed, but none the less compellingly for that." Hans-Michael Koetzle, "James Nachtwey, War Photographer," *European Photography*, no. 72 (2002): 16–18, here 16.

36. This account of the technical details is drawn from Patricia Thomson, "Photographing the Front Lines," *American Cinematographer* 83, no. 9 (2002): 20–4.

37. A. O. Scott, "Witnessing the Witness: Looking Over a Shoulder at War's Deprivation," *New York Times*, June 19, 2002, E1.

38. Hannah McBride, "Interview: Jared Moossy," *Nowhere*, 2013.

39. For instance, *Frances Ha* (Noah Baumbach, 2012) and *Department* (Ram Gopal Varma, 2012) were shot on the Canon EOS 5D Mk II.

40. De Viguerie also uses her pictures of the Arrow Boys as means to locate her previously photographed subjects, showing them to local people and asking them where they could be found.

41. Ariella Azoulay, "Getting Rid of the Distinction Between the Aesthetic and the Political," *Theory, Culture, Society* 27, nos. 7–8 (2010): 239–62, here 251.

42. Other documentaries about female photographers, such as *Pictures from a Revolution* (Susan Meiselas, Richard P. Rogers, and Alfred Guzzetti, 1991), *I'll Be Your Mirror* (Edmund Coulthard and Nan Goldin, 1995), *What Remains: The Life and Work of Sally Mann* (Steven Cantor, 2005), and *Zanele Muholi: Visual Activist* (Katherine Fairfax Wright, Malika Zouhali-Worrall, and Zanele Muholi, 2013), similarly devote substantial screen time to revealing the significance that Susan Meiselas, Nan Goldin, Sally Mann, and Zanele Muholi place on their relationships to their subjects. Seen together, these documentaries map the possible terrain of a feminist photographic practice grounded in an ethics of relationship building within the event of photography.

43. For examples of such divergent critical perspectives, see Jennifer Peeples, "Toxic Sublime: Imagining Contaminated Landscapes." *Environmental Communication* 5, no. 4 (2011): 373–92 (a positive view), and Marnin Young, "Manufactured Landscapes: The Photographs of Edward Burtynsky," *Afterimage*, May/June 2003, 8–9 (a skeptical view).

44. *Jennifer Baichwal and Edward Burtynsky with Richard Goddard*, special feature on the Mongrel DVD release of *Manufacturing Landscapes*.

45. Robert Adams, *New Topographics: Photographs of a Man-Altered Landscape* (Rochester: International Museum of Photography at George Eastman House, 1975).

46. *China* (2005), *Oil* (2009), *Water* (2013) and *Anthropocene* (2018), all published by Steidl.

47. Michael Torosian, "The Essential Element: An Interview with Edward Burtynsky," in *Manufactured Landscapes: The Photographs of Edward Burtynsky*, ed. Lori Pauli, 46–55. Ottawa: National Gallery of Canada, 2003, 52.

48. Mark Kingwell, "The Truth in Photographs: Edward Burtynsky's Revelations of Excess," in *China*, ed. Edward Burtynsky (Göttingen: Steidl, 2005), 16–19, here 17.

49. See Carol Diehl, "Toxic Sublime," *Art in America*, February 2006, 188–93; Duncan Forbes, "Edward Burtynsky's Negative Sublime," *Portfolio 47* (2008): 4–21; Mark Haworth-Booth, "Edward Burtynsky: Traditions and Affinities," in *Manufactured Landscapes: The Photographs of Edward Burtynsky*, ed. Lori Pauli (Ottawa: National Gallery of Canada, 2003), 34–9; and the 2009 exhibition at the Corcoran Gallery in Washington, DC, "Edward Burtynsky and the Industrial Sublime."

50. David Campany, "What on Earth?: Photography's Alien Landscapes." *Aperture* 211 (2013): 46–51, here 47.

51. Art-historical references abound in readings of Burtynksy's work: the quarries suggest Richard Diebkorn's angular abstractions, the shipbreaking scenes call to mind the monumental steel curves of Richard Serra, the multi-colored rectangles of the container ports allude to the chromatic grids of Ellsworth Kelly or Gerhard Richter, while the wire piles at e-waste sites evoke the tangled lines of a Jackson Pollack. See Diehl, "Toxic Sublime," 121.

52. Young, "Manufactured Landscapes," 8.

53. Manohla Dargis, "Industrial China's Ravaging of Nature, Made Disturbingly Sublime," *New York Times*, June 20, 2007, E4.

54. Gerda Cammaer, "Edward Burtynsky's *Manufactured Landscapes*: The Ethics and Aesthetics of Creating Moving Still Images and Stilling Moving Images of Ecological Disasters," *Environmental Communication: A Journal of Nature and Culture* 3, no. 1 (2009): 121–30, here 123–4.

55. DVD interview with Peter Goddard.

56. Damon Smith, "Made in China: Jennifer Baichwal and Edward Burtynsky on Their Travels Across *Manufactured Landscapes*," *Bright Lights Film Journal*, November 1, 2007.

57. Although technically this shot was produced by with a dolly, not tracks, its unambiguously straight sweep evokes the classical tracking shot.

58. Toward the end of the long take, there are some very slight variations in the speed of the camera movement, but not sufficient for the viewer to necessarily read meaning into them.

59. The artist statement that opens Burtynsky's *China* offers a similarly clear commitment to environmental protection: "In my view, China is the most recent participant to be seduced by western ideals—the hollow promise of fulfillment and happiness through material gain. The troubling downside of this is something that I am only too aware of from my experience of life in a developed nation. The mass consumerism these ideals ignite and the

resulting degradation of our environment intrinsic to the process of making things should be of deep concern to all. I no longer see my world as delineated by countries, with borders, or language, but as 6.5 billion humans living off a precariously balanced, finite planet." Burtynsky, *China*, 7.

60. Duncan Forbes notes, "The commanding view, whatever its newfound insecurity, is inadequate to the issues raised by the laboring body in the landscapes of globalization." "Edward Burtynsky's Negative Sublime," 20.

61. The series ran for two short seasons in 2003 and 2005.

62. Jon Dovey, *Freakshow: First Person Media and Factual Television* (London: Pluto Press, 2000), 27–54.

63. The title *Gursky World* (and the concept) is a play on the title of Peter Galassi's essay "Gursky's World" in *Andreas Gursky*, the catalog for the 2001 exhibition at the Museum of Modern Art, which solidified Gursky's reputation in the global art market.

Chapter 4

1. Sekula, "Reading an Archive," 154

2. Edwards, "Objects of Affect," 222–4.

3. See Okwui Enwezor, *Archive Fever: The Use of the Document in Contemporary Art* (New York/Göttingen: International Center of Photography/Steidl, 2008), and Ernst van Alphen, *Staging the Archive: Art and Photography in the Age of New Media* (London: Reaktion Books, 201).

4. *Dolce Vita Africana* was commissioned by the BBC and ZDF/Arte; *Photo Souvenir* by VPRO.

5. The exhibition, *The Mexican Suitcase: The Rediscovered Spanish Civil War Negatives of Capa, Chim and Taro*, was held at the ICP, September 24, 2010–January 9, 2011.

6. Pamela Bannos, *Vivian Maier: A Photographer's Life and Afterlife* (Chicago: University of Chicago Press, 2017), 7.

7. In her mapping of the complex dispersal of Maier's archive, Bannos indicates that many of her possessions were resold through other auction houses and are no longer traceable.

8. Rose Lichter-Mark, "Vivian Maier and the Problem of Difficult Women," *New Yorker*, May 9, 2014. As she mentions, photographer Joel Meyerowitz does offer a counterargument to this patriarchal assumption when he suggests in the film that Maier's watchfulness as a caregiver may indeed have been a key factor in her skill as a photographer.

9. Given the increasingly contested status of Maier's copyright, the documentary also works to reinforce Maloof's claim that it is his labor that has created economic value out of her legally abandoned property. For discussion of legal conflict over Maier's copyright, see Bannos, *Vivian Maier*, 272–9.

10. Rosalind Kraus, "Photography's Discursive Spaces: Landscape/View," *Art Journal* 42, no. 4 (1982): 311–19, here 316–7.

11. Abigail Solomon-Godeau, *Photography After Photography: Gender, Genre, History* (Durham, NC: Duke University Press, 2017), 147. Solomon-Godeau ends her chapter on Maier by reiterating this claim in terms of a pathological compensation: "it seems that the act of photographing the life around her was a substitute for having a life of her own" (154). This conclusion unfortunately bears out a certain tendency in the cultural narrativization of Maier that Rose Lichter-Mark so aptly dissects: "Some tellings of Maier's story suggest

that perhaps we should feel a proxy regret, that we should feel sorry <u>about</u> her solitude, her rages, her dark edges, her impecunious existence. Shall we make her a martyr, or can we allow that she may have had the life she wanted?"

12. A shorter fifty-three-minute version of the documentary is available for streaming in the United States under the title, *The Vivian Maier Mystery*.

13. Terry Castle, "New Art," *Harper's Magazine*, February 2015, 81.

14. See Castle's article for a compelling reading of Maier's queerness.

15. While Julia Scully's publication of the first book of Disfarmer photographs appeared in 1976, the aggressive commodification of his original prints as fine-art photography would not occur for almost three decades. Martin Lavut's documentary *Disfarmer: A Portrait of America* (2014) presents a similar masculinist narrative of eccentric genius as *Finding Vivian Maier* but devotes significant screen time to the politics of commodifying vernacular photography.

16. See Michelle Lamunière, *You Look Beautiful Like That: The Portrait Photographs of Seydou Keïta and Malick Sidibé* (New Haven, CT: Yale University Press, 2001), 55–6.

17. Candance M. Keller, "Framed and Hidden Histories: West African Photography from Local to Global Contexts," *African Arts* 47, no. 4 (2014): 36–47, here 44.

18. In addition to the infamous 2005 legal case over a set of Keïta negatives, Keller describes instances in which scholars have also participated in this practice of unethical appropriation of archival material (45–7).

19. Keller played a founding role in the establishment of the Archive of Malian Photography, a National Endowment for the Humanities–funded project to preserve and digitize of five important Malian photographers, including Sidibé, which also ensures that the original negatives remain in Mali. The project's website can be founded at https://amp.matrix.msu.edu/ (accessed August 10, 2022).

20. Spender's original edit of the film included two additional scenes that book-ended the documentary: his presence at the opening of the Guggenheim Bilbao's 2006 exhibition *100% Africa*, which showcased Pigozzi's African photography collection and his acceptance of the Golden Lion Award in Venice. Her commissioning editors at the BBC encouraged her to remove those two scenes that acknowledged the international art world because they felt that Sidibé "didn't need recognition from the West" (electronic communication with the author, July 31, 2020). However, due to their position, brevity, and contrast with all the other scenes, these book-ending scenes actually work more to emphasize the relocalizing strategy of the documentary.

21. Edwards, "Thinking Photography Beyond the Visual?," 39.

22. Elizabeth Edwards, "Photographs and the Sound of History," *Visual Anthropology Review* 21, no. 1–2 (2005): 27–46, here 27.

23. "Arts of Africa: From Traditional Arts to Jean Pigozzi's Contemporary Collection," Grimaldi Forum, Monaco, 2005.

24. Jean Marie Teno's essay film *Afrique, je te plumerai (Africa, I Will Fleece You)* (1992) powerfully demonstrates how post-independence nostalgia and neocolonial allegory can be marshalled to dynamically engage the political exigencies of the present.

25. Cynthia Young, "The Process of Identifying 4,500 Negatives: The Mexican Suitcase Revealed." In *The Mexican Suitcase: The Rediscovered Spanish Civil War Negatives of Capa, Chim and Taro*, ed. Cynthia Young, vol. 1, 95–115 (New York and Göttingen: International Center of Photography and Steidl, 2010), 96.

26. Steidl sold the exhibition catalog in a cardboard box designed to resemble a suitcase.

27. Randy Kennedy, "The Capa Cache," *New York Times*, January 28, 2008.

28. Trisha Ziff, interview with author, September 29, 2016. Juan Villoro also reports that Tarver received intimidating letters from the ICP claiming that he was in illegal possession of the negatives. See Javier Molina, "La maleta mexicana en México: Entrevista con Juan Villoro." *Letras Libres*, December 13, 2013, https://www.letraslibres.com/mexico/la-mal eta-mexicana-en-mexico.

29. Unless otherwise cited, my account of Ziff's recovery of the Mexican Suitcase is drawn from my 2016 interview with her, including quotations, some of which have already been published in Trish Ziff and Roger Hallas, "Challenging the Hierarchies of Photographic Histories," in *Documenting the Visual Arts*, ed. Roger Hallas (London and New York: Routledge, 2020), 191–204.

30. Tarver served as an executive producer on Ziff's documentary.

31. Ziff also dedicated her documentary to Julio.

32. For an extended discussion of this discourse of immediacy in relation to the Mexican Suitcase, see Simon Dell, "Mediation and Immediacy: The Press, the Popular Front in France, and the Spanish Civil War" in *The Mexican Suitcase: The Rediscovered Spanish Civil War Negatives of Capa, Chim and Taro*, ed. Cynthia Young, vol. 1 (New York and Göttingen: International Center of Photography and Steidl, 2010), 37–49.

33. In my interview with her, Ziff commented, "To me, a snapshot has equal interest and importance to a photograph that we consider art or photojournalism. I am interested in giving equal space to what might be termed 'high and low' photography.... We can only understand 'truth' to emerge from the coming together of all these different visions."

34. Juan Villoro amplified Ziff's concerns about the ICP's approach: "They are technically flawless. But they lack, and that never ceases to amaze me, an interest in history and context. The history of these negatives goes unnoticed. They only focus on the superstars of photography, and this is explained by the colonial vision so typical of US culture" (Molina, translation adapted from Google Translate).

35. Phillip Knightley, *The First Casualty: From Crimea to Vietnam: The War Correspondent as Hero, Propagandist, and Myth Maker* (New York: Harcourt, Brace and Jovanovich, 1975), 212.

36. See Richard Whelan, "Robert Capa's *The Falling Soldier*: A Detective Story." *Aperture* 166 (2002): 43–55.

37. Vincent Lavoie, "Robert Capa and the Turn to Forensics," in *Photography and Doubt*, ed. Sabine T. Kriegel and Andrés Mario Zervigón (London: Routledge, 2017), 121–37, here 128.

38. Dell, "Mediation and Immediacy," 39.

39. Sebastiaan Faber, *Memory Battles of the Spanish Civil War: History, Fiction, Photography* (Nashville: Vanderbilt University Press, 2018), 39.

40. Ziff employed this strategy of situating photojournalism within a wider photographic archive in her earlier curatorial project on Northern Ireland's Bloody Sunday, *Hidden Truths: Bloody Sunday*, 1972, which brought together military photography, local, and international photojournalism, forensic photography, the mass card portrait, and the family photo album.

41. See Diana Taylor, "Past Performing Future: Susan Meiselas's *Reframing History*." In *Susan Meiselas: In History*, ed. Kristen Lubben (New York and Göttingen: International Center of Photography and Steidl, 2008), 232–6.

42. Ziff uses one of these photographs as the image for the film's poster. By replacing the "Mexican Suitcase" with the image of an exile's real suitcase (taken by Seymour), this directorial choice initiates the focus of attention away from Capa and onto the history of Spanish exile.

43. In my interview, Ziff noted the irony of this "return" of the negatives to New York, given that the only possibility of their previously having been there was as part of General González's luggage on its way home to Mexico, a landing that the US government denied to Spanish exiles seeking asylum after the war.

44. Michelle L. Woodward, "Creating Memory and History: The Role of Archival Practices in Lebanon and Palestine." *Photographies* 2, no. 1 (2009): 21–35, here 24.

45. Mark Westmoreland, "Time Capsules of Catastrophic Times," *The Arab Archive: Mediated Memories and Digital Flows*, ed. Donatella Della Ratta, Kay Dickinson, and Sune Haugbolle (Amsterdam: Institute of Network Cultures, 2020), 20–34, here 29.

46. Chad Elias, "The Artist as Collector: A Dialogue on the Possibilities and Limits of an Institution," in *Akram Zaatari: Against Photography* (Barcelona: Museu d'Art Contemporani de Barcelona), 40–4, here 41.

47. Kaelen Wilson-Goldie, "Memory Games: The Arab Image Foundation," in *On Photography in Lebanon: Stories and Essays*, ed. Clémence Cottard Hachem and Nour Salamé (Beirut: Kaph Books, 2018), 147–9, here 149.

48. Elias, "The Artist as Collector," 42.

49. As Zaatari astutely notes, "There is a community of artists who share a common interest in writing history, in the tectonics of storytelling, in identifying and producing documents taking the war situation as a case or a base, not because they are interested in war as a subject, but because war is one of rare situations where notions of common logic collapse, and the notions of evidence in relation to documents and history are challenged." Eva Respini and Ana Janevski, "Interview with the Artist," in *Projects 100: Akram Zaatari* (Museum of Modern Art, 2013).

50. Wilson-Goldie, "Memory Games," 148.

51. Elias, "The Artist as Collector," 42.

52. Akram Zaatari, "History and Photographic Memory," *Journal of Visual Culture* 18, no. 2 (2019): 169–86, here 175.

53. Mark Westmoreland, "Akram Zaatari: Against Photography. A Conversation with Mark Westmoreland," *Aperture 210* (2013): 60–5.

54. Zaatari, "History and Photographic Memory," 177.

55. Anthony Downey and Akram Zaatari, "Photography as Apparatus: Akram Zaatari in Conversation with Anthony Downey," *Critical Interventions: Journal of African Art History and Visual Culture* 12, no. 2 (2018): 218–30, here 220.

56. Westmoreland, "Akram Zaatari," 63.

57. Zaatari first used this technique in his documentary *This Day* (2003) in a sequence investigating photographs of the Bedouin by Lebanese-Armenian photographer Manoug Alemian, some of which later appeared in Jibrail Jabbur's 1988 study *El Badou wal badiya* (*The Bedouins and the Desert*).

58. The contrast between flatness and dimensionality is furthered by the documentary's sound design. While the interview scenes are rich with offscreen atmospheric sounds, hardly any sounds arise from the archival scene, and any that do remain difficult to discern given the suspended flow of time in the stilled images.

59. Akram Zaatari, ed., *The Vehicle: Picturing Moments of Transition in a Modernizing Society* (Beirut: The Arab Image Foundation and Mind the Gap, 1999).

60. Karl Bassil, Zeina Maasri, and Akram Zaatari, eds., *Mapping Sitting: On Portraiture and Photography* (Beirut: Arab Image Foundation and Mind the Gap, 2002). Madani's photographs also appeared in Zaatari's 2011 exhibition *The Uneasy Subject* in Léon and Mexico City.

61. Lisa Le Feuvre and Akram Zaatari, *Hashem El Madani: Studio Practices* (London and Beirut: Photographers' Gallery, Arab Image Foundation and Mind the Gap, 2004). Accompanying many of the photographs were short quotes from Madani about the specific material and social practices he and his sitters engaged in. The studio was named after the Shehrazade Building in which it was located.

62. Respini and Janevski, "Interview with the Artist."

63. Ibid.

64. Downey and Zaatari, 224.

65. See Westmoreland, "Akram Zaatari," 62.

66. A *mawwal* is a genre of classical Arabic song in which a phrase is elongated into separate vowel syllables and repeated numerous times before the regular lyrics of the song commence. It functions as a form of lamentation or contemplation.

67. *"Twenty-Eight Nights and a Poem*: Akram Zaatari, Q&A, Berlinale Forum," February 11, 2015.

68. Batchen, "Vernacular Photographies," 262.

69. Batchen, "Whither the Vernacular?," in *Imagining Everyday Life: Engagements with Vernacular Photography*, ed. Tina M. Campt, Marianne Hirsch, Gil Hochberg, and Brian Wallis (New York and Göttingen: The Walther Collection and Steidl, 2020), 33–40, here 39.

70. "Discussion: Why Vernacular Photography?: The Limits and Possibilities of a Field," in *Imagining Everyday Life: Engagements with Vernacular Photography*, ed. Tina M. Campt, Marianne Hirsch, Gil Hochberg, and Brian Wallis (New York and Göttingen: The Walther Collection and Steidl, 2020), 61–5, here 62.

71. The documentary explains how some vendors deploy messy stacks of photographs to appeal to the pleasures of fortuitous discovery for the customer, whereas others rely on strict organization of their wares along generic and thematic categories.

Chapter 5

1. See Shearer West, *Portraiture* (Oxford: Oxford University Press, 2004), 43–69.

2. Allan Sekula, "The Body and the Archive," *October* 39 (1986): 3–64, here 14.

3. In previous work, I have also argued that the shadow archive of photographic portraiture laid the discursive and iconographic foundations for the talking head in the nonfictional moving image: "The honorific portrait of the bourgeois subject finds its correlate in nonfiction media in the authoritative figures of the newscaster and the expert witness, while the repressive portrait of the pathological subject finds its equivalent in the objectified other of documentary film and television news, which incorporates an array of figures, including the pauper, the primitive, the immigrant, the refugee, the nonwhite, the criminal, the sexual deviant, and the sick person." *Reframing Bodies: AIDS, Bearing Witness, and the Queer Moving Image* (Durham, NC: Duke University Press, 2009), 41.

4. Noa Steimatsky, *The Face on Film* (New York: Oxford University Press, 2017), 6.

5. Barthes, *Camera Lucida*, 87.

6. Hans Belting, *Face and Mask: A Double History*, translated by Thomas S. Hansen and Abby J. Hansen (Princeton: Princeton University Press, 2017), 121.

7. Hans Belting, "Image, Medium, Body," *Critical Inquiry* 31, no. 2 (2005): 302–19, here 312.

8. See W. J. T. Mitchell, *What Do Pictures Want?: The Lives and Loves of Images* (Chicago: University of Chicago Press, 2005), 28–56

9. Steimatsky, *The Face on Film*, 10.

10. Barthes, *Camera Lucida*, 28 and 96.

11. Both live-feed moving images and narrative fiction film configure presence-absence differently than does documentary film due to synchrony and suspension of disbelief.

12. I borrow the concept of "compelled photos" from Susanne Regener (cited in Tina M. Campt, *Listening to Images* [Durham: Duke University Press, 2017], 75).

13. The precise number of prisoners who were held at Tuol Sleng has been subject to significant debate. The Office of the Co-Prosecutors at the Extraordinary Chambers in the Courts of Cambodia (ECCC) has concluded that at least 18,133 people were imprisoned at S-21. See Vincent de Wilde d'Estmael, "The Uses of the Archives of the Tuol Sleng Genocide Museum and the Documentation Centre of Cambodia by the Extraordinary Chambers in the Courts of Cambodia," in *Archives and Human Rights*, ed. Jens Boel, Perrine Canavaggio, and Antonio González Quintana (New York: Routledge, 2021), 178–87, here 183.

14. Ariella Azoullay, "Photography Consists of Collaboration: Susan Meiselas, Wendy Ewald, and Ariella Azoulay," *Camera Obscura* 31, no. 1 (2016): 186–201, here 189.

15. Rachel Hughes, "The Abject Artefacts of Memory: Photographs from Cambodia's Genocide," *Media, Culture & Society* 25, no. 1 (2003): 23–44, here 25.

16. Michelle Caswell, *Archiving the Unimaginable: Silence, Memory, and the Photographic Record in Cambodia* (Madison: University of Wisconsin Press, 2014), 52.

17. After joining the Khmer Rouge, he took on the name "Duch" after an obedient schoolboy character in a well-known Cambodian children's book. See Caswell, 56.

18. Thy Phu, "Afterimages of S-21: Distant and Proximate Spectatorship and the Legacies of Cold War Human Rights." In *Photography and Its Publics*, ed. Melisa Miles and Edward Welch (London: Bloomsbury, 2020), 149–66, here 153.

19. Niven and Riley were featured in a BBC short documentary, *Secrets of S-21: Legacy of a Cambodian Prison* (Andrea Miller and David Okuefuna, 1996) that aligned their work in the S-21 archive with their own photojournalistic aestheticization of contemporary Cambodia. Both photographers are consistently framed together as they intrepidly explore the street life of Phnom Penh, the Killing Fields of Choeung Ek, and the Tuol Sleng prison in search of images (either to capture on film or to preserve). At one point in the voiceover, Riley summarizes his aestheticization of the country in clearly Orientalizing terms: "it's great place for us photographers, with the dust and the haze, the amazing array of faces, the skin, the eyes and the hair make it a great place for photographs." Even when they encounter death in contemporary Cambodia, it is bound up in the visual contemplation of landscape. Niven notices a corpse floating in a river during a journey to the countryside to find former prison guards and comments, "Life is really cheap here." Moreover, the cinematography of these scenes consistently pursues an aesthetic mimicry of their photojournalistic imagination through carefully thought-out composition and thematically resonant iconography. For example, as Niven and Riley discuss the obscurity of the

archive for ordinary Cambodians, their bodies are visually obscured behind a ventilation screen in the prison. The film concludes by consolidating its universal humanism as Niven affirms their pursuit of a higher calling through their voluntary archival work: "Instead of making photographs for newspapers which are often quickly forgotten, these photographs from the S-21 archive are timeless pictures which will last much longer than photojournalistic pictures."

20. Quoted in Hughes, "The Abject Artefacts of Memory," 36.
21. Stephanie Benzaquen, "Remediating Genocidal Images into Artworks," *re-bus 10* (Summer 2010), 209. Irish artist Matt Loughrey caused controversy in 2021 when *Vice* published several S-21 identification photographs that he had colorized. He had also digitally altered the facial expression of some of the images, including adding smiles and make up to the faces. In response to the outcry over such blatantly decontextualizing appropriation, he commented that he just wanted to "humanize the tragedy." See Seth Mydans, "Cambodians Demand Apology for Khmer Rouge Images with Smiling Faces," *New York Times*, April 13, 2021.
22. Elizabeth Becker, *When the War Was Over: Cambodia and The Khmer Rouge Revolution* (New York: Simon and Schuster, 1986).
23. Vincente Sánchez-Biosca, "Bophana's Image and Narrative," in *The Cinema of Rithy Panh: Everything Has a Soul*, ed. Leslie Barnes and Joseph Mai (New Brunswick, NJ: Rutgers University Press, 2021), 173–87, here 174–5.
24. Rithy Panh, *The Elimination: A Survivor of the Khmer Rouge Confronts His Past and the Commandant of the Killing Fields*, trans. John Cullen (New York: Other Press, 2013), 261. In an interview with Joshua Oppenheimer, Panh also relates the presence of the dead to his own status as genocide survivor, "When making the film I thought a great deal of the dead, of course. In making the film, the dead were with me, always … The very fact that I am here, to a certain degree, suggests that somebody left a place for me." Joshua Oppenheimer, "Perpetrators' Testimony and the Restoration of Humanity: *S21*, Rithy Panh," in *Killer Images: Documentary Film, Memory, and the Performance of Violence*, ed. Joram Ten Brink and Joshua Oppenheimer (London: Wallflower Press, 2012), 243–55, here 250.
25. Oppenheimer, "Perpetrators' Testimony," 244.
26. Deirdre Boyle, "Trauma, Memory, Documentary: Re-enactment in Two Films by Rithy Panh (Cambodia) and Garin Nugroho (Indonesia)," in *Documentary Testimonies: Global Archives of Suffering*, ed. Bhaskar Sarkar and Janet Walker (New York: Routledge, 2010), 155–72, here 158.
27. William Guynn, *Unspeakable Histories: Film and the Experience of Catastrophe* (New York: Columbia University Press, 2016), 172.
28. See Oppenheimer, "Perpetrators' Testimony."
29. Panh has tended to speak more generally about the function of the photographs in the regime's dehumanization of its victims than his own mobilization of them to prompt acts of bearing witness: "The photographs are very important, because the moment the photograph is taken is the first step toward putting that person to death. And as soon as the photograph is taken, that person is replaced by a number, and he has lost his or her identity." Oppenheimer, "Perpetrators' Testimony," 249.
30. Oppenheimer, "Perpetrators' Testimony," 246.
31. In one scene, Panh has one of the former guards contemplate his own identification photograph taken when he first began working at S-21. The parallel invoked here between the

identification photographs of perpetrators and victims alludes to one of the film's critical themes: the Khmer Rouge's excessive paranoia about the presence of an enemy within constructed a precarious line between comrade and traitor, since the former could quickly become the latter if named in prisoner confessions induced by torture. As Nath points out early in the film, at some point the whole country would have become implicated as the enemy within.

32. Kahn also articulates greater reflection on his actions in S-21 in another scene. As the camera pans from him across a table stacked with mugshots (including Bophana's), he confirms Arendt's argument about the "thoughtlessness" of totalitarian structures of violence: "Torture was something cold and cruel. I didn't think."

33. Quoted in Mydans, "Cambodians Demand Apology."

34. See Susan Sontag, *Regarding the Pain of Others* (New York: Farrar, Straus, and Giroux, 2003), 60–1.

35. Susana de Sousa Dias, "Weak Memories: Archives of Futurability." *Film Quarterly* 73, no. 4 (2020): 26–33, here 29.

36. Susana de Sousa Dias, "(In)visible Evidence: *The Representability of Torture*," in *A Companion to Contemporary Documentary Film*, ed. Alexandra Jushasz and Alisa Lebow (New York: Blackwell-Wiley, 2015), 482–505, here 482.

37. The title of the film refers to the 48 years of the Salazar dictatorship, Europe's longest fascist regime.

38. Bruce Jackson, *Pictures from a Drawer: Prison and the Art of Portraiture* (Philadelphia: Temple University Press, 2009), 11.

39. De Sousa Dias, "Weak Memories," 29.

40. Scott MacDonald, "Susana de Sousa Dias," *Film Quarterly* 66, no. 2 (2012): 25–34, here 28 (emphasis in original).

41. Highlighting the physical subjugation of the prisoner before the camera, the profile shots include the head brace used to guarantee uniformity of bodily position in the frame. For discussion of Bertillon's system, see Sekula, "The Body and the Archive," 25–34.

42. MacDonald, "Interview with Susana de Sousa Dias," 409.

43. De Sousa Dias, "(In)visible Evidence," 498.

44. She draws on both Rancière's "pensive image" and Deleuze's "time-image" to describe her cinematic treatment of these photographs. "(In)visible Evidence," 498–9.

45. Shoshana Felman and Dori Laub, *Testimony: Crises of Witnessing in Literature, Psychoanalysis and History* (New York: Routledge, 1992), 57.

46. De Sousa Dias, "Weak Memories," 29.

47. Azoulay, *The Civil Contract of Photography*, 384.

48. De Sousa Dias, "(In)visible Evidence," 500.

49. Felman and Laub, *Testimony*, 64.

50. De Sousa Dias, "(In)visible Evidence," 501.

51. As minister of the interior, Nicholas Sarkozy notoriously used this derogatory term in 2005 to characterize the countrywide rioting sparked by the death of two youths electrocuted while hiding from the police in an electrical substation. Moreover, he incited the discourse of ethnic cleansing by invoking the need to "*karcherise*" (power-wash) the ghettos of "*la racaille*." In an undoubted allusion to this controversy, Alastair Siddons's documentary on *Inside Out* illustrates JR's TED talk with a shot of municipal workers deploying a power-washer to remove one of JR's *Portraits of a Generation* from a Parisian wall.

52. John Tagg, *The Burden of Representation: Essays on Photographies and Histories* (Basingstoke: Macmillan, 1988), 64.

53. "The booth became an enclosure in which one could playfully try out multiple presentations of self as fleeting and inconsequential as the apparatus and its output, and a rehearsal space for a diverse set of performances in an increasingly mediated city." Richard Hornsey, "Francis Bacon and the Photobooth: Facing the Homosexual in Post-war Britain," *Visual Culture in Britain* 8, no. 2 (2007): 83–103, here 91. See also Erika Goyarrola, "Case Study on the Photo Booth," in *The Routledge Companion to Photography and Visual Culture*, ed. Moritz Neumüller (London: Routledge, 2018), 189–99.

54. JR even donated his TED Prize money to a foundation he created that runs social programs in the communities in which he has worked rather than use it to directly finance *Inside Out*. That project was initially funded by the sale of six JR prints for US$850,000. See Y-Jean Mun-Delsalle, "French Artist JR's Works Are Turning the World Inside Out," *Forbes*, September 13, 2015. Furthermore, the project guidelines suggested a US$20 per poster, which allowed projects in more affluent communities to subsidize projects elsewhere in the world that could not afford to donate. The Inside Out website does also officially recognize the Sapling Foundation (organizer of the TED Prize) as a funder.

55. Petra Eckhard, "Urban Figures, Common Ground: JR and the Cultural Practices of Perception," *European Journal of American Studies* 10, no. 3 (2015): 1–14, here 7.

56. For example, in the Shanghai installation of *Wrinkles of the City* in 2010, he pasted building-sized facial portraits of its elderly inhabitants onto the isolated houses that were the last remaining holdouts in old neighborhoods razed in the onslaught of the city's breakneck urban development.

57. Virág Molndár uses this phrase to characterize street art in general in "Street Art and the Changing Urban Public Sphere," *Public Culture* 29, no. 2 (2017): 385–414, here 395.

58. See Emmanuel Levinas, *Totality and Infinity: An Essay on Exteriority*, trans. Alphonso Lingis (The Hague: Nijhoff, 1979).

59. Claire Bishop, *Artificial Hells: Participatory Art and the Politics of Spectatorship* (London: Verso, 2012), 18–26.

60. Jennifer Orpana, "Turning the World 'Inside Out': Situating JR's Wish within Cultures of Participation," *Canadian Art Review* 39, no. 1 (2014): 66–75, 72.

61. Bertie Ferdman, "Urban Dramaturgy: The Global Art Project of JR," *PAJ: A Journal of Performance and Art* 34, no. 3 (2012): 12–26, here 25.

62. Ferdman frames this in relation to David Harvey's "Right to the City" manifesto (Urban Dramaturgy," 25).

63. Raffi Khatchadourian, "'In the Picture: An Artist's Global Experiment to Help People Be Seen," *New Yorker*, November 28, 2011. JR also deliberately elided his presence in the eponymous documentary film that he directed about the project, in order not to detract from the agency and voice of the participating women.

64. One of the running jokes of *Faces Places* (2017), his documentary collaboration with Agnès Varda, is her repeated effort to get JR to remove his sunglasses so that she can see his eyes.

65. "Group Action Guidelines," *Inside Out Project*.

66. Since the 2021 upgrade of the project website, the threshold for participation in group actions has been raised to fifty people.

67. Participants could even download a sheet of JR's signature polka-dot backdrop.

68. *Inside Out* project website, https://www.insideoutproject.net/en/. Accessed December 30, 2021.

69. As Martin Irvine *argues*, "Now working in a continuum of practice spanning street, studio, gallery, installation spaces, digital production and the Internet, street artists expose how an artwork is a momentary node of relationships, a position in a network of affiliations, configured into a contingent and interdependent order." Martin Irvine, "The Work on the Street: Street Art and Visual Culture," in *The Handbook of Visual Culture*, ed. Ian Heywood and Barry Sandywell (London: Berg, 2012), 256.

70. JR, *Inside Out* (New York: Rizzoli, 2017).

71. Slim Zeghal and Marco Berrebi, *JR: Artocratie en Tunisie* (Paris and Tunis: Alternatives/ Cérès Editions, 2011).

72. Although the group action guidelines provided no specific directions on how to use video recordings to document the actions, these locally produced videos bear striking similarities. Most run for only several minutes. They focus primarily on the act of installing the posters in public space, emphasizing the exuberance of participatory collaboration. Little contextual information is provided other than a few pieces of textual exposition or brief extracts from JR's TED Prize talk explaining the larger rationale of *Inside Out*. Interviews with participants are rare. Drawn from the conventions of the online tribute video, the shorts frequently rely on popular song to suture together the various recorded footage.

73. For an ethnographic account of TeleGhetto's media activism, see Jana Evans Braziel, *Riding with Death: Voudou Art and Urban Ecology in the Streets of Port-au-Prince* (Jackson: University Press of Mississippi, 2017), 176–202.

74. The scenes in Standing Rock document a community action focused on memorializing Ted, a young Native American teenager who took his life.

75. See Lina Khatib, *Image Politics in the Middle East: The Role of the Visual in Political Struggle* (London: I. B. Tauris, 2013).

76. Focusing on JR's projects of the late 2010s as well as his collaboration with Lys's alternative film school École Kourtrajmé, the documentary *Paper and Glue* (JR, 2021) emphasizes the importance of the collaborative process over the finished installation. Moreover, JR is consistently framed discussing his previous work within the context of initiating new collaborations. For instance, his narration of a 2017 project on the US-Mexico border is recorded during his initial meetings with a new set of collaborators, prisoners in a maximum-security facility in Tehachapi, California. This rhetorical embedding works not only to highlight the collaborative nature of his work but also situates the prisoners in the same communicative position—as listeners—as the film's viewers, subtly undermining potential othering dynamics by the latter toward the former.

77. Some of the photographers were Tunisian emigrants now living in France, such as Marco Berrebi, one of the organizers, and most were shooting and pasting outside of their own neighborhoods. For discussion of these particular dynamics, see Zeghal and Berrebi, *JR*, 26–7.

78. Many of the photographers reiterate this point in the project's photobook. For instance, Hela Ammar writes, "The Tunisian people, who had been denied the right to speak finally spoke without restraint. And it was a real pleasure to listen, explain, try to convince. For beyond the confrontation, there was also generosity." Zeghal and Berrebi, *JR*, 18.

79. Keith Moxey summarizes this distinction: "Visual studies in the UK and the US has tended to be dominated by an interpretive paradigm according to which the image is more often

than not conceived of as a *representation*, a visual construct that betrays the ideological agenda of its makers and whose content is susceptible to manipulation by its receivers. By contrast, the contemporary focus on the presence of the visual object, how it engages with the viewer in ways that stray from the cultural agendas for which it was conceived, and which may indeed affect us in a manner that sign systems fail to regulate, asks us to attend to the status of the image as a *presentation*." "Visual Studies and the Iconic Turn," *Journal of Visual Culture* 7, no. 2 (2008): 131–46, here 132–3.

Conclusion

1. Nathan Jurgenson, *The Social Photo: On Photography and Social Media* (London: Verso, 2019).
2. Martin Hand, *Ubiquitous Photography* (Cambridge, UK: Polity Press, 2012).
3. Edgar Gómez Cruz and Eric T. Meyer, "Creation and Control in the Photographic Process: iPhones and the Emerging Fifth Moment of Photography," *Photographies* 5, no. 2 (2012): 203–21, 216.
4. Paul Frosh, "The Gestural Image: The Selfie, Photography Theory, and Kinesthetic Socialibility," *International Journal of Communication* 9 (2015): 1607–28, 1610.
5. Hand, "Photography Meets Social Media: Image Making and Sharing in a Continually Networked Present," in *The Handbook of Photography Studies*, ed. Gil Pasternak (New York: Routledge, 2021), 310–26, 320.
6. Orlowski's film was widely criticized for his almost exclusive dependence of perspectives from inside the industry. See Brianna Barner, "Whose Social Dilemma?," *Docalogue*, February 2021.
7. Marquand Smith quoted in Daniel Magilow, "Shoah Selfies, Shoah Selfie Shaming, and Social Photography in Sergei Loznitsa's *Austerlitz* (2016)," *Shofar* 39, no. 2 (2021): 155–87, 158. Magilow analyzes the public debates about the appropriateness of taking selfies at the site of genocide.

Bibliography

Adams, Robert, et al. *New Topographics: Photographs of a Man-Altered Landscape*. Rochester: International Museum of Photography at George Eastman House, 1975.

Allen, Henry. "Seasons in Hell: Reflections Through Unwary Eyes." *New Yorker*, June 12, 2000, 106.

Alter, Nora. *Chris Marker*. Urbana: University of Illinois Press, 2006.

Alter, Nora. "The Political Im/perceptible in the Essay Film: Farocki's *Images of the World and the Inscription of War*." *New German Critique* 68 (1996): 165–92.

Alter, Nora. "Translating the Essay into Film and Installation." *Journal of Visual Culture* 6, no. 1 (2007): 44–57.

Amnesty International and Forensic Architecture. "Black Friday" (2015). https://blackfriday.amnesty.org/report.php.

Anderson, John. "A Photographer or an Exploiter?" *Newsday*, June 19, 2002, B10.

Arthur, Paul. "Essay Questions." *Film Comment* 39, no. 1 (2003): 58–62.

Asheim, Lester. "The Affective Film." *Journal of the University Film Producers Association* 8, no. 1 (1955): 4–9.

Attie, Jeanie. "Illusions of History." *Radical History Review* 52 (1992): 95–104.

Azoulay, Ariella. *The Civil Contract of Photography*. New York: Zone Books, 2008.

Azoulay, Ariella. *The Civil Imagination: A Political Ontology of Photography*. New York: Verso, 2012.

Azoulay, Ariella. "Getting Rid of the Distinction Between the Aesthetic and the Political." *Theory, Culture, Society* 27, nos. 7–8 (2010): 239–62.

Azoulay, Ariella. "Photography Consists of Collaboration: Susan Meiselas, Wendy Ewald, and Ariella Azoulay." *Camera Obscura* 31, no. 1 (2016): 186–201.

Azoulay, Ariella. "What Is a Photograph? What Is Photography?" *Philosophy of Photography* 1, no. 1 (2010): 9–13.

Baetens, Jan. *The Film Photonovel: A Cultural History of Forgotten Adaptations*. Austin: University of Texas Press, 2019.

Bal, Mieke. "Visual Essentialism and the Object of Visual Culture." *Journal of Visual Culture* 2, no. 1 (2003): 5–32.

Bannos, Pamela. *Vivian Maier: A Photographer's Life and Afterlife*. Chicago: University of Chicago Press, 2017.

Barner, Brianna. "Whose Social Dilemma?" *Docalogue*, February 2021. https://docalogue.com/the-social-dilemma/.

Barnhisel, Greg. *Cold War Modernists: Art, Literature, and American Cultural Diplomacy*. New York: Columbia University Press, 2015.

Baron, Jaimie. *The Archive Effect: Found Footage and the Audiovisual Experience of History*. New York: Routledge, 2014.

Barthes, Roland. *Camera Lucida: Reflections on Photography*. Translated by Richard Howard. New York: Hill and Wang, 1981.

Bassil, Karl, Zeina Maasri, and Akram Zaatari, eds. *Mapping Sitting: On Portraiture and Photography*. Beirut: Arab Image Foundation and Mind the Gap, 2002.

Batchen, Geoffrey. *Photography's Objects*. Albuquerque: University of New Mexico Art Museum, 1997.

Batchen, Geoffrey. "Vernacular Photographies." *History of Photography* 24, no. 3 (2000): 262–71.

Batchen, Geoffrey. "Whither the Vernacular?" In *Imagining Everyday Life: Engagements with Vernacular Photography*, edited by Tina M. Campt, Marianne Hirsch, Gil Hochberg, and Brian Wallis, 33–40. New York and Göttingen: The Walther Collection and Steidl, 2020.

Bate, David. "The Digital Condition of Photography." In *The Photographic Image in Digital Culture* (2nd ed.), edited by Martin Lister, 77–94. New York: Routledge, 2013.

Bazin, André. *What Is Cinema?* Edited by Hugh Gray. 2 vols. Berkeley: University of California Press, 1967, 1971.

Becker, Elizabeth. *When the War Was Over: Cambodia and The Khmer Rouge Revolution*. New York: Simon and Schuster, 1986.

Beckman, Karen, and Jean Ma, eds. *Still Moving: Between Cinema and Photography*. Durham, NC: Duke University Press, 2008.

Bellour, Raymond. "The Pensive Spectator." In *The Cinematic*, edited by David Company, 119–23. London: Whitechapel, 2007.

Belting, Hans. *Face and Mask: A Double History*. Translated by Thomas S. Hansen and Abby J. Hansen. Princeton: Princeton University Press, 2017.

Belting, Hans. "Image, Medium, Body." *Critical Inquiry* 31, no. 2 (2005): 302–19.

Bénézet, Delphine. *The Cinema of Agnès Varda*. New York: Wallflower Press, 2014.

Benson-Allott, Caetlin. "*Standard Operating Procedure*: Mediating Torture." *Film Quarterly* 64, no. 4 (2009): 39–44.

Benzaquen, Stéphanie. "Remediating Genocidal Images into Artworks." *re-bus* 10 (Summer 2010): 28–47. https://www1.essex.ac.uk/arthistory/research/pdfs/rebus/rebus_issue_5.pdf.

Bergala, Alain. "Magnum Meets the Cinema." In *Magnum Cinema: Photographs from 50 Years of Movie-making*, 7–19. London: Phaidon, 1995.

Berkowitz, Michael. *The Crime of My Very Existence: Nazism and the Myth of Jewish Criminality*. Berkeley: University of California Press, 2007.

Bhabha, Homi. "Of Mimicry and Man: The Ambivalence of Colonial Discourse." *October* 28 (1984): 125–133.

Bishop, Claire. *Artificial Hells: Participatory Art and the Politics of Spectatorship*. London: Verso, 2012.

Bluem, William. *Documentary in American Television*. New York: Hastings House, 1965.

Blümlinger, Crista. "Postcards in Agnès Varda's Cinema." In *Between Still and Moving Images*, edited by Laurent Guido and Olivier Lugon, 275–89. New Barnet: John Libbey, 2012.

Bois, Yves-Alain. "On Forensic Architecture: A Conversation with Eyal Weizman." *October* 156 (2016): 116–40.

Bopp, Petra. "Images of Violence in *Wehrmacht* Soldiers' Private Photo Albums." In *Violence and Visibility in Modern History*, edited by Jürgen Martschukat and Silvan Niedermeier, 181–97. New York: Palgrave, 2013.

Boxer, Sarah. "The Chillingly Fine Line Between Ecstasy and Grief." *New York Times*, June 9, 2000, E27.

Boyle, Deirdre. "Trauma, Memory, Documentary: Re-enactment in Two Films by Rithy Panh (Cambodia) and Garin Nugroho (Indonesia)." In *Documentary Testimonies: Global Archives of Suffering*, edited by Bhaskar Sarkar and Janet Walker, 155–72. New York: Routledge, 2010.

Brown, Elspeth H., and Thy Phu, eds. *Feeling Photography*. Durham: Duke University Press, 2014.

Burgin, Victor, ed. *Thinking Photography*. London: Macmillan, 1982.

Burtynsky, Edward. *China*. Göttingen: Steidl, 2005.

Burtynsky, Edward. *Oil*. Göttingen: Steidl, 2009.

Burtynsky, Edward. *Water*. Göttingen: Steidl, 2013.

Burtynsky, Edward, Jennifer Baichwal, and Nicholas de Pencier. *Anthropocene*. Göttingen: Steidl, 2018.

Butler, Judith. "Imitation and Gender Insubordination." In *Inside/Out: Lesbian Theories, Gay Theories*, edited by Diana Fuss, 13–31. New York: Routledge, 1991.

Caldwell, John. *Televisuality: Style, Crisis and Authority in American Television*. New Brunswick: Rutgers University Press, 1995.

Calmes, Leslie Squyres, ed. *The Letters Between Edward Weston and Willard Van Dyke*. Tucson: Center for Creative Photography, 1992.

Cammaer, Gerda. "Edward Burtynsky's *Manufactured Landscapes*: The Ethics and Aesthetics of Creating Moving Still Images and Stilling Moving Images of Ecological Disasters." *Environmental Communication: A Journal of Nature and Culture* 3, no. 1 (2009): 121–30.

Campany, David. "Introduction: When to Be Fast? When to Be Slow?" In *The Cinematic*, edited by David Campany, 10–17. London: Whitechapel, 2007.

Campany, David. *Photography and Cinema*. London: Reaktion Books, 2008.

Campany, David. "What on Earth?: Photography's Alien Landscapes." *Aperture* 211 (2013): 46–51.

Campbell, Neil, and Alfredo Cramerotti, eds. *Photocinema: The Creative Edges of Photography and Film*. Bristol: Intellect, 2013.

Campt, Tina. *Listening to Images*. Durham: Duke University Press, 2017.

Capa, Cornell. *The Concerned Photographer: The Photographs of Werner Bischof, Robert Capa, David Seymour ("Chim"), André Kertész, Leonard Freed, Dan Weiner*. New York: Grossman, 1968.

Cartier-Bresson, Henri. *The Mind's Eye: Writings on Photography and Photographers*. New York: Aperture, 1999.

Castle, Terry. "New Art." *Harper's Magazine*, February 2015, 79–83.

Caswell, Michelle. *Archiving the Unimaginable: Silence, Memory, and the Photographic Record in Cambodia*. Madison: University of Wisconsin Press, 2014.

Charney, Leo, and Vanessa Schwartz, eds. *Cinema and the Invention of Modern Life*. Berkeley: University of California Press, 1996.

Chéroux, Clément. *The Bible for Photographers*. Pamphlet published with reprint of Henri Cartier-Bresson's *The Decisive Moment*. Göttingen: Steidl, 2014.

Chéroux, Clément. "Introducing Werner Kühler." In *Imagining Everyday Life: Engagements with Vernacular Photography*, edited by Tina M. Campt, Marianne Hirsch, Gil Hochberg, and Brian Wallis, 22–32. New York and Göttingen: The Walther Collection and Steidl, 2020.

Cohen, Brianne, and Alexander Streitberger, eds. *The Photofilmic: Entangled Images in Contemporary Art and Visual Culture*. Leuven: Leuven University Press, 2016.

Corrigan, Timothy. *The Essay Film: From Montaigne, After Marker*. Oxford: Oxford University Press, 2011.

Crary, Jonathan. *Techniques of the Observer: On Vision and Modernity in the 19th Century*. Cambridge, MA: MIT Press, 1992.

Daly, Tom. "The Still Photo in Cinema." *Pot Pourri* (Summer 1977): 2–4.

Dargis, Manohla. "Industrial China's Ravaging of Nature, Made Disturbingly Sublime." *New York Times*, June 20, 2007, E4.

Darsie, Alexander. *Slide Show: Projected Images in Contemporary Art*. University Park: Penn State University Press, 2005.

de Sousa Dias, Susana. "(In)visible Evidence: The Representability of Torture." In *A Companion to Contemporary Documentary Film*, edited by Alexandra Jushasz and Alisa Lebow, 482–505. New York: Blackwell-Wiley, 2015.

de Sousa Dias, Susana. "Weak Memories: Archives of Futurability." *Film Quarterly* 73, no. 4 (2020): 26–33.

de Wilde d'Estmael, Vincent. "The Uses of the Archives of the Tuol Sleng Genocide Museum and the Documentation Centre of Cambodia by the Extraordinary Chambers in the Courts of Cambodia." In *Archives and Human Rights*, edited by Jens Boel, Perrine Canavaggio, and Antonio González Quintana, 178–87. New York: Routledge, 2021.

Delahaye, Luc. *L'Autre*. London: Phaidon, 1999.

Dell, Simon. "Mediation and Immediacy: The Press, the Popular Front in France, and the Spanish Civil War." In *The Mexican Suitcase: The Rediscovered Spanish Civil War Negatives of Capa, Chim and Taro*, edited by Cynthia Young, vol. 1, 37–49. New York and Göttingen: International Center of Photography and Steidl, 2010.

Dennett, Terry, and Jo Spence, eds. *Photography/Politics: One*. London: Photography Workshop, 1979.

Diaz, Jun. "Moving Pictures: Creating Multiplane Animation from Photographs." *DV* 11, no. 5 (2003): 26–32.

Didi-Huberman, Georges. *Images in Spite of All: Four Photographs from Auschwitz*. Translated by Shane B. Lillis. Chicago: University of Chicago Press, 2008.

Diehl, Carol. "Toxic Sublime." *Art in America*, February 2006, 188–193.

Dimendberg, Edward. "Transfiguring the Urban Gray: László Moholy-Nagy's Film Scenario 'Dynamic of The Metropolis.'" In *Camera Obscura, Camera Lucida: Essays in Honor of Annette Michelson*, edited by Richard Allen and Malcolm Turvey, 109–26. Amsterdam: University of Amsterdam Press, 2003.

"Discussion: Why Vernacular Photography?: The Limits and Possibilities of a Field." In *Imagining Everyday Life: Engagements with Vernacular Photography*, edited by Tina M. Campt, Marianne Hirsch, Gil Hochberg, and Brian Wallis, 61–5. New York and Göttingen: The Walther Collection and Steidl, 2020.

Dovey, Jon. *Freakshow: First Person Media and Factual Television*. London: Pluto Press, 2000.

Downey, Anthony, and Akram Zaatari. "Photography as Apparatus: Akram Zaatari in Conversation with Anthony Downey." *Critical Interventions: Journal of African Art History and Visual Culture* 12, no. 2 (2018): 218–30.

Drucker, Joanna. "Digital Ontologies: The Ideality of Form in/and Code Storage: Or: Can Graphesis Challenge Mathesis?" *Leonardo* 34, no. 2 (2001): 141–5.

Dubois, Philippe. *Photographie & Cinéma: De la différence à la l'indistinction*. Sesto San Giovanni: Édition Mimésis, 2021.

Dubois, Philippe. "Photography *Mise-en-Film*: Autobiographical (Hi)stories and Psychic Apparatuses." Translated by Lynne Kirby, in *Fugitive Images: From Photography to Video*, edited by Patrice Petro, 152–73. Bloomington: Indiana University Press, 1995.

Eckhard, Petra. "Urban Figures, Common Ground: JR and the Cultural Practices of Perception." *European Journal of American Studies* 10, no. 3 (2015): 1–14.

Edgerton, Gary R. *Ken Burns's America: Packaging the Past for Television*. New York: Palgrave Macmillan, 2001.

Edwards, Elizabeth. "Photographs and the Sound of History." *Visual Anthropology Review* 21, nos. 1–2 (2005): 27–46.

Edwards, Elizabeth. "Objects of Affect: Photography Beyond the Image." *Annual Review of Anthropology* 41 (2012): 221–34.

Edwards, Elizabeth. "The Thingness of Photographs." In *A Companion to Photography*, edited by Stephen Bull, 97–112. Hoboken, NJ: John Wiley, 2020,

Edwards, Elizabeth. "Thinking Photography Beyond the Visual?" In *Photography: Theoretical Snapshots*, edited by J. J. Long, Andrea Noble, and Edward Welch, 31–48. London: Routledge, 2009.

Edwards, Elizabeth, and Janice Hart, eds. *Photographs, Objects, Histories: On the Materiality of Images*. New York: Routledge, 2004.

Ehrlich, Matthew C., and Joe Saltzman. *Heroes and Scoundrels: The Image of the Journalist in Popular Culture*. Urbana: University of Illinois Press, 2015.

Elias, Chad. "The Artist as Collector: A Dialogue on the Possibilities and Limits of an Institution." In *Against Photography*, edited by Akram Zaatari, 40–4. Barcelona: Museu d'Art Contemporani de Barcelona, 2017.

Elleström, Lars. "The Modalities of Media: A Model for Understanding Intermedial Relations." In *Media Borders, Multimodality, and Intermediality*, edited by Lars Elleström, 11–48. London: Palgrave Macmillan, 2010.

Enwezor, Okwui. *Archive Fever: The Use of the Document in Contemporary Art*. New York/Göttingen: International Center of Photography/Steidl, 2008.

Enyeart, James L. *Willard Van Dyke: Changing the World Through Photography and Film*. Albuquerque: University of New Mexico Press, 2008.

Evans Braziel, Jana. *Riding with Death: Voudou Art and Urban Ecology in the Streets of Port-au-Prince*. Jackson: University Press of Mississippi, 2017.

Faber, Sebastiaan. *Memory Battles of the Spanish Civil War: History, Fiction, Photography*. Nashville: Vanderbilt University Press, 2018.

Faction Films. "Producing a Picture: Derry in Photography." In *Photography/Politics: Two*, edited by Patricia Holland, Jo Spence, and Simon Watney, 129–33. London: Commedia, 1986.

Fallon, Kris. "Archives Analog and Digital: Errol Morris and Documentary Film in the Digital Age." *Screen* 54, no. 1 (2013): 20–43.

Felman, Shoshana, and Dori Laub. *Testimony: Crises of Witnessing in Literature, Psychoanalysis and History*. New York: Routledge, 1992.

Ferdman, Bertie. "Urban Dramaturgy: The Global Art Project of JR." *PAJ: A Journal of Performance and Art* 34, no. 3 (2012): 12–26.

Finnegan, Cara A. *Making Photography Matter: A Viewer's History from the Civil War to the Great Depression*. Urbana: University of Illinois Press, 2015.

Flitterman-Lewis, Sandy. "Documenting the Ineffable: Terror and Memory in Alain Resnais's *Night and Fog*." In *Documenting the Documentary: Close Readings of Documentary Film and Video*, edited by Barry Keith Grant and Jeannette Sloniowksi, 204–22. Detroit: Wayne State University, 1998.

Forbes, Duncan. "Edward Burtynsky's Negative Sublime." *Portfolio* 47 (2008): 4–21.

Frosh, Paul. "The Gestural Image: The Selfie, Photography Theory, and Kinesthetic Sociability." *International Journal of Communication* 9 (2015): 1607–28.

Furuhata, Yuriko. *Cinema of Actuality: Japanese Avant-Garde Filmmaking in the Season of Image Politics*. Durham, NC: Duke University Press, 2013.

Gaines, Jane M. "Political Mimesis." In *Collecting Visible Evidence*, edited by Jane M. Gaines and Michael Renov, 84–102. Minneapolis: University of Minnesota Press, 1999.

Galassi, Peter. *Andreas Gursky*. New York: Museum of Modern Art, 2001.

Gilpatrick, Greg. "Manipulated Reality: *The Kid Stays in the Picture*." *Independent Film and Video Monthly* 25, no. 5 (2002): 45–6.

Gómez Cruz, Edgar, and Eric T. Meyer. "Creation and Control in the Photographic Process: iPhones and the Emerging Fifth Moment of Photography." *Photographies* 5, no. 2 (2012): 203–21.

Goyarrola, Erika. "Case Study on the Photo Booth: Proof, Appropriation, Identity." In *The Routledge Companion to Photography and Visual Culture*, edited by Moritz Neumüller, 189–99. London: Routledge, 2018.

Grant, Catherine. "Still Moving Images: Photographs and the Disappeared in Films about the 'Dirty War' in Argentina." In *Phototextualities: Intersections of Photography and Narrative*, edited by Alex Hughes and Andrea Noble, 63–86. Albuquerque: University of New Mexico Press, 2003.

Green, David. "Marking Time: Photography, Film, and Temporalities of the Image." In *Stillness and Time: Photography and the Moving Image*, edited by David Green and Joanna Lowry, 9–21. Brighton: Photoworks, 2006.

Griffiths, Alison. *Shivers Down Your Spine: Cinema, Museums, and the Immersive View*. New York: Columbia University Press, 2008.

"Group Action Guidelines." *Inside Out Project*. Accessed December 18, 2018. https://web.arch ive.org/web/20150701164745/http://www.insideoutproject.net:80/sites/all/themes/inside out/documents/Group_Action_Guidelines.pdf.

Guerin, Frances. "The Ambiguity of Amateur Photography in Modern Warfare." *New Literary History* 48, no. 1 (2017): 53–74.

Guerin, Frances. *Through Amateur Eyes: Film and Photography in Nazi Germany*. Minneapolis: University of Minnesota Press, 2012.

Guido, Laurent, and Olivier Lugon, eds. *Between Still and Moving Images*. New Barnet: John Libbey, 2012.

Guynn, William. *Unspeakable Histories: Film and the Experience of Catastrophe*. New York: Columbia University Press, 2016.

Hallas, Roger. "Introduction." In *Documenting the Visual Arts*, edited by Roger Hallas, 1–20. London: Routledge, 2020.

Hallas, Roger. "Photojournalism, NGOs, and the New Media Ecology." In *Sensible Politics: The Visual Culture of Nongovernmental Activism*, edited by Meg McLagan and Yates McKee, 94–114. New York: Zone Books, 2012.

Hallas, Roger. *Reframing Bodies: AIDS, Bearing Witness, and the Queer Moving Image*. Durham, NC: Duke University Press, 2009.

Hámos, Gusztáv, Katja Pratschke, and Thomas Tode, eds. *Viva Fotofilm: Bewegt/Unbewegt*. Marburg: Schüren Verlag, 2009.

Hand, Martin. "Photography Meets Social Media: Image Making and Sharing in a Continually Networked Present." In *The Handbook of Photography Studies*, edited by Gil Pasternak, 310–26. New York: Routledge, 2021.

Hand, Martin. *Ubiquitous Photography*. Cambridge, UK: Polity Press, 2012.

Haworth-Booth, Mark. "Edward Burtynsky: Traditions and Affinities." In *Manufactured Landscapes: The Photographs of Edward Burtynsky*, edited by Lori Pauli, 34–9. Ottawa: National Gallery of Canada, 2003.

Hayles, N. Katherine. "Translating Media: Why We Should Rethink Textuality." *Yale Journal of Criticism* 16, no. 2 (2003): 263–90.

Hebard, Andrew. "Disruptive Histories: Toward a Radical Politics of Remembrance in Alain Resnais's *Night and Fog*." *New German Critique* 71 (1997): 87–113.

Heyman, Therese Thau. *Seeing Straight: The f.64 Revolution in Photography*. Oakland, CA: Oakland Museum, 1992.

Hirsch, Joshua. *Afterimage: Film, Trauma and the Holocaust*. Philadelphia: Temple University Press, 2003.

Holland, Patricia, Jo Spence, and Simon Watney, eds. *Photography/Politics Two*. London: Commedia, 1986.

Horak, Jan Christopher. *Making Images Move: Photographers and Avant Garde Cinema*. Washington, DC: Smithsonian Institution, 1997.

Hornsey, Richard. "Francis Bacon and the Photobooth: Facing the Homosexual in Post-war Britain." *Visual Culture in Britain* 8, no. 2 (2007): 83–103.

Hughes, Rachel. "The Abject Artefacts of Memory: Photographs from Cambodia's Genocide." *Media, Culture & Society* 25, no. 1 (2003): 23–44.

Hürlimann, Annemarie, and Alois Martin Müller, eds. *Film Stills: Emotions Made in Hollywood*. Ostfildern: Hatje Cantz, 1993.

Irvine, Martin. "The Work on the Street: Street Art and Visual Culture." In *The Handbook of Visual Culture*, edited by Ian Heywood and Barry Sandywell, 236–78. London: Berg, 2012.

Jackson, Bruce. *Pictures from a Drawer: Prison and the Art of Portraiture*. Philadelphia: Temple University Press, 2009.

Jacobs, Steven. *Framing Pictures: Film and the Visual Arts*. Edinburgh: Edinburgh University Press, 2011.

Jacobs, Steven. "The History and Aesthetics of the Classical Film Still." *History of Photography* 34, no. 4 (2010): 373–86.

Jazdon, Mikolaj. "Starring Photos: On Polish Iconographic Films Made from Photos." *Kwartalnik Filmowy*. Special Issue (2013): Polish Film Scholars on Polish Cinema: 140–58.

Jeffay, Tory. "Flat Out Formalism: *Strong Island* as Trans of Color Critique." *New Review of Film and Television Studies* 19, no. 2 (2021): 217–38.

Jones, David. "The Canadian Film Board Unit B." In *New Challenges for Documentary*, edited by Alan Rosenthal and John Corner, 79–93. 2nd ed. Manchester: Manchester University Press, 2005.

JR. *Inside Out*. New York: Rizzoli, 2017.

Jurgenson, Nathan. *The Social Photo: On Photography and Social Media*. London: Verso, 2019.

Kennedy, Randy. "The Still-Life Mentor to a Filmmaking Generation." *New York Times*, October 19, 2006.

Kennedy, Randy. "The Capa Cache." *New York Times*, January 28, 2008.

Katz, Robert. "Documentary in Transition: Part 1: The United States." *Hollywood Quarterly* 3, no. 4 (1948): 425–33.

Keller, Candace M. "Framed and Hidden Histories: West African Photography from Local to Global Contexts." *African Arts* 47, no. 4 (2014): 36–47.

Khatchadourian, Raffi. "'In the Picture: An Artist's Global Experiment to Help People Be Seen." *New Yorker*, November 28, 2011. https://www.newyorker.com/magazine/2011/11/28/in-the-picture-raffi-khatchadourian.

Khatib, Lina. *Image Politics in the Middle East: The Role of the Visual in Political Struggle*. London: I. B. Tauris, 2013.

Kingwell, Mark. "The Truth in Photographs: Edward Burtynsky's Revelations of Excess." In *China*, edited by Edward Burtynsky. Göttingen: Steidl, 2005, 16–19.

Kinsey, Tammy. "*War Photographer* (2001)." *The Moving Image* 3, no. 2 (2003): 108–11.

Kirschenbaum, Matthew G. *Mechanisms: New Media and the Forensic Imagination*. Cambridge, MA: MIT Press, 2008.

Kittler, Friedrich. *Film, Gramophone, Typewriter*. Translated by Geoffrey Winthrop-Young and Michael Wutz. Stanford: Stanford University Press, 1999.

Klinger, Barbara. "Beyond Cheap Thrills: 3D Cinema Today, the Parallax Debates, and the 'Pop Out.'" In *3D Cinema and Beyond*, edited by Dan Adler, Janine Marchessault, and Sanja Obradovic, 186–99. Toronto: Public Books, 2013.

Knightley, Phillip. *The First Casualty: From Crimea to Vietnam: The War Correspondent as Hero, Propagandist, and Myth Maker*. New York: Harcourt, Brace and Jovanovich, 1975.

Koehler, Robert. "War Photographer." *Variety*, June 17, 2002, 27.

Koetzle, Hans-Michael. "James Nachtwey, War Photographer." *European Photography*, no. 72 (2002): 16–18.

Krauss, Rosalind, "Photography's Discursive Spaces: Landscape/View." *Art Journal* 42, no. 4 (1982): 311–19.

Lamunière, Michelle, *You Look Beautiful Like That: The Portrait Photographs of Seydou Keïta and Malick Sidibé*. New Haven, CT: Yale University Press, 2001.

Lancioni, Judith. "The Rhetoric of the Frame: Revisioning Archival Photographs in *The Civil War*." *Western Journal of Communication* 60, no. 4 (1996): 397–414.

Lane, Philip J., Jr. "NBC-TV's Project 20: An Analysis of the Art of the Still-in-Motion Film in Television." Ph.D. dissertation, Northwestern University, 1969.

Langford, Martha. *Suspended Conversations: The Afterlife of Memory in Photographic Albums*. Montreal: McGill-Queen's University Press, 2001.

Lavoie, Vincent. "Robert Capa and the Turn to Forensics." In *Photography and Doubt*, edited by Sabine T. Kriegel and Andrés Mario Zervigón, 121–37. London: Routledge, 2017.

Le Feuvre, Lisa, and Akram Zaatari, eds. *Hashem El Madani: Studio Practices*. London and Beirut: Photographers' Gallery, Arab Image Foundation and Mind the Gap, 2004.

Lee, Anthony W., and Elizabeth Young. *On Alexander Gardner's Photographic Sketch Book of the Civil War*. Berkeley: University of California Press, 2008.

Levinas, Emmanuel. *Totality and Infinity: An Essay on Exteriority*. Translated by Alphonso Lingis. The Hague: Nijhoff, 1979.

Lichter-Mark, Rose. "Vivian Maier and the Problem of Difficult Women." *New Yorker*, May 9, 2014, https://www.newyorker.com/culture/culture-desk/vivian-maier-and-the-problem-of-difficult-women.

Lindeperg, Sylvie. *"Night and Fog": A Film in History*. Translated by Tom Mas. Minneapolis: University of Minnesota Press, 2014.

Lindeperg, Sylvie. "The Strange Twentieth-Century Album." *L'Atalante: International Film Studies Journal* 12 (2011): 20–7.

Linfield, Susie. *The Cruel Radiance: Photography and Political Violence*. Chicago: University of Chicago Press, 2010.

Lister, Martin, ed. *The Photographic Image in Digital Culture*. 2nd ed. New York: Routledge, 2013.

Lopate, Phillip. "In Search of the Centaur." In *Beyond the Document: Essays on Nonfiction Film*, edited by Charles Warren, 243–70. Middleton, CT: Wesleyan University Press, 1996.

López, Ana. "Calling for Intermediality." *Cinema Journal* 54, vol. 1 (2014): 135–41.

Lubben, Kristen. "An Interview with Susan Meiselas." In *Susan Meiselas: In History*, edited by Kristen Lubben, 128–73. New York and Göttingen: International Center of Photography/Steidl, 2008.

Lupton, Catherine. *Chris Marker*. London: Reaktion Books, 2004.

MacDonald, Scott. "Interview with Susana de Sousa Dias." *Rethinking History* 18, no. 3 (2014): 400–12.

MacDonald, Scott. "Susana de Sousa Dias." *Film Quarterly* 66, no. 2 (2012): 25–34.

Magilow, Daniel H. "Shoah Selfies, Shoah Selfie Shaming, and Social Photography in Sergei Loznitsa's *Austerlitz* (2016)." *Shofar* 39, no. 2 (2021): 155–87.

Magnin, André. *Malick Sidibé*. Zürich: Scalo, 1998.

Manovich, Lev. *The Language of New Media*. Cambridge, MA: MIT Press, 2001.

McBride, Hannah. "Interview: Jared Moossy." *Nowhere*, 2013, https://nowheremag.com/2013/02/interview-jared-moosy/.

Mitchell, W. J. T. "There Are No Visual Media." *Journal of Visual Culture* 4, no. 2 (2005): 257–66.

Mitchell, W. J. T. *What Do Pictures Want?: The Lives and Loves of Images*. Chicago: University of Chicago Press, 2005.

Molina, Javier. "La maleta mexicana en México: Entrevista con Juan Villoro." *Letras Libres*, December 13, 2013, https://www.letraslibres.com/mexico/la-maleta-mexicana-en-mexico.

Molndár, Virág. "Street Art and the Changing Urban Public Sphere." *Public Culture* 29, no. 2 (2017): 385–414.

Moroz, Sarah. "Socialism and cha-cha-cha." *The Guardian*, December 10, 2015. https://www.theguardian.com/artanddesign/2015/dec/10/agnes-varda-photographs-cuba-salut-les-cubains.

Moxey, Keith. "Visual Studies and the Iconic Turn." *Journal of Visual Culture* 7, no. 2 (2008): 131–46.

Muellner, Nicholas. "The New Interval." In *The Versatile Image: Photography, Digital Technologies and the Internet*, edited by Alexandra Moschovi, Carol McKay and Arabella Plouviez, 75–85. Leuven: Leuven University Press, 2013.

Müller, Jürgen E. "Intermediality and Media Historiography in the Digital Era." *Acta Universitatis Sapientiae, Film and Media Studies* 2 (2010): 15–38.

Mun-Delsalle, Y-Jean. "French Artist JR's Works Are Turning the World Inside Out." *Forbes*, September 13, 2015. https://www.forbes.com/sites/yjeanmundelsalle/2015/09/13/french-artist-jrs-works-are-turning-the-world-inside-out/#7e2da93517f5.

Murphy, Denis. "*Men at Lunch/Lónsa Spéir* (Seán Ó Cualáin, 2012)." *Estudios Irlandeses* 8 (2013): 226–8. http://www.estudiosirlandeses.org/reviews/men-at-lunch-lonsaspeir-sean-o-cualain-2012/.

Mydans, Seth. "Cambodians Demand Apology for Khmer Rouge Images with Smiling Faces." *New York Times*, April 13, 2021.

Nachtwey, James. *Inferno*. London: Phaidon, 2000.

Nardelli, Matilde. "End(u)ring Photography." *Photographies* 5, no. 2 (2012): 159–77.

Negroponte, Nicholas. *Being Digital*. New York: Knopf, 1995.

Nichols, Bill. "Feelings of Revulsion and the Limits of Academic Discourse." *Jump Cut* 52 (2010). https://www.ejumpcut.org/archive/jc52.2010/sopNichols/index.html.

Nichols, Bill. *Representing Reality: Issues in Documentary Representation*. Bloomington: Indiana University Press, 1991.

O'Donoghue, Darragh. "Home Video: *Men at Lunch*." *Cineaste* 39, no. 3 (2014): 67–9.

Olin, Margaret. *Touching Photographs*. Chicago: University of Chicago Press, 2012.

Oppenheimer, Joshua. "Perpetrators' Testimony and the Restoration of Humanity: *S21*, Rithy Panh." In *Killer Images: Documentary Film, Memory, and the Performance of Violence*, edited by Joram Ten Brink and Joshua Oppenheimer, 243–55. London: Wallflower Press, 2012.

Orpana, Jennifer. "Turning the World 'Inside Out': Situating JR's Wish within Cultures of Participation." *Canadian Art Review* 39, no. 1 (2014): 66–75.

Panh, Rithy. *The Elimination: A Survivor of the Khmer Rouge Confronts His Past and the Commandant of the Killing Fields*. Translated by John Cullen. New York: Other Press, 2013.

Pankenberg, Volker. *Farocki/Godard: Film as Theory*. Amsterdam: University of Amsterdam Press, 2015.

Peeples, Jennifer. "Toxic Sublime: Imagining Contaminated Landscapes." *Environmental Communication* 5, no. 4 (2011): 373–92.

Pethő, Ágnes. *Cinema and Intermediality: The Passion for the In-Between*. Newcastle: Cambridge Scholars Press, 2011.

Phu, Thy. "Afterimages of S-21: Distant and Proximate Spectatorship and the Legacies of Cold War Human Rights." In *Photography and Its Publics*, edited by Melisa Miles and Edward Welch, 149–66. London: Bloomsbury, 2020.

Pinney, Christopher. *Camera Indica: The Social Life of Indian Photographs*. London: Reaktion, 1997.

Pollock, Giselda, and Max Silverman, eds. *Concentrationary Cinema: Aesthetics as Political Resistance in Alain Resnais's Night and Fog*. New York: Berghahn Books, 2010.

Rascarolli, Laura. *The Personal Camera: Subjective Cinema and the Essay Film*. New York: Wallflower Press, 2009.

Raskin, Richard. *Nuit et Brouillard by Alain Resnais: On the Making, Reception and Functions of a Major Documentary Film*. Aarhus: Aarhus University Press, 1987.

Reichardt, Mark, Holly Edwards, and Erina Dugganne, eds. *Beautiful Suffering: Photography and the Traffic in Pain*. Williamstown, MA: Williams College Museum of Art, 2007.

Respini, Eva, and Ana Janevski. "Interview with the Artist." In *Projects 100: Akram Zaatari*. Museum of Modern Art, 2013. https://www.moma.org/interactives/exhibitions/projects/wp-content/uploads/2013/05/Interview-Akram-Zaatari1.pdf.

Ricciardelli, Lucia. *American Documentary Filmmaking in the Digital Age: Depictions of War in Burns, Moore, and Morris*. New York: Routledge, 2014.

Rony, Fatimah Tobing. *The Third Eye: Race, Cinema and Ethnographic Spectacle*. Durham, NC: Duke University Press, 1996.

Rosler, Martha. *Decoys and Disruptions: Selected Writings, 1975–2001*. Cambridge, MA: MIT Press, 2004, 245–58.

Rossaak, Eivind, ed. *Between Stillness and Motion: Film, Photography, Algorithms*. Amsterdam: University of Amsterdam Press, 2011.

Roston, Tom. *Ken Burns: The Kindle Singles Interview*. Amazon Services, 2014.

Rudolph, Jörg, Frank Drauschke, and Alexander Sachse. *Hingerichtet in Moskau: Opfer des Stalinismus aus Berlin 1950–1953*. Berlin: Der Landesbeauftragter für die Stasi-Unterlagen, 2007.

Sánchez-Biosca, Vincente. "Bophana's Image and Narrative." In *The Cinema of Rithy Panh: Everything Has a Soul*, edited by Leslie Barnes and Joseph Mai, 173–87. New Brunswick, NJ: Rutgers University Press, 2021.

Saxton, Libby. *No Power Without an Image: Icons Between Photography and Film*. Edinburgh: Edinburgh University Press, 2020.

Schmid, Marion. *Intermedial Dialogues: The French New Wave and the Other Arts*. Edinburgh: Edinburgh University Press, 2019.

Scott, A. O. "Witnessing the Witness: Looking Over a Shoulder at War's Deprivation." *New York Times*, June 19, 2002, E1.

Sekula, Allan. "Reading an Archive: Photography Between Labour and Capital." In *Photography/Politics: Two*, edited by Patricia Holland, Jo Spence, and Simon Watney, 153–61. London: Commedia, 1986.

Sekula, Allan. "The Body and the Archive." *October 39* (1986): 3–64.

Silverman, Kaja. *The Threshold of the Visible World*. New York: Routledge, 1996.

Smith, Damon. "Made in China: Jennifer Baichwal and Edward Burtynsky on Their Travels Across *Manufactured Landscapes*." *Bright Lights Film Journal*, November 1, 2007. http://brightlightsfilm.com/made-china-jennifer-baichwal-edward-burtynsky-travels-across-manufactured-landscapes/#.WgoK847k7XU.

Solomon-Godeau, Abigail. *Photography After Photography: Gender, Genre, History*. Durham, NC: Duke University Press, 2017.

Sontag, Susan. *On Photography*. New York: Farrar, Straus, and Giroux, 1977.

Sontag, Susan. *Regarding the Pain of Others*. New York: Farrar, Straus, and Giroux, 2003.

Statzer, Mary, ed. *The Photographic Object, 1970*. Berkeley: University of California Press, 2016.

Steimatsky, Noa. *The Face on Film*. New York: Oxford University Press, 2017.

Stewart, Garrett. *Between Film and Screen: Modernism's Photo Synthesis*. Chicago: University of Chicago Press, 1999.

Stutesman, Drake. "Connectivity: An Interview with Susan Meiselas." *Framework: The Journal of Cinema and Media* 51, no. 1 (2010): 61–78.

Sutton, Damian. *Photography, Cinema, Memory: The Crystal Image of Time*. Minneapolis: University of Minnesota Press, 2009.

Tagg, John. *The Burden of Representation: Essays on Photographies and Histories*. Basingstoke: Macmillan, 1988.

Taylor, Diana. *The Archive and the Repertoire: Performing Cultural Memory in the Americas*. Durham, NC: Duke University Press, 2003.

Taylor, Diana. "Past Performing Future: Susan Meiselas's *Reframing History*." In *Susan Meiselas: In History*, edited by Kristen Lubben, 232–6. New York and Göttingen: International Center of Photography and Steidl, 2008,

Thelen, David. "The Movie Maker as Historian: Conversations with Ken Burns." *Journal of American History* 81, no. 3 (1994): 1031–50.

Thomson, Patricia. "Photographing the Front Lines." *American Cinematographer* 83, no. 9 (2002): 20–4.

Thomson, Patricia. "Sundance 2002: New Directions: 'The Kid Stays in the Picture.'" *American Cinematographer* 83, no. 4 (2002): 102–6.

Tibbetts, John C. "The Incredible Stillness of Being." *American Studies* 37, no. 1 (1996): 117–33.

Toplin, Robert Brent. *Ken Burns's The Civil War*. New York: Oxford University Press, 1996.

Torosian, Michael. "The Essential Element: An Interview with Edward Burtynsky." In *Manufactured Landscapes: The Photographs of Edward Burtynsky*, edited by Lori Pauli, 46–55. Ottawa: National Gallery of Canada, 2003,

Trachtenberg, Alan. *Reading American Photographs: Images as History, Matthew Brady to Walker Evans*. New York: Hill and Wang, 1990.

Trachtenberg, Alan. "Weegee's City Secrets." *E-rea* 7, no. 2 (2010). http://journals.openedition.org/erea/1168.

"*Twenty-Eight Nights and a Poem*: Akram Zaatari, Q&A, Berlinale Forum." February 11, 2015. https://www.youtube.com/watch?v=mt_iETNouYM.

Ungar, Steven. "Quality Wars: The Groupe des Trente and the Renewal of the Short Subject in France, 1953–1963." *South Central Review* 33, no. 2 (2016): 30–43.

van Alphen, Ernst. *Staging the Archive: Art and Photography in the Age of New Media*. London: Reaktion Books, 2014.

Vause, Mikel. "Capturing the American Experience: A Conversation with Ken Burns." *The Contemporary West* 23, no. 1 (2006). https://www.weber.edu/weberjournal/Journal_Archives/Archive_D/Vol_23_1/KenBurnsConv.html.

Vignaux, Valérie. "*Salut les Cubains* d'Agnès Varda ou cinécriture et cinema politique." In *Varda/Cuba*, edited by Clément Chéroux and Karolina Ziebinska-Lewandowska, 147–51. Paris: Editions du Centre Pompidou, 2015.

Walker, Ian. "The Problematic Possibilities of Documentary." In *A Companion to Photography*, edited by Stephen Bull, 371–91. Oxford: Wiley Blackwell, 2020.

Weizman, Eyal. "Before and After Images: Eyal Weizman's The Image Complex." 2016. https://thephotographersgalleryblog.org.uk/2016/05/22/the-image-complex/.

Weizman, Eyal. *Forensic Architecture: Notes from Fields and Forums*. Berlin: Hatje Kantz, 2012.

Weizman, Eyal. "Interview with Eyal Weizman." *International Review of the Red Cross* 98, no. 1 (2016): 21–35.

Weizman, Eyal. "Introduction: Forensis." In *Forensis: The Architecture of Public Truth*, edited by Forensic Architecture, 9–32. Berlin: Sternberg Press, 2014.

Weizman, Eyal. "Theory Talk #69." 2015. http://www.theory-talks.org/2015/03/theory-talk-69.html.

West, Shearer. *Portraiture*. Oxford: Oxford University Press, 2004.

Westmoreland, Mark R. "Akram Zaatari: Against Photography. A Conversation with Mark Westmoreland." *Aperture* 210 (2013): 60–5.

Westmoreland, Mark R. "Time Capsules of Catastrophic Times." In *The Arab Archive: Mediated Memories and Digital Flows*, edited by Donatella Della Ratta, Kay Dickinson, and Sune Haugbolle, 20–34. Amsterdam: Institute of Network Cultures, 2020.

Whelan, Richard. "Robert Capa's *The Fallen Soldier*: A Detective Story." *Aperture* 166 (2002): 43–55.

Wilkinson, Alec. "Picturing Auschwitz." *New Yorker*, March 17, 2008, 48–55.

Williams, Linda. "Cluster Fuck: The Forcible Frame in Errol Morris's *Standard Operating Procedure*." *Camera Obscura* 25, no. 1 (2010): 28–67.

Wilson, Emma. "Material Remains: *Night and Fog*." *October* 112 (2005): 89–110.

Wilson-Goldie, Kaelen. "Memory Games: The Arab Image Foundation." In *On Photography in Lebanon: Stories and Essays*, edited by Clémence Cottard Hachem and Nour Salamé, 147–9. Beirut: Kaph Books, 2018.

Winston, Brian. *Claiming the Real II: Documentary: Grierson and Beyond*. London: Palgrave Macmillan, 2008.

Woodward, Michelle L. "Creating Memory and History: The Role of Archival Practices in Lebanon and Palestine." *Photographies* 2, no. 1 (2009): 21–35.

Wyver, John. *Vision On: Film, Television and the Arts in Britain*. London: Wallflower, 2007.

Young, Cynthia. "The Process of Identifying 4,500 Negatives: The Mexican Suitcase Revealed." In *The Mexican Suitcase: The Rediscovered Spanish Civil War Negatives of Capa, Chim and Taro*, edited by Cynthia Young, vol. 1, 95–115. New York and Göttingen: International Center of Photography and Steidl, 2010.

Young, Marnin. "Manufactured Landscapes: The Photographs of Edward Burtynsky." *Afterimage* 30, no. 6 (May/June 2003): 8–9.

Zaatari, Akram. "History and Photographic Memory." *Journal of Visual Culture* 18, no. 2 (2019): 169–86.

Zaatari, Akram, ed. *The Vehicle: Picturing Moments of Transition in a Modernizing Society*. Beirut: The Arab Image Foundation and Mind the Gap, 1999.

Zeghal, Slim, and Marco Berrebi, *JR: Artocratie en Tunisie*. Paris and Tunis: Alternatives/Cérès Editions, 2011.

Ziebinska-Lewandowska, Karolina. "Socialisme et cha-cha-cha." In *Varda/Cuba*, edited by Clément Chéroux and Karolina Ziebinska-Lewandowska, 7–12. Paris: Editions du Centre Pompidou, 2015.

Ziff, Trisha. *Hidden Truths: Bloody Sunday, 1972*. Santa Monica, CA: Smart Art Press, 1998.

Ziff, Trisha. "Photographs at War." In *The Media and Northern Ireland*, edited by Bill Rolston, 187–205. London: Macmillan, 1991.

Ziff, Trisha, and Roger Hallas, "Challenging the Hierarchies of Photographic Histories." In *Documenting the Visual Arts*, edited by Roger Hallas, 191–204. London and New York: Routledge, 2020.

Zimmermann, Patricia. *States of Emergency: Documentaries, Wars, Democracies*. Minneapolis: University of Minnesota Press, 2000.

Index